Paul

Love Mom
XMAS 96.

BRYN FRANK

SHORT WALKS IN ENGLISH TOWNS

WITH PHOTOGRAPHS BY
DERRY BRABBS
AND MAPS BY
HUBERT PRAGNELL

ARTUS BOOKS

ENDPAPERS *Elm Hill, Norwich*

HALF-TITLE PAGE (P.1) *Merton Street, Oxford*

TITLE PAGE (P.2) *The Circus, Bath*

CONTENTS

Introduction   6

Bath   8

Cambridge   26

Canterbury   46

Chester   64

Lincoln   84

Norwich   102

Oxford   120

Salisbury   140

Shrewsbury   154

York   170

Index   188

A map for each town is to be found two pages after the beginning of the chapter.

INTRODUCTION

It is ten o'clock on a bitterly cold night in 'uphill Lincoln'. Several small candlelit restaurants and wine bars are open but not doing much business. Tempting though a plate of lasagne and a glass of chianti are, I know they would break the spell. Here, on top of the highest hill in Lincolnshire and in the lee of one of our finest cathedrals, I stop in my tracks to absorb a complete stillness I would not have thought possible in the heart of a major English city. Floodlit and shimmering, with a pin-cushion of stars behind it, the cathedral shines out over half this unsung county. A medieval mystic would not be disappointed.

Three months later in York, frost is as hard to imagine as football hooligans in Lincoln – though the city has had its share. Photographers are out to capture yet again the biggest pictorial cliché in England: the daffodils that adorn the earthworks on which the city walls were built. But then they can hardly be expected to photograph the ghosts of the Roman legionnaires said to frequent the deepest recesses of some of the city's most ancient buildings.

In Oxford, in June, a cocktail of exceptionally warm weather, the strangely soporific throb of traffic over four-hundred-year-old stone walls, and too much local beer makes tourists as well as undergraduates light-headed. In Cambridge, in late autumn, leaves drift down from the trees, which, pretty as they are, tend to camouflage the city's architectural masterpieces. The surrounding fenland is bleak and very much an acquired taste, which makes Cambridge seem particularly cosy and self-contained.

The mood is everything. A flat tyre on the inner ring road, a surly bus driver between railway station and hotel, a concoction of arterial roads, one-way systems, and office developments that dwarf medieval church towers and once-proud coaching inns, all can conspire to hide the best of our towns and cities from the average passer-by.

Exploring ten towns and cities in depth and at different times of the year, I deliberately took my time. Detail became all-important: here was a flower-filled cul-de-sac graced by wrought-iron railings, there a museum in which on a Saturday afternoon at the height of the tourist season I was the only visitor, here a teashop in an excavated Roman cellar, there a river-boat landing I had never imagined. There was much more than met the eye merely perusing a town plan.

The best of our towns and cities do not exist in isolation but as part of the counties in which they stand. Only the London commuter thinks that England is simply an urban sprawl. No town is an island: that black and white half-timbered house that has stood for three hundred years or more may originally have been put up by a family concern still based in a nearby village; the poultry cross under which townspeople have sheltered from the rain for perhaps five hundred years still has tomato growers and game dealers from the surrounding countryside selling their wares; the workaday bus station is a terminus for a score of single-deckers that have spent the morning threading their way through outlying villages with names straight out of *This England*.

The favourite golden rule of most city guides is, 'Look up, above first floor level'. I would add, 'Take it slowly, talk to the people, read up the history and go at different times of the day.' Short walks taken in small doses can be long in enjoyment.

Several of the places referred to in this book as towns are technically cities. Local councillors should not get hot under the collar, however: the man in the high street, even in a provincial city, will tend to say 'town', and we have used the word loosely. Apart from which, there is a very fine line between the two, and many a well-informed visitor to this country is miffed to discover that being in possession of a cathedral does not make a town a city. Nor is size much of a guide.

We have also used the word 'short' advisedly. To some readers, the ascent of Lincoln's Steep Hill will be something to knock off between the late hotel breakfast and early pub lunch. To others the two-mile circumnavigation of Chester's city walls can be spun out to last the whole day. But roughly the walks in themselves last between two and three hours, although those times do not build in much room in which to stand and stare. Inevitably some walks are longer than others in terms of distance, and in Oxford and Cambridge, for example, if you actually visit the colleges on our recommended route, their quads and courts will effectively double the distance.

The three-dimensional maps do not conform to strict principles. They, too, are simply a guide, reflecting as far as is practical the main points of interest on or near the walking route, and sometimes beyond it. They could not be done to a precise scale: in towns as closely packed as some of these are, with buildings to look up at and admire and squares to stroll around, even our eagle's eye view has to be a little selective.

BATH

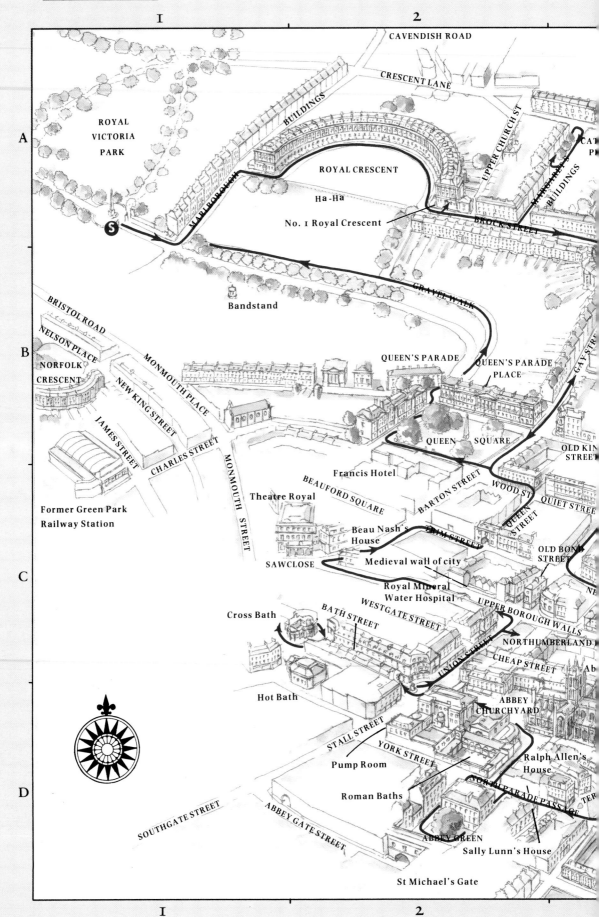

CAVENDISH ROAD

CRESCENT LANE

ROYAL VICTORIA PARK

BUILDINGS

UPPER CHURCH ST

CAT P

BUILDINGS

A

ROYAL CRESCENT

Ha-Ha

No. 1 Royal Crescent

BROCK STREET

MARLBOROUGH

S

GRAVEL WALK

Bandstand

BRISTOL ROAD

NELSON PLACE

MONMOUTH PLACE

NEW KING STREET

QUEEN'S PARADE

QUEEN'S PARADE PLACE

GAY STRE

B

NORFOLK CRESCENT

JAMES STREET

CHARLES STREET

QUEEN SQUARE

OLD KIN STREET

Former Green Park Railway Station

MONMOUTH STREET

Francis Hotel

Theatre Royal

BEAUFORD SQUARE

BARTON STREET

WOOD ST

QUIET STREET

QUEEN STREET

OLD BOND STREET

Beau Nash's House

TRIM STREET

SAWCLOSE

Medieval wall of city

N

C

Royal Mineral Water Hospital

UPPER BOROUGH WALLS

Cross Bath

BATH STREET

WESTGATE STREET

UNION STREET

NORTHUMBERLAND

CHEAP STREET

Ab

Hot Bath

ABBEY CHURCHYARD

STALL STREET

Pump Room

YORK STREET

Ralph Allen's House

Roman Baths

NORTH PARADE PASSAGE

TER

D

SOUTHGATE STREET

ABBEY GATE STREET

ABBEY GREEN

Sally Lunn's House

St Michael's Gate

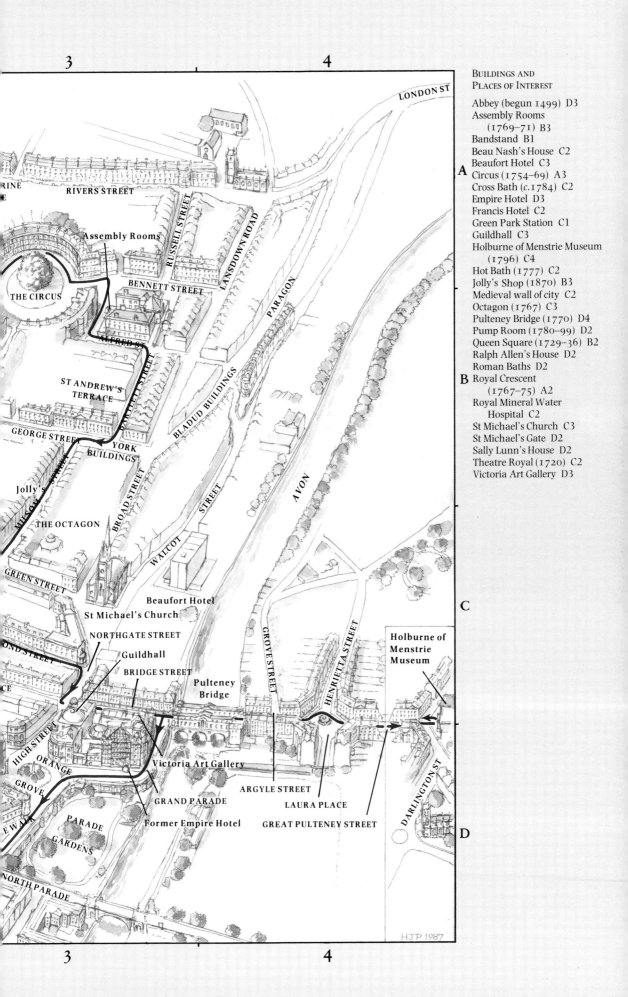

3   **4**

LONDON ST

RIVERS STREET

Assembly Rooms

RUSSELL STREET

LANSDOWN ROAD

THE CIRCUS

BENNETT STREET

PARAGON

ALFRED ST

ST ANDREW'S
TERRACE

BLADUD BUILDINGS

GEORGE STREET

YORK
BUILDINGS

BROAD STREET

AVON

Jolly's

WALCOT STREET

THE OCTAGON

GREEN STREET

Beaufort Hotel

St Michael's Church

GROVE STREET

HENRIETTA STREET

Holburne of
Menstrie
Museum

NORTHGATE STREET

Guildhall

BRIDGE STREET

Pulteney
Bridge

ND STREET

CE

HIGH STREET

Victoria Art Gallery

ORANGE

GROVE

GRAND PARADE

ARGYLE STREET

LAURA PLACE

DARLINGTON ST

E WALK

PARADE
GARDENS

Former Empire Hotel

GREAT PULTENEY STREET

NORTH PARADE

HJP 1987

3   **4**

BUILDINGS AND
PLACES OF INTEREST

Abbey (begun 1499) D3
Assembly Rooms
   (1769–71) B3
Bandstand B1
Beau Nash's House C2
Beaufort Hotel C3
Circus (1754–69) A3
Cross Bath (c.1784) C2
Empire Hotel D3
Francis Hotel C2
Green Park Station C1
Guildhall C3
Holburne of Menstrie Museum
   (1796) C4
Hot Bath (1777) C2
Jolly's Shop (1870) B3
Medieval wall of city C2
Octagon (1767) C3
Pulteney Bridge (1770) D4
Pump Room (1780–99) D2
Queen Square (1729–36) B2
Ralph Allen's House D2
Roman Baths D2
Royal Crescent
   (1767–75) A2
Royal Mineral Water
   Hospital C2
St Michael's Church C3
St Michael's Gate D2
Sally Lunn's House D2
Theatre Royal (1720) C2
Victoria Art Gallery D3

Daniel Defoe once remarked that people went to Bath to commit 'the worst of all murders – to kill time'. That was at the beginning of the 1700s, when Bath was just beginning to be recognized as a spa. It was then a shabby place if supposedly a healthy one, and bore little resemblance to the present-day city. If killing time is still a crime, the mitigating circumstances at Bath now include the sound of a Beethoven trio in the Grand Pump Room, the effect of early morning sun on the unique Pulteney Bridge, and a visit to the Circus. This is not a circus with performing animals – unless you include dogs that lift their legs on five great plane trees that probably should not be there at all – but the greatest monument to the skills of the architects John Wood and his son, who helped to transform Bath into one of the most striking and harmonious cities in Europe.

'Plant a tree in '73' ran a slogan. It referred to 1973, but unfortunately for Bath it seems to have applied to 1873 (or thereabouts) as well, because for all their good intentions the Victorians actually undermined the plans of the great architects and designers who, in the eighteenth century, made Bath what it largely is today. The Woods might turn in their graves if they saw the trees in the middle of the Circus, and Queen Square, and Abbey Green, and elsewhere in the city. But this is to quibble a little. For with or without trees Bath is the sort of place that prompts you to choose a clean shirt and give your hair an extra brush before setting out for a stroll. And stroll you should: Bath is not as hostile towards the car as some cities, but it demands to be seen on foot.

There is ample car parking away from the city centre, but the Royal Victoria Park, on the western side of the city, just north of the A4 Bristol road, is well positioned for an exploration of the best of Bath and has roadside parking. Assuming you use this, turn left out of the Royal Victoria Park into the very handsome Marlborough Buildings and walk uphill. Notice that some of the terraced houses have been cleaned, while others still have their traditional covering of soot. Bath stone is notoriously soft, and thus easy to cut and dress. It can only be effectively cleaned by jets of water on its surface. More drastic treatment renders it pockmarked and badly weathered. There is an age-old argument about whether Bath stone is grey or golden. I would settle for cream, but there are also splashes of yellow and ironstone-orange. Almost every street is harmonious, however, and even the 1930s Post Office building in Northgate Street does not jar too badly.

It is the little details, which vary from one house to another, that help make Bath's best streets what they are. Here in Marlborough Buildings you can glimpse a typical Regency balcony with hanging plants or window boxes, while over there hang a pair of real shutters; here again are two handsome laurel trees, and across the road is a highly polished brass doorbell. John Wood the Younger was responsible for the Royal Crescent. He began the project in 1767 and completed it in 1775, probably inspired by Bernini's colonnade around the Piazza San Pietro in Rome. The massive curve of thirty imposingly tall, terraced houses (among the earliest terraced houses ever designed in Britain) are outwardly divided by 114 great Ionic columns. The Royal Crescent Hotel, exactly in the centre of the Crescent, whispers its presence; the name appears discreetly on two angular flower pots, albeit in gold lettering. Inside, substantial table lamps, flower displays and good silver on damasked dining tables in the lower ground floor restaurant add a touch of elegance.

Do not neglect to leave your calling card at Number 1 Royal Crescent, which is absolutely charming. It is technically a museum, decorated and furnished in painstakingly precise Georgian style by the Bath Preservation Trust, but it is actually much more. Given the right fancy dress you could easily be transported back to the eighteenth century, and be convinced that you are part of Bath society in its heyday. Go right to the top of the house, which most people avoid, to the gallery landing where there is no access to the rooms. The sound of a voice floats upwards: 'No need to climb up there – there's nothing to see!' But looking down is fun and there are some interesting items to see, among them a chair that was made for an Irish giant called Patrick Cotter O'Brian, who was exhibited in Bath in the eighteenth century. He was 8ft 3ins tall. Photography is not allowed. While I was there somebody walked into the dining room and asked if they could take a photograph. The answer was no, and they left without even looking at the beautiful room. People love the fact that some of the food laid out on the formal dining room table is real. ('What time do we eat?' asks a visitor in a deep Southern drawl, and gets a very polite reply. But how many times has the guide heard the joke?)

The lawn in front of the Royal Crescent ('Private, Subscribing Residents Only') is peppered with daisies, while the greenery beyond is peppered with language students. Turn left out of No. 1, Royal Crescent, and walk along Brock Street towards the Circus, but before that detour left into the tempting little pedestrian precinct called Margaret's Buildings. A circuit of Catherine Place, at the end of Margaret's Buildings, would also do no harm, for this square, where copper beeches and other trees crowd the garden in the middle, combines the formality of Bath with the practicality of a London square. Margaret's Buildings has some smart shops, where the needs of the twentieth century are not neglected: a car showroom and a laundrette blend in with a ceramics gallery, an antiquarian bookshop and the obligatory antique shops. Return to Brock Street, which links the Royal Crescent and the Circus, and turn left towards the Circus. The most dominant features of the Circus are the five massive plane trees – each about a hundred years old – which reduce the size of the surrounding terraced houses. The latter really do form a circle, from which three roads, including Brock Street, fan out. The Circus was designed to offer equally balanced views from each of the three streets running into it. Either road is tempting to take (Gay Street goes downhill, towards Queen Square) but our route continues into Bennett Street and towards the Assembly Rooms.

The Circus, a plaque informs us, was conceived by John Wood senior and John Wood junior, and built between 1754 and 1769. Notice that the doors are uniformly white, but that the carvings on the stone frieze between the first and second floors, almost all of which are original, are each unique and display motifs associated with the sciences and the arts. The carved stone acorns at the top probably refer to the Bladud legend. According to this, the restorative properties of Bath's springs were discovered when a ninth-century BC leper, Bladud, a son of King Lud and father of King Lear, cured himself of sores by immersing himself in a warm swamp. His pigs had found it because of the large numbers of acorns in the area. From that moment, it is said, Bath never looked back. The warm springs, whose source is said to be rain-water from the Mendip Hills south-west of Bath, now gush to the surface in the heart of the city at a rate of

100,000 gallons a day. The fact that the water tastes metallic and not particularly pleasant (or as Dickens's Sam Weller put it, 'of warm flat irons') may be one reason why people feel it does them good. Quite recently, there was a period when it was not possible either to bathe or drink the waters on account of there being 'something nasty in the water', but the problem has now been resolved and only the dilapidated condition of the spa itself – development plans are afoot – prevents bathing. The Pump Room water is safe to drink.

If you turn into the forecourt of the Assembly Rooms, now the Museum of Costume, notice how handsome the backs of the houses in this part of the Circus are. The forecourt also boasts seats, a phone, an information panel and tubs of brightly coloured flowers – a civilized rendezvous for families who cannot agree on which part of the city they want to see. Each year, at the Museum of Costume, a 'Dress of the Year' is chosen for contemporary fashion for future display, which keeps the exhibition fresh and interesting, as well as helping the visitor to relate his own experience to the items on show. However, what really makes the museum attractive to me is its setting in the basement of what used to be Bath's Upper Assembly Rooms, which put two original 'lower' Assembly Rooms, closer to the Avon, into the shade. Assembly Rooms epitomized what Beau Nash, uncrowned King of Bath in the first half of the eighteenth century, wanted to achieve – a genteel, civilized, and cosmopolitan venue for society, in which there were dances, gaming tables, and a room in which to take tea. And they are still used for something approaching their original purpose – though antique fairs and civic receptions tend to predominate.

Richard, or 'Beau', Nash was born in Swansea in 1674 and arrived in Bath in 1705, three years after a successful visit by the hugely overweight but health-conscious Queen Anne. Her visit had pointed the city towards a future – prosperous or not, depending on the entrepreneurs – as a health spa. Nash found a shabby provincial town and set about transforming it. By sheer force of personality and remarkable energy he was able to organize the lives of wealthy and influential visitors and local residents, paternalistically laying down rules of etiquette. He was both a roué and a gentleman, and was self-seeking but had a social conscience. He helped to found the Royal Mineral Hospital where treatment for poor people was free, and under a different guise it is still in use today. Nash died in relative poverty, but hundreds of people attended his funeral in 1761, for it was under his influence that the city's great architects and entrepreneurial businessmen flourished.

Turn left out of the Assembly Rooms into Alfred Street, and then right into Bartlett Street, walking downhill. This is antique hunting country. Prices are generally high but not necessarily for the larger items that are less easily transportable by tourists inspired by Bath's antiquity. Notice, a few yards further along Alfred Street from where you turn into Bartlett Street, a pub called the Assembly Inn. Only when you spot it do you realize how scarce pubs are in this part of the city. The traffic sounds coming from Paragon (street) ahead of you will seem very noticeable after quiet enclaves that evoke images of Georgian dandies strolling about in their finery. At the end of Bartlett Street, turn right into George Street and then left into Bath's most famous and historically best recorded shopping street. This is Milsom Street. The city council has kindly placed four more seats here at your disposal. But look to your right as you turn into Milsom Street, towards the western end of George Street, and you will see what, up to the 1960s at least, was one of the very few nationally regarded restaurants outside London, The Hole in the Wall.

This part of George Street makes no particular impact during the day, but at night – especially when it is warm and people spill out onto the pavement from one of the nearby pubs, and two or three of the ubiquitous antique shops are illuminated from within – it takes on a more distinctive character with its walkway high above the road. Try not, anyway, to miss Bath at night. If the city can take first prize in the 'Britain in Bloom' contest for granted, it would do pretty well in any 'Britain by Night' competition. Also, when shadows fall, you might fall for the place if you have found daytime Bath a little too beautiful to be true. The floodlighting strongly reminded me of certain mid-European cities that have avoided redevelopment more by luck than judgement – especially Vienna and Prague. It is a pity, however, that the shops are not open, for they would do very well. Nevertheless, this is certainly the time to read restaurant menus, and to plan your assault on antique shops.

I watched a pair of old ladies toiling up Milsom Street, and the sight made me think of Bath chairs. These resembled modern invalid carriages but were pulled by the nose by attendants who used to position themselves at strategic points in the city even as late as the 1930s. I spoke to a taxi driver who last recalled seeing some at about the time he joined up, soon after war broke out in 1939. Bath chairs were the successors of the sedan chairs that appear almost like part of the street furniture in old engravings of Bath. (There is, incidentally, a well-preserved sedan chair in the museum at No. 1 Royal Crescent.) Jane Austen, who knew Bath well and stayed in several locations in the town, refers to Milsom Street in her books: in *Northanger Abbey* Isabella Thorpe saw the 'prettiest little hat you can imagine' in a shop window, and in *Persuasion* Sir Walter Elliott 'counted eighty-seven women go by without there being a tolerable face among them'. Jane Austen, incidentally, disliked the way in which some Bath stone gleamed white in the sun – an interesting insight into the effect produced by what then must have been comparatively new buildings.

Milsom Street is named after Daniel Milsom, a property developer whose building plots became shops; the most famous shopkeeper of that period was James Jolly (est. 1831), who was primarily a draper.

Jolly's shop front, which dates from about 1870, dominates the street (the back of the shop can be seen from Gay Street). There are quite a few modern fascias here, but these are generally understated and blend in with the Georgian and Victorian buildings. Awnings and flags add colour against the stone, which is mainly grey. Car parking is also permitted. On the left hand side as you walk down the street, roughly opposite Quiet Street, but hidden away, is the Octagon chapel, in which the original accommodation was so comfortable that some pews even had their own fireplaces. It is now the headquarters of the Royal Photographic Society, and also used as the National Centre of Photography.

If you do not mind looking like a tourist, or taking your chances amid the city centre traffic, you can take a horse-drawn carriage ride around the town from the bottom of Milsom Street. A white horse and the hunting pink of the coachman make an impressive combination. As he waits for more customers one coachman tells me about the questions tourists ask him and what their main preoccupations are. He is sympathetic: it is, after all, hard to get to grips with a place like Bath in a short time. It seems that most people think that Beau Nash was Bath's chief architect, that the Roman Baths as we see them today have been in more or less continuous use for nearly two thousand years, and that the Royal Crescent is in the very centre of the city. One of the jaunts he offers takes passengers over Pulteney Bridge and along Great Pulteney Street to the Holburne of Menstrie Museum, which is also part of my suggested route.

Turn left into New Bond Street and then right into Northgate Street, looking briefly back along Northgate Street towards the Beaufort Hotel. Although it now seems to have settled quite peaceably into the Bath scene, this was once a highly controversial and unsympathetic modern instrusion, or so it was claimed. The problem was clearly that Georgian architecture can be aped only to a certain extent, and that modern developers have to find their own style. Roughly opposite the

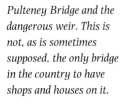

Pulteney Bridge and the dangerous weir. This is not, as is sometimes supposed, the only bridge in the country to have shops and houses on it.

Beaufort Hotel, just behind the post office which was built in the 1930s in Georgian style, is a pub called The Oliver, after the inventor of the Bath Oliver biscuit. As you turn right into Northgate Street, the abbey with its spectacular clerestory windows, is straight ahead. But take the road to the left, where you will see the familiar blue-and-white sign pointing towards the Victoria Street Gallery and the Holburne Museum. Before you turn, however, notice on the right some rather pleasing modern buildings in Upper Borough Walls and, in contrast on the left, a narrow alleyway with the backs of houses towering above it – a rare shabby corner behind the smart façades. A detour is also recommended, taking in the covered market adjacent to the Guildhall, whose Banqueting Room, if it is not being used for a function, is also worth seeing. It has been called the most elegant room in Bath, which is saying something. It is almost as impressive as the remarkable second-hand paperback stall in the covered market.

Bridge Street contains the Victoria Art Gallery and Library. There is a statue of the elderly Victoria over the library. Erected by 'the women of Bath' in 1901, it probably came too late to atone for a real or imaginary slight to the royal personage on Bath's famous Gravel Walk, which I describe later in the route.

The only thing I have against the Pulteney Bridge, which is accessible from the covered market, is that you have to enter the little shops that line it to look down on the River Avon. Otherwise this seems to be a perfectly ordinary (or, for Bath, ordinarily pretty street) rather than one of only two bridges in England with houses built on it. It was designed by Robert Adam in 1770, and it was his only contribution to the Bath scene. His design was inspired by Andrea Palladio, the Italian renaissance architect who was one of the first European architects to show an appreciation of Roman buildings and be influenced by them. Over the bridge Bridge Street gives way to the very stylish Argyle Street. Look to the left and you might spot Northanger Court, recalling Jane Austen's novel that so effectively captures the early nineteenth-century atmosphere of the city. There is a good general store, a grocer's and an impressive Nonconformist church on the same side of the road.

Argyle Street, in turn, opens into Laura Place, with a fountain in the centre, bordered by silver birch trees, which are most unusual in an English city square. The original plan, in 1805, was to erect a Nelson's column to celebrate the victory at Trafalgar, but this was never realized. Ahead is the Holburne Museum, which makes a very good excuse to walk the length of Great Pulteney Street. This is still one of Bath's smartest addresses, and its previous residents have included William Wilberforce, Napoleon III, Louis XVIII, Lord Macaulay, and Jane Austen. The museum, which lies at the end of the street, was actually built as the Sydney Hotel in 1796. Its curious name comes from Sir Thomas William Holburne, whose collection it mainly houses, together with that of his family connections in Menstrie, in Scotland. Among the many items on display are paintings by several English Masters, including Gainsborough, Stubbs and Turner.

If you retrace your steps along Great Pulteney Street, over the bridge and left into Grand Parade, you will see the parapet directly in front of you where people like to lean over and watch the activity on the Avon far below: pleasure boats filling up, canoeists bobbing over the weir, and swimmers risking their lives – this is a notoriously

The Holburne of Menstrie Museum is perhaps the finest building in this part of Bath, which was developed as a result of the Pulteney Bridge's construction.

dangerous stretch of the river. There is also a very good view here of the south side of the Pulteney Bridge. Continue along Grand Parade as far as Orange Grove, which was cleverly renamed by Beau Nash in honour of William of Orange's visit in 1735. However, he made sure that William, later king, contributed generously to Bath both financially and fashionably. The remarkable building on the right as you approach Orange Grove is the Empire Hotel, built in 1901, whose speculative builder announced to the city council after the initial plans had been passed that he was 'taking it for granted that there are no restrictions as to height'. The best thing that can be said in its favour is that it underlines the beauty of most of the rest of the city. The greenery to the left of the Grand Parade, below Orange Grove, is called Parade Gardens and always boosts Bath's prowess in the annual 'Britain In Bloom' contest. But the city has won this so many times that nowadays it is only allowed to enter every other year.

Walk south of Orange Grove into the western end of North Parade. This leads into North Parade Passage, which two hundred years ago used to be known as Lilliput Alley. Free of traffic, and wider than its former name might suggest, it is a good bet that many people who stroll down it are heading for Sally Lunn's House, a teashop that takes its name from a woman who sold cakes here around 1670. At the top of the four-storeyed, bow-windowed building is a detail that most seekers after the buns called 'Sally Lunns' seem to miss. It is the figure of an owl. The connection is thus: owls in attic rooms acted as a defence against small animals that infiltrated the wig frames used to store and protect the elaborate wigs of the time. These were sometimes two feet high, waxed into shape and then worn for weeks at a time.

Just to the north of Sally Lunn's House, though well tucked away and accessible only in office hours, is what remains of Ralph Allen's House. You will reach it if you turn right at the end of North Parade Passage, right into York Street and then right again past a souvenir

An essential stop on most visitors' itineraries, Sally Lunn's House was a cake-shop in the seventeenth century and is now a teashop selling buns called 'Sally Lunns'.

shop. Ralph Allen (1694–1764) could hardly have been cast in a more different mould than Beau Nash. From very humble beginnings he had done well to become the local postmaster. He then worked out a way to simplify the rather makeshift postal system in operation at the time. Again going to the heart of the matter he realized that Bath was about to become a fashionable resort, and it would need public buildings and better housing. He therefore bought a number of stone quarries, and had his own house refaced in this stone, which convinced people of its possibilities. If you walk back towards the end of York Street you can glimpse the folly Allen built on one of Bath's hills to the east. This is Sham Castle, which is merely a façade but is floodlit to great effect on summer evenings.

From Ralph Allen's House turn left and left again down towards Abbey Green, which is a gem, though not improved by the Victorian obsession with tree planting. The big plane tree is all right in itself and shady on a hot day, but nevertheless completely unnecessary, diminishing the pretty houses surrounding it. Look out for a couple of details often missed: the new archway on the far side of Abbey Green, St Michael's Gate, whimsically named after the trademark of the Marks and Spencer store at the southern end of Abbey Green, and in the north-west corner a 'crinoline grill' against a shop front, which, looking like a cow-catcher on a train, prevented the delicate balance of crinoline hoops from being upset and thus upending skirts. The device is fairly easy to date, as crinolines were in fashion in Bath

between 1856 and 1867. As you walk north out of Abbey Green and cross York Street, look to your left, where the tops of Victorian statues that adorn the Roman Baths are visible. The fact that they can be seen from this level indicates how far below the present road surface the Roman Baths were.

The spas that are taken for granted in both western and eastern Europe are a novelty to most English visitors, which may account for the carnival atmosphere in Abbey Churchyard. I joined the throng of summer afternoon visitors to the Roman Baths, queueing at the entrance to the Pump Room in which people were already jostling for tables for afternoon tea. I peered curiously into the Pump Room, and remembered that tours, guided or otherwise, ended up there, whether or not I wanted a plate of Bath buns and a pot of Earl Grey. A few people gazed wistfully at the green waters of the King's Bath as if they would not mind taking a dip there and then. It transpired that they were actually waiting for the fifteen-minute dissertation from one of the liveliest guides (I tagged on just in time) I have heard. A great loss to fourth-form schoolboys somewhere, I thought: I learned more about why, when the Romans bathed here, there was sometimes screaming and cursing (mainly due to inexperienced armpit-pluckers) and why army engineers made the best plumbers (so sophisticated was the system), than I would have done in the best reference library in the city. That it was delivered at breakneck speed did not in the least detract. It is easy to imagine the effect on Roman soldiers of

invigorating hot springs that for a few blissful minutes at least recalled a home base where the living was easy; native troops more used to the British climate had not yet been fully absorbed into the army. There had previously been a Celtic shrine here, to the goddess Sulis, and the Roman invaders incorporated the name into Aquae Sulis, which is how Bath appears on Roman maps. It was the discovery in 1727 of a life-size head from a statue of the Roman goddess Minerva, whose name had been coupled with Sulis in Roman times, that was the first clue to what lay beneath the surface. The baths were used for hundreds of years after the Romans left, but the original structure was obscured – partly because of neglect by the Saxons, who called the place Akemanceaster, or 'sick man's town'. A later name was Hoke Bathum, hence 'Bath'. It must have assumed considerable importance during the tenth century, for the Saxon king Edgar was crowned here in 973. He apparently built a church of which there is now no trace, but a Norman cathedral was built, of which a few stones remain, incorporated into the abbey.

Watching a few gallons' worth of the many thousands that bubble up every day must have had an effect, because the first thing I did on leaving the Roman baths, via the Pump Room, was to disappear into the Crystal Palace pub in Abbey Green. This was not entirely by chance: I had asked for advice about pubs in the Tourist Information Centre, and although they are not officially allowed to favour one pub above another there was some raising of eyebrows and reading between the lines . . . .

After leaving the Pump Room and the Roman Baths, cross Stall Street in a detour towards what, in Nash's day, was perhaps the most important corner of the city. For at the end of Bath Street in Cross Bath or one of two other semi-public baths people took *to* the waters. Bathing went out of fashion in the early nineteenth century, when sea bathing became all the rage, and never really regained popularity. There was a brief flurry of interest when, in the 1880s, the Roman baths were discovered, but even that was temporary. The name Cross Bath refers to an ancient cross that stood beside the spring, and was one of three in the heart of the city. The sites of the original baths are presently undergoing extensive renovation.

Samuel Pepys was not impressed when he visited the Cross Bath at 4 a.m. one day in 1668, in order to avoid the crowds. He underwent the somewhat uncomfortable treatment there but, at the time, going to the bath was really more a matter of enjoying oneself rather than being treated for medical disorders. As Pepys indicated it probably did

*Sculpture on the west front
of Bath Abbey
commemorating a dream of
Bishop King, who began
building the present
structure on the remains of
a Norman church in 1499.
In the dream he saw angels
ascending and descending a
ladder from heaven and
heard a voice say, 'Let a
King restore the church'.*

more harm than good to mix in the same water with so many unwashed bodies. There was also a bizarre custom whereby unlikely objects were thrown into the water by spectators – like astonished piglets and hydrophobic cats. On the left of Bath Street, opposite Cross Bath, are the remains of the Hot Bath, or the old Royal Bath, of 1777, and both of these will be incorporated in extensive restorations to the original spa now going on.

Retrace your steps along Bath Street to Stall Street, turn left and walk uphill towards where Westgate Street and Cheap Street – the latter name an Anglo-Saxon throwback rare in Bath – cross west to east. Walk a little further north, into Union Street, then turn right into Northumberland Place. At first glance Northumberland Place and Union Passage look as if they are part of a purpose-built shopping precinct, but these bustling narrow streets are the genuine article. In a café in Union Passage I sampled a Bath bun (which differs from a Sally Lunn in that it is much smaller, glazed and contains currants and peel, whereas a Sally Lunn is on the sweet side but can be eaten with a savoury topping) and browsed among second-hand jazz records. Elsewhere in the warren of small streets I could have sampled home-made fudge, booked a cheap return flight to Corfu, and had my shoes soled and heeled, which by now began to look like a necessary requirement. If this hectic little commercial corner of Bath did not exist, it might be necessary to invent it as a healthy contrast to the formal terraces and classical lines of the spa years.

Turn left into Upper Borough Walls and walk due west. On the left you will see what used to be the Royal Mineral Water Hospital. Much frequented by sufferers from aches and pains, it is still a treatment centre today. Just a few yards past here, on the right-hand side in Westgate, are some remains of Bath's medieval walls. The castellations, however, are merely a Victorian accoutrement.

Continue westwards along Upper Borough Walls, and into Sawclose. I had expected the Theatre Royal to exude formality and so I was surprised to find it encircled by workaday Bath, with a snack bar across the road, a garage forecourt, and a very lively pub nearby. That pub, the Garrick's Head, occupies with part of the Theatre itself what used to be Beau Nash's house when he was at the height of his success. When times were harder (he died in relative poverty, reduced to selling off trinkets presented to him by the 'great' and 'good') he lived next door, round the corner in Sawclose, in what is now Popjoy's Restaurant. The restaurant is named (roughly!) after his most devoted mistress Juliana Papjoy, and the house, built in 1720, has been restored internally to its original colours.

From Sawclose walk up Barton Street as if towards Queen Square, look briefly into Beauford Square on the left for a fine view of what is now the back of the Theatre Royal, but then turn right along Trim Street, which is all too often overlooked. Named after a prosperous businessman called George Trim, it is cobbled, elegant and quite unspoilt. Turn left under the bridge that neatly closes off Queen Street, and walk up this pretty cobbled street with its small antique shops and cosy candlelit restaurants. From here, turn left into Wood Street, which leads into Queen Square.

In Queen Square, with the Francis Hotel behind you and a tall obelisk ahead, the palatial building that you can see through the trees actually consists of seven separate properties, although it was designed to look like one. The obelisk of 1738 in the middle of the square was erected by Beau Nash in memory of Frederick Prince of Wales, son of George II, who was killed after being struck on the head by a tennis ball – which in those days would have been made of wood covered with flannel. It was repaired in 1977 to celebrate the twenty-fifth year of the Queen's reign and, by happy coincidence, the 250th anniversary of the creation of the square by John Wood the Elder. The great trees in the square are of several varieties, but, as is so often the case in Bath, it is the plane trees that dominate.

The Francis Hotel was rebuilt in the early 1950s on the site of several houses that were bombed in the infamous 'Baedecker' raids of 25 and 26 April 1942, in which 417 people were killed. The south side of Queen Square was one of the worst-hit places in the city. Several buildings here contain solicitors' and accountants' offices, and on the west side of the square is the site where William Oliver lived. He died here in 1764. His great skill was to recognize that most of Bath's visitors were suffering the effects of excessive (and conspicuous) food consumption. He introduced the 'Bath Oliver' biscuit, consisting mainly of water and oatmeal, as the main part of a crash diet, and it made his fortune. In one of Bath's smarter hotels I ordered the cheeseboard after dinner, which came with Bath Olivers. A nice local touch, but rather bland.

The walk actually takes us north, across Queen Square Place and past Queen's Parade (notice how the house at No. 1 Queen's Parade has retained its Georgian lines and how much more elegant it is than the Victorianized houses adjacent). But first, make a detour up Gay Street, noticing on the right Old King Street, where cars are parked. This leads to the rear of Jolly's, the famous shop mentioned earlier, which fronts on to Milsom Street. Notice particularly at No. 41, on the right and on a corner, the celebrated 'powder room', distinctive for its blue-and-white Delft-tiled alcove. This is the only surviving example of a place in which gentleman's wigs were prepared. The house itself was built by John Wood the Elder for himself in 1740.

At the top of Queen's Parade turn right into Queen's Parade Place and left into Gravel Walk, described by Jane Austen in *Northanger Abbey*. It is recorded that Victoria, later Queen, was humiliated here when opening Victoria Park in 1830 as a girl of eleven. A breeze along Gravel Walk caused her skirts to billow out, which was greeted by great ribaldry, and this is said to be the reason she never revisited the city. The event caused her to be nicknamed locally 'bandy legs'. From Gravel Walk there are views of the backs of the houses in Brock Street, and their gardens. Primitive water closets used to lie at the bottom of these gardens, and the custom among ladies was to go out to 'pluck a rose'. Not a far cry from 'powder my nose'! Gravel Walk emerges into the park, from where you can look up to the Royal Crescent, and get a good view of the ha-ha below which cattle used to graze. Behind you is a bandstand on which there are summer Sunday afternoon concerts, and to the left, on the far side of the Royal Crescent, stretches the Royal Victoria Park.

It may seem like heresy, but I recommend a bus ride to round off your visit. In summer a frequent, open-topped, double-decker service provides a gargoyle's eye view of the best of the city, and travelling up and down a couple of the seven hills that Bath, like Rome, was built on, puts the city into topographical perspective. My only regret, however, is that as far as I know it is not possible to 'do' Bath from a sedan chair. Eager entrepreneurs take note!

Looking up Queen Street from Trim Street, which was named after an owner of the land on which the street was developed. The archway is generally known as Trim Bridge.

CAMBRIDGE

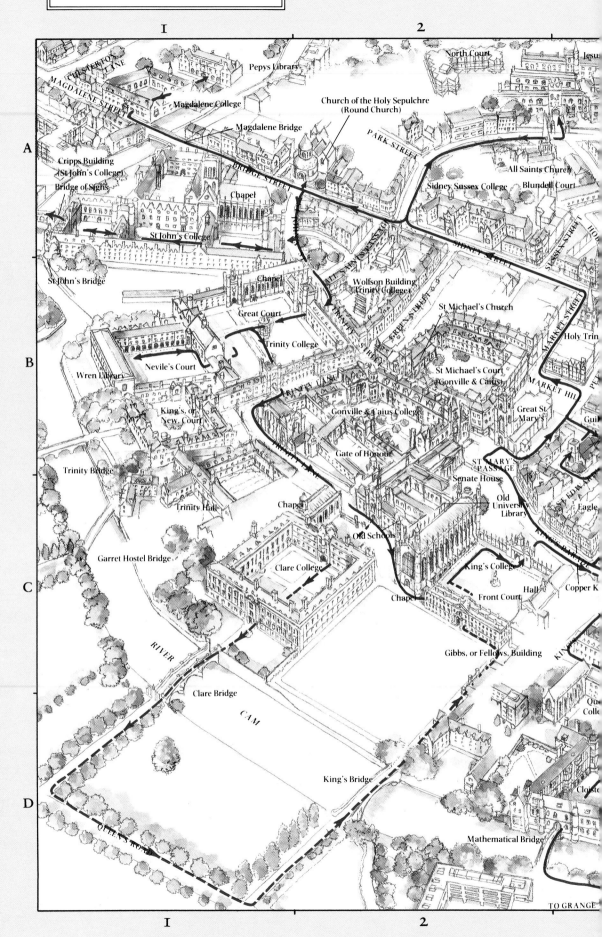

CAMBRIDGE

Chesterton Lane

Magdalene Street

Magdalene College

Pepys Library

Magdalene Bridge

Church of the Holy Sepulchre (Round Church)

PARK STREET

North Court

Jesu

Cripps Building (St John's College)

Bridge of Sighs

Chapel

BRIDGE STREET

Sidney Sussex College

All Saints Church

Blundell Court

St John's College

St John's Bridge

Chapel

Wolfson Building (Trinity College)

St Michael's Church

SIDNEY STREET

SUSSEX STREET

HOB

Great Court

Trinity College

Nevile's Court

Wren Library

King's, or New, Court

Trinity Bridge

Trinity Hall

Garret Hostel Bridge

RIVER

Clare Bridge

CAM

Clare College

Chapel

Old Schools

St Michael's Court (Gonville & Caius)

Gonville & Caius College

Gate of Honour

Senate House

Old University Library

King's College

Front Court

Hall

Copper K

Gibbs, or Fellows, Building

Mathematical Bridge

King's Bridge

QUEEN'S ROAD

TO GRANGE

MARKET STREET

MARKET HILL

Great St Mary's

Holy Trin

Guil

Eagle

St Mary's Passage

Chapel

Que Coll

Cloiste

KING

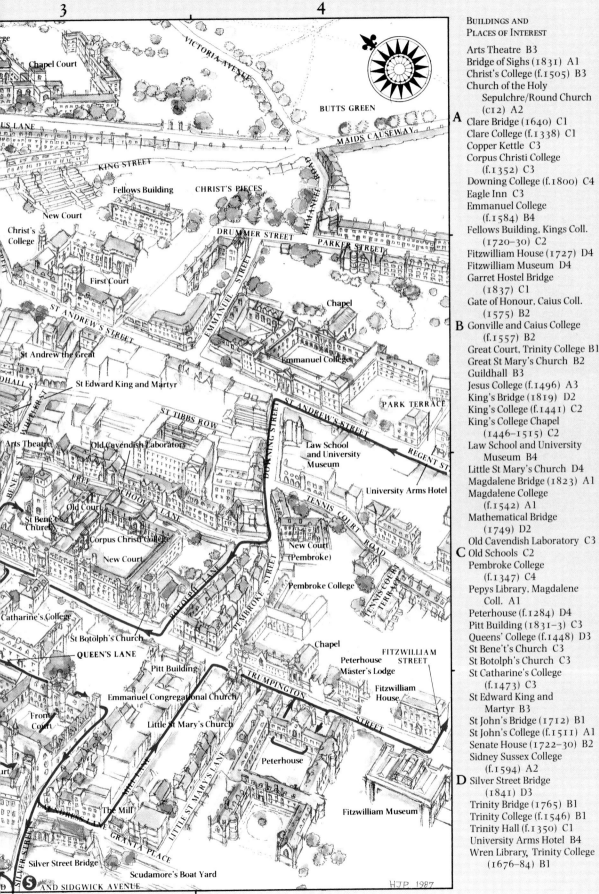

3   4

VICTORIA AVENUE

Chapel Court

BUTTS GREEN

US LANE

MAIDS CAUSEWAY

KING STREET

Fellows Building   CHRIST'S PIECES

New Court

Christ's College

DRUMMER STREET

PARKER STREET

First Court

ST ANDREW'S STREET

Chapel

St Andrew the Great

Emmanuel College

St Edward King and Martyr

PARK TERRACE

ST TIBBS ROW

Arts Theatre

Old Cavendish Laboratory

ST ANDREW'S STREET

Law School and University Museum

REGENT ST

BENE'T ST

FREE SCHOOL LANE

Old Court

University Arms Hotel

St Benet's Church

TENNIS COURT ROAD

Corpus Christi College

New Court

New Court (Pembroke)

Catharine's College

Pembroke College

St Botolph's Church

TENNIS COURT TERRACE

QUEEN'S LANE

Pitt Building

Chapel

FITZWILLIAM STREET

Peterhouse Master's Lodge

Emmanuel Congregational Church

TRUMPINGTON

Fitzwilliam House

Front Court

Little St Mary's Church

STREET

The Mill

Peterhouse

GRANTA PLACE

LITTLE ST MARY'S LANE

Fitzwilliam Museum

SILVER STREET

Silver Street Bridge

Scudamore's Boat Yard

S   AND SIDGWICK AVENUE

HJP 1987

3   4

BUILDINGS AND
PLACES OF INTEREST

Arts Theatre B3
Bridge of Sighs (1831) A1
Christ's College (f.1505) B3
Church of the Holy
    Sepulchre/Round Church
    (c12) A2

A Clare Bridge (1640) C1
Clare College (f.1338) C1
Copper Kettle C3
Corpus Christi College
    (f.1352) C3
Downing College (f.1800) C4
Eagle Inn C3
Emmanuel College
    (f.1584) B4
Fellows Building, Kings Coll.
    (1720–30) C2
Fitzwilliam House (1727) D4
Fitzwilliam Museum D4
Garret Hostel Bridge
    (1837) C1
Gate of Honour, Caius Coll.
    (1575) B2

B Gonville and Caius College
    (f.1557) B2
Great Court, Trinity College B1
Great St Mary's Church B2
Guildhall B3
Jesus College (f.1496) A3
King's Bridge (1819) D2
King's College (f.1441) C2
King's College Chapel
    (1446–1515) C2
Law School and University
    Museum B4
Little St Mary's Church D4
Magdalene Bridge (1823) A1
Magdalene College
    (f.1542) A1
Mathematical Bridge
    (1749) D2
Old Cavendish Laboratory C3

C Old Schools C2
Pembroke College
    (f.1347) C4
Pepys Library, Magdalene
    Coll. A1
Peterhouse (f.1284) D4
Pitt Building (1831–3) C3
Queens' College (f.1448) D3
St Bene't's Church C3
St Botolph's Church C3
St Catharine's College
    (f.1473) C3
St Edward King and
    Martyr B3
St John's Bridge (1712) B1
St John's College (f.1511) A1
Senate House (1722–30) B2
Sidney Sussex College
    (f.1594) A2

D Silver Street Bridge
    (1841) D3
Trinity Bridge (1765) B1
Trinity College (f.1546) B1
Trinity Hall (f.1350) C1
University Arms Hotel B4
Wren Library, Trinity College
    (1676–84) B1

A wind-up gramophone, a picnic hamper, a two-litre bottle of warm German plonk, a couple of willow trees, and a large chunk of the Cambridgeshire sky as viewed from the bottom of a punt – all of this may be accepted in mitigation for a misspent youth. Any Cambridge student who fails final exams and says 'too many afternoon teas in Grantchester' may get, if not a pass, at least a murmur of understanding. So if you are going to waste time try to do it on the Backs at Cambridge. You do not, as a matter of fact, have to be a member of the university to enjoy it, although of course it helps.

Cambridge has been called 'silicon city' because of the recent influx of prosperous electronic industries which has threatened to alter its character and has certainly driven many local people into far-flung housing estates because of the price of city property. But it still has parties of tourists stopping undergraduates on Clare Bridge (the prettiest of all the bridges over the Cam) and vainly asking them to pose in their finery for photographs, not realizing of course that the everyday wearing of gowns has long since disappeared. It still has college porters waiting (and waiting) to be asked that age-old apocryphal question about how they get King's College lawn looking like a billiard table, to which the answer is: 'It's easy madam. You just cut and roll, cut and roll, cut and roll for about three hundred years.'

With good reason traditionalists are particularly concerned about the effect of the internal combustion engine on the city. A vintage open-topped Rolls looks good on a bright summer morning in the forecourt of King's College, but a traffic jam clogging up Trumpington Street outside Pembroke College and Peterhouse and the sound of revving engines penetrating even the dark recesses of Peterhouse's seventeenth-century chapel are less attractive. I suspect that part of the appeal of those eighteenth-century engravings of Cambridge's older colleges is simply the absence of cars.

So I recommend parking well out of the city centre prior to exploring Cambridge, and ideally would choose the west side of the city, which has plentiful and free roadside parking and is yet still very much part of the Cambridge people expect to find, rather than just suburbia. An advantage of parking in Grange Road, Sidgwick Avenue or West Road is that they offer the best, most civilized way into the city and are unspoilt by the detritus of the late twentieth century. Here is a chance to absorb the ambience of tree-shaded, red-brick, late-Victorian and Edwardian avenues that are roughly Cambridge's equivalent of North Oxford. For in both universities the lifting in the late nineteenth century of the regulations that forbade dons to marry created a need for substantial family houses within striking distance of the principal colleges.

Grange Road lies beyond the University Library, which was built in the early 1930s in a style that might have caused Cambridge's earlier architects to spin in their graves. The distinctive tower in which books are stored on twelve storeys is known colloquially as 'the brick pin'. Being here gives the visitor the excuse to see Robinson College, whose stark red-brick exterior belies the huge spread of landscaped gardens behind it. This, the most recent of Cambridge colleges, was endowed by the late Cambridgeshire-born multi-millionaire David Robinson.

Starting from near Robinson College walk towards the junction with Sidgwick Avenue. On the right are the grounds of the Cambridge University Rugby Football Club, and on the left are the buildings and playing fields of King's College School, from which are drawn the boy sopranos of the King's College Chapel choir. On the left is Selwyn College, comparatively isolated among the older colleges, though admittedly brought more into the fold by the existence of Newnham, Robinson and some outlying college buildings. The abolition of the requirement for heads of colleges to be members of the Church of England worried some traditionalists, and Selwyn (after George Selwyn, a bishop of Lichfield) was founded in 1882 with the proviso – still applying today – that its master is in holy orders.

Turn left into Sidgwick Avenue, with Newnham College on your right after you turn. Though the mystique of Newnham, the second of the women's colleges to be built, has somewhat evaporated since most Cambridge colleges have now become accessible to both men and women, it is still the most chic. Its Sidgwick Avenue face does not do justice to the charm of its late-nineteenth-century neo-Dutch, red-brick and white-painted buildings on the more secluded side.

If you are intent on seeing 'the real Cambridge', rather than what is served up for tourists, be in Sidgwick Avenue on a weekday lunchtime during term, when the lecture rooms of the functional 1960s purpose-built Arts and History Faculties disgorge several hundred cyclists, with only a minority on foot. The Sidgwick site is windswept, much of the paint is peeling, and economics seem to have taken precedence over style and imagination. But the once highly controversial History Faculty Library, designed by James Stirling and built between 1964 and 1969, is to my mind worth a detour across the concrete, though it has to be admitted that it has been most closely compared with the rear view of a Manchester warehouse.

At the junction of Sidgwick Avenue and Queen's Road, Silver Street begins. On the right, facing the rather nondescript 1930s Fisher Building, is a clutch of houses, one of which occupies an entertaining niche in Cambridge's more recent history, though it is probably overlooked by ninety-nine visitors out of a hundred. For Newnham Grange, whose twentieth-century neighbour is Darwin College, housing about a hundred graduate students, was the home of Gwen Raverat, grand-daughter of Charles Darwin. She wrote a delightful account of domestic Cambridge life in her book *Period Piece*.

Silver Street Bridge is a popular vantage point for newly arrived visitors who have parked in or around Grange Road or Queen's Road. It also has the advantage of fairly salubrious new underground public

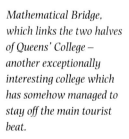

Mathematical Bridge, which links the two halves of Queens' College – another exceptionally interesting college which has somehow managed to stay off the main tourist beat.

lavatories. This is a rather unsung part of the Cambridge scene: an open stretch of river – windswept in winter – a second low bridge under which ducks make the transition from the Upper River to the Cam proper, the Anchor and the Mill pubs, and the less than beautiful Graduate Centre, just beyond which is the modern and attractive Garden House Hotel and Scudamore's Boat Yard. In summer this is a honeypot for would-be punters and in winter it presents a rather haunting picture of moored and upturned punts.

Queens' College is content to reveal only its plainest side to passers-by. However, if you walk through the porter's lodge off Silver Street and cross the Mathematical Bridge over the Cam you will be rewarded by what, for many people, is the prettiest college in Cambridge. After St John's Bridge of Sighs and the elegant Clare Bridge, the Mathematical Bridge is probably the most written about of all the bridges over the Cam. Though for some reason often attributed to Sir Isaac Newton (who was a student at Trinity College) it was actually built in 1749, more than twenty years after Newton died, to an ancient Chinese design. No nails were used – which does sound somewhat like a Newton *tour de force* – and the bridge was rebuilt twice (with nails!).

I walked through Queens' on a winter afternoon during the last few minutes that it was open to the public and when the visitors had retreated to tea and scones in King's Parade. The shadows and the quiet greatly enhanced the atmosphere. The combination of two courts in particular is impressive. Old Court, or Front Court, was built all of a piece in 1446–8, making it the oldest completely original court in the university. Cloister Court, less geometrically formal, complements the older one. To do justice to Queens' College the best route is to walk through Cloister and Old Court and then to leave the college via the original gatehouse, turning right into Queens' Lane and right again into Silver Street.

Walk a few yards in the direction of Silver Street Bridge, but turn left almost immediately down Laundress Lane, behind the Anchor pub; the Mill, the other of the two pubs that dominate this corner of Cambridge, will be directly ahead. Modest Laundress Lane has been in use for hundreds of years, and as the name suggests it is where many Cambridge washerwomen used to congregate, and near where they used to lay out their clean washing to dry on the principal island adjacent to the bridge. The laundrywomen are long gone, and the little passage is now dominated by a cycle repair and hire shop. Opposite that, though seemingly inches rather than feet away, is the Centre for Asian Studies. A sign at the Mill end of Laundress Lane reads 'No Thoroughfare For Carriages or Horses, 24th March, 1857'. Notice the inn sign hanging outside the pub – a rare example of an accurate representation of the scene outside a pub.

It seems in high summer as if all human life is at the Mill, and the practice of taking pints of Tolly Cobbold ale onto the bridge while watching the world go by may perhaps have inspired many a non-punter to chance his arm. Rank beginners are usually spotted by their inclination to spin round and round, and while few actually fall in, the likelihood that one or two will do so, in the space of a long lunch hour, adds extra spice for onlookers. Although a punt is hardly a serious means of transport, it is a half-hearted tourist who does not attempt to grasp the principle of punting. Scudamore's will oblige, though there are queues at the balmiest time when the sun is high over King's College Chapel and shadows are cool under Clare Bridge. Because of

Punts by Silver Street Bridge, with old and new buildings of Queens' College in the background. This is the most popular point on the Cam from which to hire a punt.

the current in the Mill Pool large signs warn against swimming. Cambridge punters stand Venetian-style and pole from a built-in platform in the stern, appropriate when they pass under the Bridge of Sighs at St John's, where one has to duck under the low arch unless travelling dead centre.

From the Mill, walk up Mill Lane past Miller's Yard on the right, a new shop and office development cleverly tucked away, then go past the Mill Lane lecture rooms and turn right into Trumpington Street with Pembroke College diagonally across the road. To the left as you turn is the original Cambridge University Press building, better known as the Pitt Building. It is such a close emulation of a grandiose Perpendicular church that newly arrived undergraduates used to be directed to the 'freshmen's church' as a practical joke. It is called the Pitt Building because it was built from money left over from a massive response to erect a statue to William Pitt, which now stands in the Pembroke College grounds. In 1784 Pitt became Prime Minister at the age of twenty-five, just a couple of years after coming down from Pembroke.

Another claim to fame of this low-profile but most interesting college is that its original mid-fourteenth century court was just 90 × 50ft. Happily for the passer-by the oldest existing, unchanged part of Pembroke is its fourteenth-century entrance arch. The deliberately simple chapel, topped by its hexagonal lantern, is attributed to Wren and was begun in the same year (1663) as his Sheldonian Theatre at Oxford.

Cross again to the west side of Trumpington Street and look out for Little St Mary's Lane, on your right, and Little St Mary's Church, or, more officially, St Mary's the Less. The terraced houses of Little St Mary's Lane – mainly whitewashed brick houses of the eighteenth and nineteenth centuries – are typical ingredients of that Cambridge magic which blends domestic informality with dramatic architecture. Little St Mary's Church was originally St Peter's-without-Trumpington Gate. It was rebuilt in 1340–50. There is a memorial on the north wall to the Rev. Godfrey Washington, a Fellow of Peterhouse (vicar between 1705 and 1729) and a distant relative of Laurence Washington, who lived at Sulgrave, in Northamptonshire. The memorial bears the Washington coat of arms, from which the stars and stripes evolved.

Peterhouse (you do not say 'college'), originally called St Peter's, is handy for the visitor, extremely attractive despite some unsympathetic Victorian renovations, and easy to encompass in just a few minutes. It is the oldest college (1284) and the second smallest after Corpus Christi with 213 students to Corpus Christi's 212. Among its famous figures was the poet Thomas Gray, author of *Elegy, written in a Country Churchyard*, who turned his back on Peterhouse in 1756 and crossed the road to reside in Pembroke, which he could see from his rooms across the road. Being exceptionally afraid of fire, he kept a rope in his room as an escape route (a device still used in certain colleges). A gang of especially rowdy undergraduates pretended the college was on fire, deeply upsetting Gray; he did not use the rope but gave up Peterhouse for good. The iron bar he had installed to take his weight can still be seen. As soon as you pass the porter's lodge there is a feeling of intimacy and harmony, in part due to the chapel arcade, beyond which are high railings. As at Corpus Christi, the students originally used a convenient town church, in this case Little St Mary's Church, but this was abandoned in the 1630s after the consecration of the chapel.

This part of Cambridge is rather sedate, comparatively uncommercialized, and only demands half-closed eyes to see it as it was two or even three hundred years ago. Yet as you leave Peterhouse and Pembroke you might think that the best of Cambridge lies to the north and that you might just as well turn back. All too many people do, which is why Fitzwilliam Street, Downing College and even the impressive Fitzwilliam Museum are comparatively neglected. Unvisited by generations of undergraduates, and ignored by the greater

Looking into Peterhouse from Trumpington Street. James Mason, the film star, studied here, achieving success in undergraduate theatre and also obtaining a First.

mass of the townspeople, the Fitzwilliam Museum hides an astonishing world of beauty behind its stern neo-classical façade. Founded in 1816, it is one of the oldest public museums in Britain. It is particularly remarkable for its Rembrandt etchings, its medieval illuminated manuscripts, its paintings of the English School and its Greek and Roman antiquities.

From here cross the road to Fitzwilliam Street, whose tightly knit, early nineteenth-century houses are particularly easy on the eye. Several of them are occupied by undergraduates and graduate students. At the end of Fitzwilliam Street cross Tennis Court Road for the westerly entrance to Downing College. You have to fiddle your way through functional iron gates, and from this angle the college could not be more unprepossessing. Just far enough away from the core of the university to seem almost rural, it is in fact deliberately in campus style and is said to have been the inspiration of the University of Virginia, whose plan it preceded by about ten years. Some Cambridge colleges, though quite beautiful, can sometimes seem claustrophobic, especially those smaller courts that get little sun. Downing's spacious grounds, however, are set off by its neo-classical buildings. No fewer than 213 years elapsed between the creation of Sidney Sussex (1594), the last of a spate of fifteenth- and sixteenth-century colleges, and Downing, the next Cambridge college to be built. Pleasant though it is, Downing is only a shadow of what it was originally intended to be. Earlier plans for the college were put on ice for almost fifty years, and the final go-ahead coincided with a turn-of-the-century vogue in Greek architecture.

As you reach the college's main gate in Regent Street, turn left. The University Arms Hotel and the inviting entrance to Parker's Piece are then across the road. The hotel's restaurant looks out on to Parker's Piece and its acres of greenery – it is exactly a mile all the way round – much used by schoolboy cricketers and townspeople walking their dogs. An advantage of a walk through Downing is that it makes the

Downing College was designed campus-style, breaking away from the tightly enclosed courtyard tradition. It lies roughly between the Fitzwilliam Museum and Parker's Piece.

transition from 'gown' to 'town' more harmoniously than any other college: Emmanuel College, for example, is wholly in the commercial part of the city, Christ's, Magdalene and Jesus are on the edge of it, and the much-vaunted gardens of Sidney Sussex are surrounded by the more or less continual buzz of traffic.

And so to St Andrew's Street, with its supermarkets, cinemas, Indian and Chinese restaurants. Emmanuel, the next college on the route, is not one of the colleges with a high public profile, but it is worth a stop, especially as it is hard to miss, situated as it is exactly where Downing Street leaves St Andrew's Street at right angles. Known colloquially as 'Emma', the college was founded in 1584 to prepare men for the Protestant ministry. Because of early seventeenth-century intolerance towards the Puritans, many Emmanuel men were among the New England settlers. One of these was John Harvard, who graduated in 1632.

Downing Street is dull, lined by giant, functional university buildings, which were mostly built in the late nineteenth century for the science and engineering departments. It is also likely to have a queue of cars waiting to get into the Lion Yard car park. But it leads down a very slight gradient into the much more charming Pembroke Street, past the northern end of Tennis Court Road. Pembroke Street curves just enough to make it interesting and it is full of intrigue after dark. The street lights seem softer, shadows kinder. But day or night, do not walk its whole length. Instead, fork right into Free School Lane and then sharp left into Botolph Lane, which runs towards Trumpington Street parallel with the lower half of Pembroke Street.

St Botolph's Church is on your right as you walk down Botolph Lane – known to students at Pembroke, St Catharine's, and Corpus Christi, among others, as 'Botolph's Crack'. Opposite the church and on the corner of Silver Street are four shops that could not be more appropriate to the Cambridge scene if they tried: a formal robe makers (and hirer of gowns for ceremonial occasions), a wine merchant, a cycle shop and a luxury delicatessen. At the end of Botolph Lane, turn right. Adjacent to the shops and set well back from the road, St Catharine's shares the distinction with Sidney Sussex and one of the Gonville and Caius (pronounced keys) courts of being open to the street. This allows even normally energetic visitors to tick it off their list without finding their way through the porter's lodge and into the main court. It was not always orientated towards Trumpington Street, and the original plan was for the gate (only occasionally open) on Queens' Lane to be the main one. The rather sombre, dark brick Jacobean buildings were largely designed by Robert Grumbold in 1674. There is, incidentally, a memorial to him in St Botolph's.

Notice, between St Catharine's and King's College, King's Lane, which stands roughly on the site of perhaps the best-known livery stable in England, though long since disappeared. This is where a wealthy entrepreneur and carrier called Thomas Hobson used to offer only what in his opinion was the most rested horse for hire, horses being used as casually as buses or taxis are today. He would brook no argument, hence the phrase 'Hobson's Choice'.

Corpus Christi, opposite, is far from being the oldest college, appearing seventh in the league table of antiquity (if one includes colleges that were later absorbed by other colleges, such as two that were swallowed up by Trinity). But its Old Court is a remarkable if not completely original survivor from about 1300 – the best preserved

LEFT *The chapel of Corpus Christi College, overlooking New Court. The second smallest college after Peterhouse, Corpus Christi is one of a clutch of colleges on the south side of Cambridge, effectively separated from those in the north by King's.*

BELOW *Residential King's College buildings close to the river, on the opposite side of the lawn from King's College Chapel.*

medieval court in Oxford or Cambridge – though, to my mind, it is forbidding and strangely unattractive, for the grey brown 'Cambridge clunch' is not one of England's most lovely building materials. In one respect Corpus Christi (generally known as 'Corpus') was unique: there was originally no chapel, and the students made their religious observance at St Bene't's (short for St Benedict's) Church, which even now is readily accessible via a lane leading from the Old Court.

It might be assumed that King's College would dominate King's Parade to the exclusion of all else, but this famous street is surprisingly harmonious and its piecemeal development has worked far better than any town planner might have guessed. Stand on the corner of the nineteenth-century Gothic National Westminster Bank to take in King's Parade from its southerly end, but then detour up Benet Street just a matter of yards in order to see St Bene't's Church and, opposite on your left, the unique Eagle pub and Eagle Yard. The striking pub sign depicts an eagle in flight – another example of Cambridge's better-than-average pub signs. The gallery that runs the length of the main part of the pub dates from about 1820, a rare survivor of the galleries that were used instead of internal passages when space was limited. (The George, in London's Southwark, is comparable.) St Bene't's Church wears its great antiquity modestly, but it is worth remembering that its tower was standing long before William the Conqueror came to the conclusion that King Harold was an upstart. Inside, the church is much more spacious than it seems from the street. It was *re*built in the 1300s.

Return to King's Parade and turn right. Remaining, for the moment on the right-hand, easterly side of the road allows both a better perspective on King's College and, beyond it, the Old Schools and the

Gonville and Caius College and its tower, with Great Court, Trinity, behind and St John's Chapel beyond – seen from Great St Mary's Church. The undergraduate rooms in the tower, looking down King's Parade, afford some of the best views in Cambridge.

Senate House. You can also browse in any one of three bookshops and pop into the Copper Kettle for a snack. One of the Copper Kettle's claims to fame is its traditional willingness to put up undergraduate posters ('Much Ado in Punk Dress', 'Milton's *Comus* performed for the first time since 1931', etc.). As the later stage of the walk actually takes us through King's and a couple of adjacent back streets and tucked-away colleges, stay on the east side of King's Parade. If the neo-Gothic screen dividing the college from the street (which has been much improved by recent cleaning) looks intricate and spiky, consider the effect it has had over the years on the night climbers of Cambridge. Though they have been fairly quiet during the last few years, the stunts of Cambridge's night climbers occasionally put the pinnacles of King's College Chapel on the front pages of not just the Cambridge Evening News but the national newspapers too. The most spectacular climb in recent memory was the hoisting of the celebrated 'Peace in Vietnam' banner, which bridged the 50ft gap between the two pinnacles.

None of King's Parade's individual shops and houses are remarkable in their own right, but they make a perfect foil for King's, the adjacent Old Schools – the oldest heart of the university proper – and the Senate House, which is the venue for degree ceremonies and other formal occasions. Behind and to the side of the Senate House is one of the most distinctive college towers in Cambridge, which arises from

the south front of Tree Court at Gonville and Caius (generally known as Caius). Lucky the undergraduates with one of the rooms that enjoy a bird's eye view of King's Parade.

In such a tightly knit line of half-timbering, stucco and red brick, to come upon a miniature traffic-free boulevard, adjacent to Great St Mary's Church, is a surprise. Yet it repeats one of Cambridge's recurring themes: the cheek-by-jowl development of several centuries, usually very harmonious, relieved by half unexpected open spaces that seem almost wasteful. At certain times the tower of Great St Mary's is accessible, and it offers the best panoramic views of the university and the Backs.

The Senate House end of King's Parade makes a contrast with the hustle and bustle of the six-day-a-week market ahead of you. But, before plunging into that, should it appeal, turn right, parallel again with King's Parade and right again as far as the bijou Church of St Edward King and Martyr and into St Edward's Passage, which forks round it. It is a shame to miss this peaceful little backwater, with its second-hand bookshops and St Edward's Church, which so few people seem to know but which has such poignant memories of three English martyrs who preached there at the time of the Reformation. Thomas Bilney, Robert Barnes and Hugh Latimer were burnt at the stake in 1531, 1540 and 1555 respectively. An extra bonus is the Arts Theatre self-service buffet, reached via steep flights of stairs at the side of the Arts Theatre. It is not quite a club, not quite a café, but much more than a coffee bar. At a lower level is the Arts Theatre restaurant, where many a visiting dignitary has been entertained by the committees of college societies.

Cambridge market place has been much altered over the years but it was a favourite subject among early engravers, and you have a good chance of picking up a print of it. Although buildings have come and gone, in most of the prints there is still the unmistakable outline of Henry VI's King's College Chapel rising up to the left of Great St Mary's Church. The south-east corner of the market place leads to a modern shopping centre; better to walk east along Market Street, and thence left into Sidney Street.

The only porter who smiled as I strolled through a college's main gate was the one at Sidney Sussex, on a quiet afternoon out of term time – perhaps he was pleased that the college had a visitor. Founded in 1594, the college was built on the site of a thirteenth-century friary that had been dissolved in 1538, and on Henry VIII's instructions part of the friary's fabric was re-used on the building of Trinity College. The friendly porter presides in a lodge between two separate courts on Sidney Street, and there is much that meets the eye, especially the pleasant gardens. Easily the most famous member is Oliver Cromwell, which is ironic in view of the fact that the college was largely pro-monarchy during the Civil War of 1642–7, even though its sympathies prior to the war had been Puritan. One result was the eviction of its Master and Fellows, and Oliver Cromwell did not intercede on behalf of his old college. The college has retained three portraits of him, including the famous 'warts and all' picture.

If Sidney has only a small claim to fame among the colleges, at least in comparison with half a dozen 'musts', and therefore receives scant attention, Jesus does not deserve its comparative obscurity, though it probably enjoys it. To see Jesus, turn right into Jesus Lane, noticing after you turn the Pitt Club on your left, and then, tucked slightly away down a road off to the left, the unprepossessing façade of the university theatre. Jesus has benefitted from its location. It has had room to breathe and expand, and has a rich variety of architecture. The chapel, of medieval origin but heavily restored by Pugin in 1846–9, is perhaps the best example of Victorian Gothic in Cambridge, with windows by Burne-Jones and a ceiling by William Morris. Yet Jesus may be best known for the crocuses in its Fellows' Garden. These are so celebrated that the door to Jesus Lane is traditionally left ajar in spring so passers-by can peep in.

Return to Sidney Street, and do not miss the Round Church at the end of the street on your right. This is the last remaining Norman round church in England and also the oldest, dating from about 1130. Only part of it is actually round – happily the part that is seen from the main road. Opposite – in dramatic contrast – are the late-Victorian chapel of St John's College and, just beyond that, a 1930s residential wing of the college, of which the less said the better.

Do not dwell too closely on what you see of St John's at this juncture – it does get better (although it has to be admitted that St John's is regarded as an architecturally rather sombre and severe college) – but continue along Bridge Street to Magdalene Bridge and Magdalene College. Magdalene Bridge has a functional air about it, and its surroundings had been somewhat ravaged by development when I walked across it, but the bridge, or rather bridges on that site, have

The Bridge of Sighs over the Cam links the nineteenth-century New Court of St John's College with its older buildings (on the right). Closed to the public for a number of years, the bridge is now open again.

played an important part in Cambridge's history. Quays and warehouses once extended here for a couple of hundred yards, and the roadway to the south of the bridge is still called Quayside.

Try to see Magdalene when the sun shines, for the effect of it on the red brick of the First Court and on the colours of the coats of arms above staircase doors is magical. This is the only one of the older foundations across the river. Samuel Pepys was one of many outstanding former students. He bequeathed his great library to the college, containing his diary written in his own version of shorthand. Beyond the Pepys Library is the garden, but new flats on the other side of the river detract from any sense of seclusion.

Cross Magdalene Street with care – though it is actually doubtful whether it is busier or noisier than in Pepys's time – and you will find yourself at the entrance to a spacious arrangement of more recent Magdalene buildings, through which one can reach the newest and much praised part of neighbouring St John's College. Most prominent here is the 1960s Cripps Building, whose size gives a clue to the scale of the college. It has 550 students (compared with Corpus Christi's 212). To reach St John's, however, it is best to retrace your steps over Magdalene Bridge and down Bridge Street, then turn right into St John's Street, which continues into Trinity Street. Just past the imposing chapel turn right into the college by the main gate. The gatehouse is generally reckoned to be Cambridge's best. Like Christ's, St John's was founded by Margaret Beaufort, mother of Henry VII, and her coat of arms is in position over the main door. Both the arms and the door are original. (Almost directly opposite St John's is All Saints' Passage, actually a two-pronged affair, the prong on each side of a triangular green with trees leading to the main stem that joins Sidney Street at right angles.)

St John's is the second largest college in the university after Trinity and is full of variety. With a degree of monastic calm, even on a workaday morning, it manages to overcome the demoralizing effect of the Victorian chapel that is so much at odds with the rest of the college. Though even that has the status of a Cambridge landmark and its choir is very highly regarded. If you walk through two courts you will come to the Bridge of Sighs. For some years this was closed to the public, but it may be that the college grew tired of glum groups of tourists denied access to such a famous landmark. Over the bridge lie New Court (new that is in the 1830s), which you reach via a rather dark and echoing arrangement of corridors and via cloisters overlooking the most placid and spacious part of the Backs, and beyond that the modern buildings.

Retrace your steps again, and from one impressive gatehouse turn right through another – this time Trinity's, whose entrance yard offers a bit of space to offset the extreme narrowness of Trinity Street, along which Cambridge's blue double-deckers trundle within inches of ancient gables with never a scratch. Notice, by the way, the somewhat weather-beaten statue of Henry VIII, who effectively founded Trinity by amalgamating two existing colleges in 1546; he is holding a chair leg instead of a sceptre. What began as an undergraduate joke is now a part of Cambridge tradition. Even more bizarre, the king is wearing a crown on top of his hat!

Trinity is less self-consciously grand than King's, but also secure in the knowledge that its Great Court is perhaps the most impressive of its kind in the world. Great Court is a far cry from the quiet backwaters of some of the colleges. The gatehouse and the porter's lodge are

BELOW LEFT Christ's College gateway, sporting Margaret Beaufort's coat of arms. Famous in recent years for its history scholars and its rugby prowess, the college has to contend with the proximity of chain stores and heavy traffic.

probably the busiest in Cambridge, but I have noticed that visitors bustle through and seem to slow down to a sedate pace, perhaps overawed by the scale of their surroundings. Trinity is often compared with Oxford's Christ Church, and it is worth noting that in creating it Henry VIII probably aimed to outdo the discredited Cardinal Wolsey, who founded Christ Church.

It is a tourist board cliché that overseas visitors ask 'Where is the university?' I know of one former undergraduate who used to point to Trinity. Historically and architecturally it will probably do as well as any, especially if the visitors make their way across the court, admiring the fountain as they go, and walk up the steps to the hall, in order to reach Nevile's Court and the Wren Library. I say 'walk': to scale the steps in one leap is a traditional challenge for athletes. The fountain, by the way, is supplied by water from a mile away, via an underground conduit built in 1325, and this is supplemented by a well. Wren had originally wanted his library to be circular – thus anticipating Oxford's Radcliffe Camera – but it quickly found favour as it stands. The library is very skilfully designed, for though huge it does not overpower the buildings adjacent to it.

The whole scene at this point – the river by the Wren Library as it curves slightly before touching on St John's, the library itself, the self-confident if rather elongated New Court of St John's, and the apparent calmness, in any weather conditions, of the Backs here (less intimate

BELOW *Great Court, Trinity College – the largest court and the largest college in both Cambridge and Oxford. Rooms here are highly sought after.*

and more formal than further upstream) – is all so impressive that anything else is likely to be an anti-climax. For nothing like this exists in Oxford, and there is not much to compete with it in the whole of Europe. It has long been admired, though it was not always salubrious. In fact there used to be a constant sewage problem along this stretch of the river. It is recorded that when Queen Victoria visited Trinity in the company of one master, Dr Whewell, she asked about the pieces of paper floating down the river, to which he replied, being able to think on his feet, 'Ma'am, those are notices people have torn down warning that bathing is prohibited.'

Walk back through Nevile's Court from the library, open to the public for a token charge and very good too, and leave Trinity by turning right into Trinity Lane. Within a few yards you are outside the main gate of Trinity Hall, an exquisite, rather tucked-away college, always rather fashionable, with a reputation for turning out urbane lawyers and good English literature graduates. It butts onto the river, with a pretty and little-known terrace.

There is nothing tucked-away about King's College, which you get to by walking south past the gates of imposing and rather formal-looking Clare College and then, if the gates are open, by slipping into the north side of King's. If that north gate is closed, as it often is, you have a ready-made excuse to walk through Clare, over Clare Bridge, through wrought-iron gates that must be the most photographed in the east of England, and, if you have the energy, all the way round via

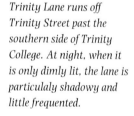

Trinity Lane runs off Trinity Street past the southern side of Trinity College. At night, when it is only dimly lit, the lane is particulaly shadowy and little frequented.

ABOVE *Clare Bridge, looking away from the college. The River Cam is at its shallowest here and the bottom is composed mainly of gravel, making it the easiest place for punting.*

Queen's Road and then left onto a west-east footpath, which in turn leads back towards King's. One reason for making this detour is for the sake of your camera, because the view from the Queen's Road end of the footpath is a calendar classic: the west front of King's College Chapel (with or without scaffolding), the huge Fellows Building to its right as you look, and, on the left, part of the residential eighteenth-century buildings of Clare.

The chapel was built of limestone mostly brought to Cambridge by river from quarries owned by the college in Yorkshire. The construction began in 1446, by 1515 the roof was on and during the next fifteen years Flemish glaziers added the windows. And then in 1535 Henry VIII made a gift to the college of the choir stalls and the elaborately carved screen. For all its black-and-white severity the Fellows Building by James Gibbs is able to hold its own with the chapel, but few visitors seem to enter it and the neon lights which illuminate the interior are much less appealing than the softer glow of distantly seen desk lamps in garrets and senior common rooms of really ancient college buildings. Leave by the main gate and turn right into King's Parade.

Roughly opposite the National Westminster Bank turn right into King's Lane and follow this to its end, turning left into – appropriately enough – Queens' Lane. On the right is the old gate to Queens' college, and directly ahead Silver Street and thus, beyond the river, Grange Road. Or you could walk just a few yards to the corner of Trumpington Street and Pembroke Street and buy a dozen of those crumpets from Fitzbillies tea shop without which no afternoon tea in college is complete. They may not taste quite as good as they do in rooms overlooking Great Court, Trinity, but they do convey nostalgia. Perhaps, on reflection, the best Cambridge souvenir would be a postcard of the Backs with butter stains on it.

CANTERBURY

CANTERBURY

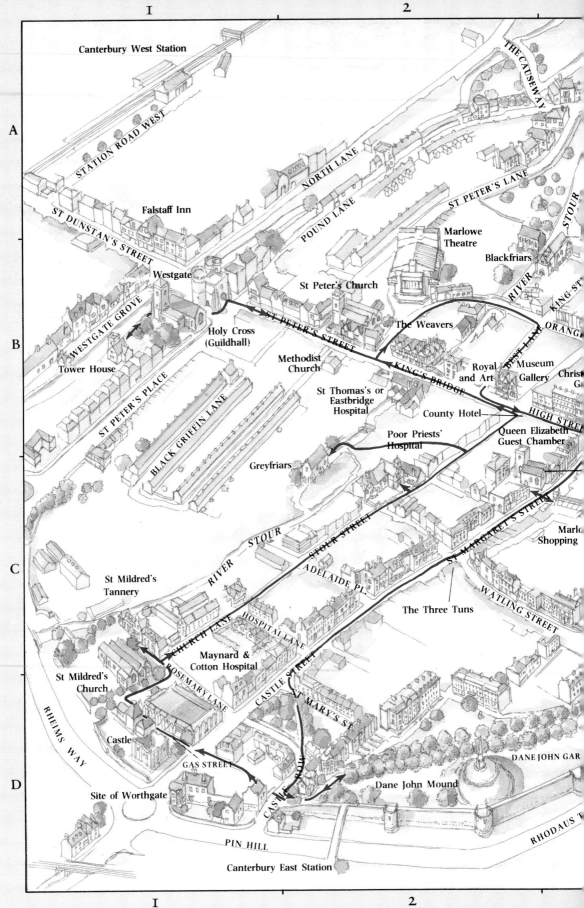

Canterbury West Station

STATION ROAD WEST

ST DUNSTAN'S STREET

Falstaff Inn

Westgate

WESTGATE GROVE

Tower House

Holy Cross (Guildhall)

ST PETER'S PLACE

BLACK GRIFFIN LANE

Methodist Church

St Peter's Street

ST PETER'S STREET

St Peter's Church

NORTH LANE

POUND LANE

ST PETER'S LANE

Marlowe Theatre

Blackfriars

The Weavers

RIVER STOUR

KING ST

ORANGE

BEST LANE

KING'S BRIDGE

Royal Museum and Art Gallery

Christ G

St Thomas's or Eastbridge Hospital

County Hotel

HIGH STREET

Poor Priests' Hospital

Greyfriars

Queen Elizabeth Guest Chamber

St Mildred's Tannery

RIVER STOUR

STOUR STREET

ADELAIDE PL.

CHURCH LANE

HOSPITAL LANE

Maynard & Cotton Hospital

St Mildred's Church

ROSEMARY LANE

The Three Tuns

ST MARGARET'S STREET

WATLING STREET

Marlo Shopping

RHEIMS WAY

Castle

GAS STREET

CASTLE STREET

CASTLE ROW

ST MARY'S ST

Site of Worthgate

PIN HILL

Canterbury East Station

Dane John Mound

DANE JOHN GAR

RHODAUS T

THE CAUSEWAY

A

B

C

D

1

2

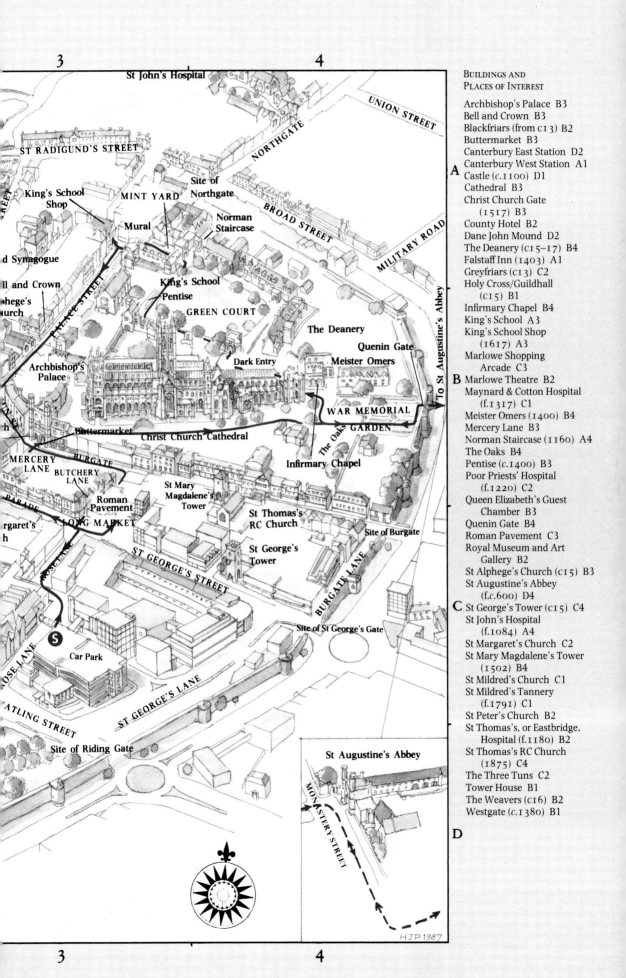

St John's Hospital

UNION STREET

NORTHGATE

ST RADIGUND'S STREET

Site of
Northgate

BROAD STREET

King's School
Shop

MINT YARD

MILITARY ROAD

Mural

Norman
Staircase

d Synagogue

King's School
Pentise

GREEN COURT

The Deanery

ll and Crown
hege's
urch

Quenin Gate

Meister Omers

Archbishop's
Palace

Dark Entry

To St Augustine's Abbey

h

WAR MEMORIAL
GARDEN

Buttermarket

Christ Church Cathedral

The Oaks

MERCERY
LANE

BURGATE

Infirmary Chapel

BUTCHERY
LANE

Roman
Pavement

St Mary
Magdalene's
Tower

St Thomas's
RC Church

rgaret's
h

PARADE

LONG MARKET

St George's
Tower

Site of Burgate

BURGATE LANE

ST GEORGE'S STREET

Site of St George's Gate

ROSE LANE

S

Car Park

ST GEORGE'S LANE

ATLING STREET

ROSE LANE

Site of Riding Gate

St Augustine's Abbey

MONASTERY STREET

HJP 1987

BUILDINGS AND
PLACES OF INTEREST

Archbishop's Palace B3
Bell and Crown B3
Blackfriars (from c13) B2
Buttermarket B3
Canterbury East Station D2
Canterbury West Station A1
Castle (c.1100) D1
Cathedral B3
Christ Church Gate
    (1517) B3
County Hotel B2
Dane John Mound D2
The Deanery (c15–17) B4
Falstaff Inn (1403) A1
Greyfriars (c13) C2
Holy Cross/Guildhall
    (c15) B1
Infirmary Chapel B4
King's School A3
King's School Shop
    (1617) A3
Marlowe Shopping
    Arcade C3
Marlowe Theatre B2
Maynard & Cotton Hospital
    (f.1317) C1
Meister Omers (1400) B4
Mercery Lane B3
Norman Staircase (1160) A4
The Oaks B4
Pentise (c.1400) B3
Poor Priests' Hospital
    (f.1220) C2
Queen Elizabeth's Guest
    Chamber B3
Quenin Gate B4
Roman Pavement C3
Royal Museum and Art
    Gallery B2
St Alphege's Church (c15) B3
St Augustine's Abbey
    (f.c.600) D4
St George's Tower (c15) C4
St John's Hospital
    (f.1084) A4
St Margaret's Church C2
St Mary Magdalene's Tower
    (1502) B4
St Mildred's Church C1
St Mildred's Tannery
    (f.1791) C1
St Peter's Church B2
St Thomas's, or Eastbridge,
    Hospital (f.1180) B2
St Thomas's RC Church
    (1875) C4
The Three Tuns C2
Tower House B1
The Weavers (c16) B2
Westgate (c.1380) B1

A

B

C

D

PAGES 46–7 *The copper gilt effigy of Prince Edward, the Black Prince (1330–76), wearing full armour, in the Trinity Chapel in the cathedral.*

My most telling moment in Canterbury Cathedral came as I paused below the flight of worn steps from the south choir aisle leading up to the Trinity Chapel that was once the shrine to Thomas Becket. I had been on my feet for many hours. Every other yard of this marvellously historic city had stopped me in my stride: here a dramatically contorted Roman pavement, there a wine-cellar-cool medieval hospice, here an ornate banqueting room where Elizabeth I is said – almost certainly wrongly – to have entertained a visiting dignitary, there a low-ceilinged inn mentioned by Charles Dickens. A dapper white-bearded guide was explaining to his charges as I passed that 'real pilgrims making their way to the tomb of Thomas Becket, murdered for his opposition to the crown by Henry II in 1170, would have ascended these steps on their knees.' One or two people self-consciously rubbed their legs. At such moments the drama of this huge and intricate church comes home. Some English cathedrals seem merely decorative, but Canterbury Cathedral is so rich in superlatives and so overpowering that, along with the cathedral precinct and the adjacent buildings of the King's School, most of them originally monastic, it has become a small, rather otherworldly city in its own right.

For all its privations, it is said that the medieval world was rich in colour. I was reminded of this while sitting in the Buttermarket in the midst of an uninhibited, multi-coloured polyglot crowd of pilgrims predominantly from France and northern Europe. Once through Christ Church Gate – by far the best approach to the cathedral – they seemed slightly more subdued. By the time most of them had snaked towards the Convent Garden (a reminder of how London's Covent Garden got its name) they seemed quite awe-struck.

That afternoon, for the first time in England, I dusted off my schoolboy French after being accosted first by a party of teenagers, who appeared to be from Caen – appropriately as it turned out – and whose English was worse than my French, and then by a couple who probably spoke good English but seemed shy about using it. It brought home how close France once must have seemed to England, and in contrast how alien and inhospitable the north of England must have seemed when the cathedral was built and when the Becket pilgrimages were at their height in the thirteenth and fourteenth centuries. But I heard North Country accents, from a family who were obviously on a detour *en route* for the ferry at Dover. For Canterbury is essential visiting. Seldom is so much encapsulated in such a small city, and it is no exaggeration to say that there can be no proper understanding of English history without a visit here.

Canterbury is fairly well endowed with car parks. One of the most central is the Watling Street car park, close to the Marlowe Shopping Arcade, and there is a convenient multi-storey car park across the road too. Follow Rose Lane (passing the Marlowe Arcade on your left) towards Longmarket, a central traffic-free piazza. Just a few yards from here, though well hidden from view behind a baker's shop and rather overlooked, is the Roman Pavement. It is not surprising if this is only visited by a small proportion of Canterbury's pilgrims. Its entrance is, to say the least, discreet, and could at first glance be a public lavatory. Downstairs you are in a dark, different world, and for the price of a newspaper can commune with the ghosts of Roman settlers. Notice especially how far below the present level of the road – about 8ft – it is. The pavement was probably part of the floor of one of the rooms of a courtyard building dating from about AD 100. That it is warped and misshapen has nothing to do with some Roman version of crazy golf, but is due to the way the earth settled during the course of two thousand years. Astonishingly the mosaics retain some vestiges of their early colouring. These Roman remains were discovered in 1945 during cleaning and rebuilding after the wartime bombing of Canterbury.

Emerge into the daylight, cross Parade and turn left into St Margaret's Street, going down a slight incline. Nothing historic here, you might think, especially if you turn into the modern and attractive Marlowe Arcade (opened in 1985), though St Margaret's Church, roughly opposite the Marlowe Arcade, has one of the best brasses in Canterbury, to a fifteenth-century mayor called John Wynter. The church is to become the setting for 'The Thomas Becket Pilgrimage of Chaucerian England', an audio-visual reconstruction of Chaucer's *Canterbury Tales* on similar lines to York's Jorvik Viking Centre. Turn right at The Three Tuns pub then immediately left into Castle Street. This is like a little Canterbury suburb in its own right, with guesthouses, cafés and greengrocers. A conspiratorial knot of King's School boys were sitting around a formica table in a café; the university, being on a hill beyond the city's ancient Westgate, does not seem to impinge on the city, but the pupils of King's School – one of England's oldest public schools – are very evident in term time. When you reach St Mary's Street on the left, turn into the small tree-shaded park and follow the path that crosses this diagonally. It is attractive because the houses on all sides are on a human scale. Nothing dominates, though a pub beckons, and your eye might also be attracted by the terrace, on your right as you cross the park, of modern Georgian-style houses.

Bear right and follow Castle Row, but turn first left into Dane John Gardens. Most visitors who get this far assume the name has something to do with Danish invaders, but it probably derives from the word 'donjohn', from dungeon, or castle keep. Canterbury's rather unregarded but very striking Norman castle lies at the top of Castle Street and thus only a few yards from the entrance to Dane John Gardens. The gardens are dominated by the Dane John Mound, which was probably part of a pre-Roman defensive system or perhaps an elaborate burial chamber. It stands hard by a well-preserved (or,

Dane John Mound, the memorial to Alderman Fitzsimmons and part of the city walls. The name Dane John probably derives from the word for dungeon.

rather, well-restored) stretch of Canterbury's medieval walls, which obviously came after the Dane John Mound as they changed course in order to accommodate it. Along the walls, every few hundred yards, are fourteenth-century bastions. The gardens are rather too much of a thoroughfare to be picnic territory, and probably too early in this itinerary, but do walk the length of the avenue of lime trees and admire the stuccoed Regency houses with frilly balconies. The gardens were laid out by one Alderman Fitzsimmons in 1790, and the obelisk at the top of the mound is a memorial to him.

Leave Dane John Gardens by the way you came in and cross a car park towards the castle. (This is a fairly capacious long-stay car park, cheaper than the one in Watling Street, though less convenient for a well co-ordinated route, shopping expeditions, or visits to the cathedral or the Tourist Information Centre.) I suspect that not one visitor to the cathedral in a hundred sees Canterbury Castle, dating from the early twelfth century. It dominates Gas Street. If people living in the neat, orange-brick modern town-houses that face the flinty, weed-covered and outwardly very substantial keep are not inspired by the sight, they should remember that the alternative, without the castle, would be a view of heavy traffic on the ring road that lies just beyond it. Some of the houses have taken their names from this excellent location: 'Castle Keep' and 'Castle View' among them. The castle was captured by Wat Tyler in the Peasants' Revolt of 1381 (more as a gesture, probably, than for any tactical reason), but it was three hundred years old even then, having been built by William the Conqueror. Once the site covered over 4 acres, but the keep (the fifth largest in England) is all that remains. Like some of the army pill boxes built in England in 1940 in anticipation of an invasion, it resisted attempts to demolish it; the walls are 11ft thick in places.

Gas Street residents also happen to live close to one of Canterbury's most remarkable churches. For at the end of that unromantic-sounding lane, and to the right, is St Mildred's. The name alone indicates how old the church must be, as no Norman or later Christians would have approved a dedication to a Saxon saint (Mildred was a great-great-granddaughter of the Saxon King Ethelbert, who in 597 welcomed a party of missionaries from Rome). It is the oldest church inside Canterbury's original city walls, which are among the best preserved in England. Here, in 1626, Isaak Walton – author of the still-read *The Compleat Angler* – was married, but this was a quiet incident in a chequered history, for St Mildred's survived two fires, a flood and the loss of its tower, and also seems to have come through the modern development of this corner of the city unscathed. It is not even redundant, but very much a fully functioning parish church.

Now pick up Church Lane and Stour Street, which run roughly parallel with Canterbury's river, noticing on the left just past St Mildred's an imposing, flint-built, former church school, now adapted for housing. Separate accommodation was originally arranged for boys at one end and girls at the other, with the headmaster's house in the middle. Just past Rosemary Lane you pass on the left a tannery, built in 1791 and still functioning, and then, a few yards further along on the right, the low-key buildings of Maynard and Cotton's Hospital – that is, a hospice, or almshouses. I would have wandered past this without noticing it if it had not been for a glimpse through a high wrought-iron gateway of the kind of traditional English garden

that would not disgrace Ann Hathaway's cottage in Stratford-upon-Avon – all hollyhocks, lupins and foxgloves. It was originally founded by a medieval merchant, Maynard, who as an official coiner literally had a licence to make money, but most of the red-brick building dates from about 1708, when Leonard Cotton, a wealthy pewterer, enlarged the original foundation.

I was surprised to find such rich pickings in such a quiet backwater as sleepy Stour Street, but the best was yet to come. First there was the Canterbury Heritage Centre, a state-of-the-art museum constructed in and around what was originally the Poor Priests' Hospital, a thirteenth-century almshouse for retired unmarried clergy, which was opened as a fully fledged visitor centre by the Queen and Duke of Edinburgh in 1987. And then there were the remains of a Franciscan Friary, which is literally in a backwater. I would not say that the Heritage Centre would substitute for a visit to Canterbury itself but it might be a close-run thing. There are too many lovely and evocative exhibits to detail here, though I especially remember the artist's impression of *Roman Canterbury abandoned* (Durovernum, as they knew it, was left to its own devices by the Romans in AD 410); an illuminated scale model of the cathedral that will stop you in your tracks – part of a set-piece describing its rebuilding after a great fire in 1174; and a panel describing the preparation of illuminated manuscripts, for which Canterbury was very well known, including in particular the method used for making inks: red ink from grinding lead steeped in vinegar, and black from oak galls and iron sulphate. And at least from the window of the room devoted to Chaucer and the medieval Canterbury pilgrims there is the view of the remaining Franciscan Friary, with, beyond that, the city's imposing medieval Westgate and in the distance some of the buildings of the University of Kent.

Still in Stour Street, immediately opposite the private garage of the County Hotel – Canterbury's biggest – turn into a doorway marked 'To Greyfriars' (the sign is only small). Follow the path towards the

*The ancient Poor Priests'
Hospital in Stour Street is
now a spacious and
imaginatively laid-out
visitor centre. It was
opened by the Queen and
the Duke of Edinburgh in
1987.*

river and thence to what remains of the Franciscan Friary that was
founded here in 1224, two years before the death of St Francis of
Assisi (notice, some distance away from the building, which now
incorporates a chapel, a private house called 'Assissi (sic) Cottage').
The shallow and rather incongruous arches of the old red brick bridge
over the Stour suggest that the river bed has risen considerably. Part
of the building used to be a prison, taking the overflow from the prison
in the city's Westgate. A lay member of the Franciscan order gave me
an unofficial guided tour, pointing out prisoners' graffiti, discovered
only after extensive cleaning. A home-made calendar, perhaps four
hundred years old, was beautifully scripted, but some days of the week
are misspelt. He also lifted a trap door: behold, the river running
below. 'Boats used to come under here to deliver goods. And there was
probably a bit of fishing done too.' But the river seemed too shallow for
fishing or boating. Then I remembered that the Roman pavement is
about 8ft below the present road surface, and that before silting up the
river would have been perhaps 7–8ft deep. Canterbury's Stour flows
in a broad loop through Kent from the South Downs to the sea at
Pegwell Bay. The tidal section of the river was navigable until near the
end of the last century, and the local port was at Fordwich nearby.

Return to Stour Street, turn left, alongside the County Hotel, and then left again into King's Bridge, a continuation of the High Street. The building that became a hotel has seen a lot of history, for the High Street used to be part of the main London-to-Dover road. Richard II would certainly have passed by in the 1380s, and you might have bribed somebody for a window seat to see Henry VIII and Elizabeth I and their entourages. The County was originally the house of a Jewish money-lender, effectively a merchant banker, who probably died around 1215. It was over three hundred years before a wine licence was granted, in 1588, and the building became the Saracen's Head. It later became a Post House – not a modern Trusthouse Forte version, though the hotel is owned by that group – and thus one of the liveliest, noisiest buildings in the city, where news of the outside world would come hot off the stage coach.

Just a few yards along King's Bridge you are once more approaching the River Stour. Walk slowly so as not to miss on the left St Thomas's Hospital, also known as Eastbridge Hospital. This was founded in 1185, to provide accommodation (strictly one night only) for poor pilgrims in Canterbury to see Becket's tomb. The cool and damp undercroft cannot have done a lot for knees still needing to negotiate the steps up to the Trinity Chapel. Chaucer would almost certainly have known the hospital (or hostel) when he was writing his *Canterbury Tales*, in about 1387–8, as records show the building was fully used then. It has had a chequered history since that time, but have reverted in part to its original use (the undercroft, built in 1190, had beds for a dozen genuine pilgrims) and there are now a number of very small flats for elderly people. When I called in there was a photographic exhibition which included pictures of the aftermath of flooding by the Stour: the river is clearly not the innocent it appears at first sight to be.

Immediately over the bridge you cannot mistake the half-timbered Weavers' houses, named after the Huguenots who settled here in the sixteenth and seventeenth centuries and whose descendants still hold Sunday services in French in the cathedral. This is one of two points from which you can pick up small boats to explore a short stretch of the river; you walk through what is now – appropriately – a knitwear shop, and buy your ticket beside the little waterside garden.

Continue up King's Bridge Street and then (with the distinctive Westgate ahead of you) into St Peter's Street. Notice a street on the right called The Friars. I took Westgate for granted, not realizing it is possible to climb it until I saw small figures waving at nobody in particular from the top. For the sake of the price of a bar of chocolate it seemed churlish not to give it a try, and it was less daunting to climb to the top of it than I had first assumed. From the middle of the eighteenth century the prison in it was mainly occupied by debtors and petty criminals, and there was everyday and informal contact between prisoners and passers-by via a ground-floor grille.

Against all the odds, and especially the demands of development, Westgate has remained in position. It dies a little every time a juggernaut goes by. It would have been knocked down in the nineteenth century if the petition of a travelling fair owner had been granted, but the mayor at the time used his casting vote against the plan. It probably originated as a late Roman gateway, but was replaced in about 1380. It was partly paid for by one Archbishop Simon of Sudbury, who was murdered shortly after in the Peasants'

LEFT *The Weavers' houses and pleasure boats on the Stour. You walk through a shop in the houses – selling, appropriately, wool – to pick up a boat.*

RIGHT *Westgate from Westgate Gardens. If Chaucer did visit Canterbury in the late fourteenth century, which is disputed, he would have seen Westgate as a brand-new, pristine building.*

Revolt of 1381. So, assuming Chaucer did actually travel to Canterbury (which has been disputed) he would have seen a pristine building. From the battlements on the east side of the Westgate roof you can look across almost on equal terms to the partly cleaned west front of the cathedral.

Notice the Falstaff Inn, in St Dunstan's Street, looking west from the top of the Westgate. This was built in 1403 to provide accommodation for pilgrims and other travellers who arrived in Canterbury after curfew, when the gates were locked. It was originally known as the White Hart, but the name was changed in 1783. Opposite this, at No. 71, is a building with three gates mentioned by Dickens in *David Copperfield*. Westgate stands in the middle of St Peter's Street, so watch out for traffic. Cross into Westgate Gardens, which *is* picnic country. The River Little Stour runs alongside, and a bonus as you stroll into the heart of the gardens is the row of white-painted, timber-framed houses on the far side of the river. Not a tile is out of place, not a single weed protrudes from any of the hanging flower baskets. A striking building within the gardens, by the river, is the Tower House, a nineteenth-century brick and flint house presented to the city in 1936 and used as the Mayor's Parlour.

Retrace your steps past Westgate and back down St Peter's Street, then turn left into The Friars, mentioned above. On your left is the Marlowe Theatre, modest enough from this angle but, as seen from the top of Westgate, expensively remodelled and extended. It used to be the Odeon Cinema, and was opened in 1984 in its new guise in time for the first Canterbury Festival. The theatre commemorates Christopher Marlowe (1564–93), who was born in Canterbury and christened in St George's Church, the tower of which still stands near Longmarket. A close contemporary of Shakespeare, his plays include *Tamburlaine, Dr Faustus* and *The Jew of Malta*.

Walk along The Friars and over the river bridge. To the left is Blackfriars, the remains of a Dominican Friary best seen by detouring up St Peter's Lane (off to the left between The Friars and Westgate), or in close-up from one of the river boats. Look back from the bridge towards the Canterbury Tales pub on the left-hand side of the road. It bears a date of origin on its side of 1386. Such inscriptions are always later additions, and by accident or design 1386 is just one year before Chaucer is thought to have written *Canterbury Tales*. Turn sharp right into Best Lane and near where this joins the High Street at right angles pause outside an Italian restaurant. Look down into the yard and you will see a glass-covered well, a rare survivor.

Turn left into the High Street. As you turn into the High Street you are a few paces from the Royal Museum and Art Gallery. If you have any sense of nostalgia, this is the best kind of municipal gallery – a little bit gloomy, a little bit unsophisticated, and not in the Canterbury Heritage league. The biggest room is devoted to the history of the local regiment nicknamed 'The Buffs'. Just a few yards further along the High Street, on the opposite side of the road, is the Queen Elizabeth Guest Chamber. If you do walk up the stairs for a plate of what by all accounts they do best, which is roast-of-the-day and two veg, you have a more legitimate reason to study the room's elaborately coloured, moulded reliefs and heraldic emblems. Tradition says that Queen Elizabeth entertained the Duke of Alençon here when this was a small inn, but it does not actually sound like her style, not least because she was famously loathe to part with money even for her own travelling expenses: a visit from the Queen could literally ruin a noble host.

I bought a pound of expensive cherries in a shop next door – Kent claims to be the garden of England, after all – and listened to the sound of Al Jolson emanating from a second-hand bric-à-brac shop and bookseller in an adjacent passageway. I then crossed the High Street to go down Mercery Lane, the most romantic street in Canterbury, whose views of Christ Church Gate and the cathedral rising above it gets the cameras clicking. This debouches into Buttermarket. Here are seats where you can watch a good proportion of Britain's several million annual tourists go by, press your chocolate flake deeper into your ice cream and reflect on the bull- and bear-baiting that once took place here. The slaughterhouses of Butchery Lane were just along the road, and apparently bull and bear meat – the latter unknown in Britain today, but still eaten in some countries – was made more tender by the excitement and fear created in the animals.

Christ Church Gate is worth sitting down for. Illiterate pilgrims would have 'read' it as we read cartoons. Like some details inside the cathedral, it recalls the bright colours of the medieval world. It has suffered both from rather heavy restoration and from vandals, but contains just enough clues to its glorious past to make it exceptionally interesting. Parliamentary forces, for example, removed a statue of Christ from a large niche – now empty. In a curious act of destruction in the 1930s a turret was removed to enable the cathedral clock to be seen from a local bank, but some restoration work was done to compensate. The highly decorative gate was originally put up to commemorate the marriage of Prince Arthur, eldest son of Henry VII, to Catherine of Aragon, daughter of the King and Queen of Spain. Their heads, in tiny stone effigies, can be seen in the gate well above head height on your right as you walk through towards the cathedral. The gate was nearly twenty years in the making. It is said the king lost interest after the untimely death of his son in 1502. The extravagantly vaulted roof contains a Tudor rose, signifying the joining of Yorkist and Lancastrian factions at the end of the Wars of the Roses. The double-fronted house on your left, immediately after you walk through the gate, was originally the gatekeeper's cottage. Even today

The west window of Canterbury Cathedral has late-twelfth-century stained glass in the lowest two rows, including a famous representation of Adam 'delving', or digging, in the centre of the bottom row.

the main gates of the cathedral precinct are opened and closed respectively in the morning and the evening.

This is a suitably dramatic approach to what is not only the most significant English cathedral but architecturally the most intricate and many-sided: the nave, of about 1400, is Perpendicular, the choir is early French-Gothic, and the principal crypt Romanesque. I think one of the reasons why visitors are so often deeply impressed is, simply, the charm of its different levels: the choir above the nave, the high altar and the Trinity Chapel higher again, followed by the corona close to where Thomas Becket's body lay in a shrine after his murder. It all has an intriguing, labyrinthine quality, which makes it impossible just to look in and say you've 'done' the cathedral. The effect on medieval pilgrims as they approached the corona lit by high windows, their way illuminated by candles and oil lamps, is not hard to imagine. And below all this are the crypts, mysterious, shadowy and moving – effectively a second, underground cathedral.

Favourite places for picknickers and parties of French students to congregate seem to be 'The Oaks', a large patch of greenery on your right as you start to leave the cathedral precincts and approach Convent Garden, better known as the Kent War Memorial Garden. Most of what is now grass was originally the monks' fish pond, and several monks would have been employed full time tending the fish stocks. Walk through the Cemetery Gate into the War Memorial Garden, where people do not sit on the grass (it is always beautifully manicured, and more often than not I have seen gardeners at work). Also notice the bilberry tree, partly supported by a specially devised crutch. It is said to have been planted by Charles II. One of the gardeners told me that in the autumn the ground is covered with fat bilberries. I was suitably impressed, and only afterwards wondered why nobody picked them. Walk round the War Memorial Garden towards Quenin Gate, built in 1170 and named after Queen Bertha. Here you can pass through the city wall and make a very interesting detour to St Augustine's Abbey. To reach this impressively ruined abbey, cross Broad Street and go down Lady Wootton's Green opposite. Turn right at the end into Monastery Street, then turn left into pleasant, tree-lined Longport and the entrance to the abbey is on the left.

St Augustine's is the oldest Anglo-Saxon abbey in England. Founded in about AD 599, it was planned as an impressive burial place for the Archbishops of Canterbury and the Kings of Kent. Part of its distinction arose because it was also used as a residence for monks sent from Rome to convert the English to Catholicism. It was an unlikely survivor of the Viking invasions and, perhaps inspired by this, Archbishop Dunstan re-dedicated an enlarged abbey in 978. Its later prosperity was its downfall, because at the time of the dissolution of the monasteries in 1538 Henry VIII cast covetous eyes on it. He retained the abbots' lodging as a royal palace, and later, on the same site, elaborate renovations were made to existing buildings to house Anne of Cleves *en route* to meet her new husband, although she stayed only one night, 29 December 1539. Nothing more dramatic caused the ultimate ruin of the abbey than a storm in 1703, which dealt the death blow to an increasingly unsafe structure. It is as elegant as any of the ruins in the hands of English Heritage, with its tended lawns and finely detailed walls.

BELOW *The War Memorial Gardens, with Bell Harry Tower and the cathedral in the background. Notice on the right the wooden support for part of the rare bilberry tree.*

One of several half-timbered houses in Palace Street, No. 17, Conquest House, dates from the seventeenth century and contains a twelfth-century undercroft where according to tradition the four knights and their followers plotted the murder of Becket.

As I walked back from the abbey towards Quenin Gate, ice cream sellers under an avenue of chestnut trees were doing a good trade. A second-hand book dealer was open later in the day than I would have expected, and T-shirted tourists were gazing intently at restaurant menus, presumably planning their assault on escargots and jugged hare later in the evening. It is unlikely, however, that they would have eaten better than the inhabitants of the abbey in its heyday – life inside the great religous houses was much less austere than most people imagine today.

Retrace your steps to the cathedral, then bear right past the east end. At this point only a tutored eye can differentiate between those buildings that belong to the King's School and those that have no connection with it. The solid and handsome great house on the right, called Meister Omers, was built in about 1400 by a Prior Chillenden. One of the King's School's greatest assets, the house has among its claims to distinction an 18ft-wide fireplace in the kitchen. Its main function was as a guest house for important visitors to the cathedral, and by the standards of the time the accommodation is said to have been sumptuous. The evocative ruins on your right as you walk away from this down a slight incline, with the cathedral on your left, are the Infirmary Chapel, in which aged or sick monks who were too ill to go to chapel could attend mass.

Turn right, noticing on the left the slightly out-of-place Cotswold stone of the cathedral library that replaced the one damaged in the bombings of 1942. It proved impossible to get a supply of the Caen stone of which the cathedral was originally built, and yellow Cotswold stone was chosen as second best. Next you come to 'Dark Entry'. It is a passage, not as daunting as it sounds, said to be haunted by the ghost of Nell Cook, who was accused of poisoning the canon she worked for and was walled up after being condemned to death. I emerged from Dark Entry into a scene of pure nostalgia: dark-jacketed sixth-formers strolled insouciantly across the greensward of Green Court. Knots of lesser mortals, girls as well as boys, tennis rackets akimbo, soaked up the late afternoon sun. Green Court was where much of the day-to-day business of the monastery which was the original basis for Canterbury Cathedral went on. It is busy enough today, except when it dozes out of term time.

Take the footpath to your left, to see a side of the cathedral many visitors miss. It is much more functional – rather like seeing the underside of a steam engine – and reveals such details as a comparatively sophisticated water tower that was revolutionary in medieval times. Ahead of you is the Pentise, a covered way built, at about the time the *Canterbury Tales* was being written, by Prior Chillenden, who looked after the creature comforts of guests in Meister Omers. The Pentise was built to keep them dry while walking between the Court Gate and Cellarers Hall. Not only is the King's School an exceptionally ancient public school, it also has a set of magnificent buildings. The most unwilling pupil can hardly fail to be impressed by the Norman staircase, just north of the north-west corner of Green Court. This is all that remains of the entrance to a great hall, long gone. Its magnificence can be imagined just by looking at the massive twelfth-century stone stairway in which classic decorative Norman arches seem impressively matter of fact.

Leave Green Court by the north-west corner, passing Mint Yard, formerly known as Almonry Yard. A chapel that was one of the first buildings of the school after its foundation by Henry VIII has now disappeared. Happily, there is no anticlimax as you leave the King's School by Mint Yard and turn left into Palace Street. It is an uncommercialized, workaday link between the academic but noticeably unstuffy atmosphere of the school and the much more hectic Buttermarket. Before starting along Palace Street, cross the road and detour briefly into King Street to look at the bizarre, brightly coloured mural at the back of a house which stands on the corner of King Street and Palace Street. In Palace Street you cannot miss the black-painted King's School Shop, a tourist attraction in its own right. The gable bears the date 1617, and though it looks like 'The House That Jack Built', it is perfectly safe inside: the eye-catching misshapen front door was pushed out of position over many generations by settlement and pressure from other houses in the same terrace.

Continue along Palace Street. On the right is the Bell and Crown pub. A notice outside lists all the landlords since the licence was granted in 1862 (Thomas Newman was the first). Also listed are the archbishops whose palace used to stand opposite. According to the landlord the benign Archbishop Ramsey (1961–74) was a frequent customer. A few yards further on, also on the right, the Canterbury Centre occupies what used to be St Alphege's Church. On a warm afternoon when tourists clustered round Christ Church Gate ten deep I looked in here and it was cool and deserted. It is not a commercial venture but an increasingly well-known setting for exhibitions devoted to Canterbury's past.

At the end of Palace Street fork left up Sun Street. If you look up above the Captain's Cabin shop you will spot the unlikely ornament of a bright red parish pump that used to stand in the street. Local tradition says that housewives who used to congregate around this were so incensed at the idea of its disappearance when main drainage came that a sympathetic city council reinstated it, albeit at a different level. I was able to find no more convincing explanation! The sparkling blue-and-gold Sun Hotel on the right as you walk up Sun Street was built in 1503 and is also referred to in Dickens's *David Copperfield*. It was a successor to an even older inn and was originally used by servants at the monastery from which the cathedral arose. Sun Street ends by Christ Church Gate. Continue straight along Burgate, then turn right into Butchery Lane, where a bull's head with illuminated red eyes is a striking feature just above head height on the right. Here you are a few yards from Longmarket and then the Watling Street car park.

Yard for yard this walk is the shortest in this book. It is, however, probably the most closely packed after Oxford and Cambridge. In an age of theme parks and *son et lumière* Canterbury does not need any of it. Put the whole thing under a perspex roof (the cathedral's great Bell Harry Tower might, of course, not fit) – its ancient streets, its doll-like timber-framed houses, its surprisingly quiet back streets and the equally surprising amount of greenery, and its hostelries that can tell many a six-hundred-year-old or older tale – and it would be a historian's Disneyland. And if the first thing the visitor on foot does on reaching the Buttermarket even before looking up to admire the ornate Christ Church Gate is to take off his shoes and give himself a surreptitious foot massage, at least he will only be doing what pilgrims must have done more or less openly for the last eight hundred years or more.

The King's School Shop, at the end of Palace Street, lies directly opposite the Mint Yard entrance to the school. Though misshapen, it is structurally safe.

CHESTER

CHESTER

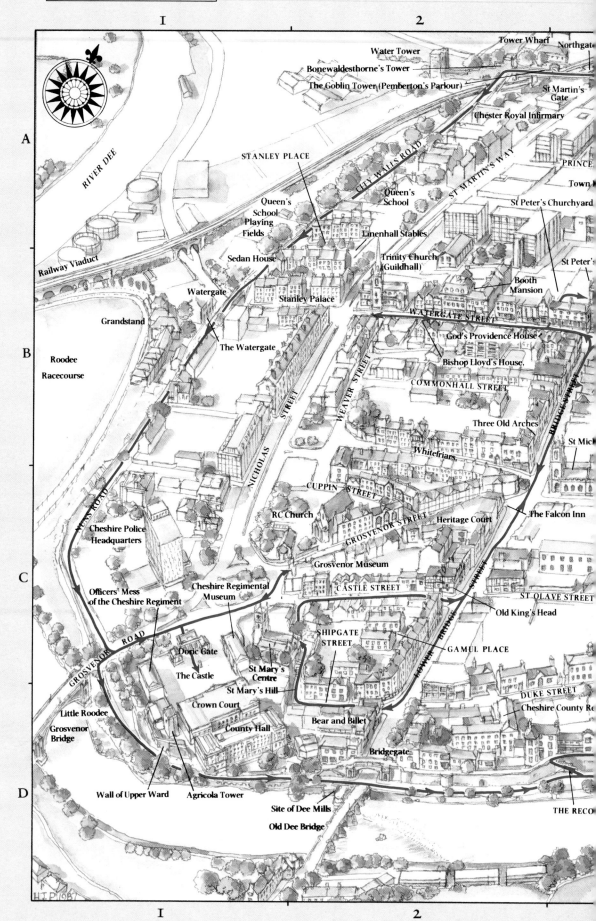

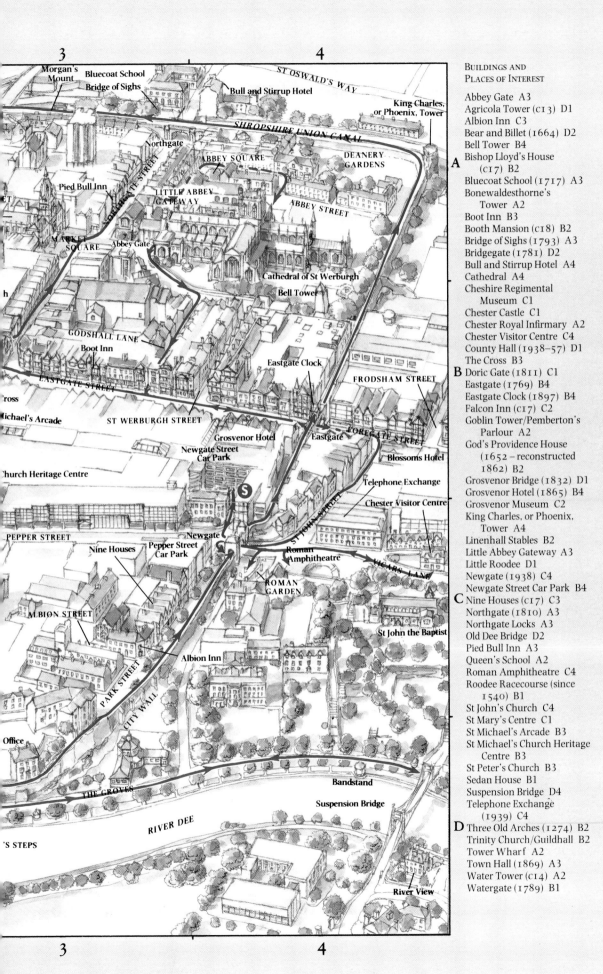

Morgan's Mount
Bluecoat School
Bridge of Sighs
Bull and Stirrup Hotel
ST OSWALD'S WAY
King Charles, or Phoenix, Tower
SHROPSHIRE UNION CANAL
Northgate
ABBEY SQUARE
DEANERY GARDENS
Pied Bull Inn
LITTLE ABBEY GATEWAY
ABBEY STREET
MARKET SQUARE
Abbey Gate
Cathedral of St Werburgh
Bell Tower
GODSHALL LANE
Boot Inn
EASTGATE STREET
Eastgate Clock
FRODSHAM STREET
Cross
Michael's Arcade
ST WERBURGH STREET
Grosvenor Hotel
Newgate Street Car Park
Eastgate
FOREGATE STREET
Blossoms Hotel
Church Heritage Centre
Telephone Exchange
Chester Visitor Centre
PEPPER STREET
Newgate
Pepper Street Car Park
Nine Houses
Roman Amphitheatre
VICARS LANE
ST JOHN'S STREET
ALBION STREET
ROMAN GARDEN
St John the Baptist
Office
Albion Inn
PARK STREET
CITY WALL
THE GROVES
Bandstand
Suspension Bridge
RIVER DEE
River View
'S STEPS

BUILDINGS AND
PLACES OF INTEREST

Abbey Gate A3
Agricola Tower (C13) D1
Albion Inn C3
Bear and Billet (1664) D2
Bell Tower B4
Bishop Lloyd's House (C17) B2
Bluecoat School (1717) A3
Bonewaldesthorne's Tower A2
Boot Inn B3
Booth Mansion (C18) B2
Bridge of Sighs (1793) A3
Bridgegate (1781) D2
Bull and Stirrup Hotel A4
Cathedral A4
Cheshire Regimental Museum C1
Chester Castle C1
Chester Royal Infirmary A2
Chester Visitor Centre C4
County Hall (1938–57) D1
The Cross B3
Doric Gate (1811) C1
Eastgate (1769) B4
Eastgate Clock (1897) B4
Falcon Inn (C17) C2
Goblin Tower/Pemberton's Parlour A2
God's Providence House (1652 – reconstructed 1862) B2
Grosvenor Bridge (1832) D1
Grosvenor Hotel (1865) B4
Grosvenor Museum C2
King Charles, or Phoenix, Tower A4
Linenhall Stables B2
Little Abbey Gateway A3
Little Roodee D1
Newgate (1938) C4
Newgate Street Car Park B4
Nine Houses (C17) C3
Northgate (1810) A3
Northgate Locks A3
Old Dee Bridge D2
Pied Bull Inn A3
Queen's School A2
Roman Amphitheatre C4
Roodee Racecourse (since 1540) B1
St John's Church C4
St Mary's Centre C1
St Michael's Arcade B3
St Michael's Church Heritage Centre B3
St Peter's Church B3
Sedan House B1
Suspension Bridge D4
Telephone Exchange (1939) C4
Three Old Arches (1274) B2
Trinity Church/Guildhall B2
Tower Wharf A2
Town Hall (1869) A3
Water Tower (C14) A2
Watergate (1789) B1

PAGES 64–5

Approaching Northgate on the Chester city walls. The two-mile-long red-sandstone walls that add so much to Chester's character were established in the Middle Ages on Roman foundations.

I once went to Chester on a Saturday morning by train. The town was jam-packed, and City Road, linking the station and Chester proper, resembled the approach to Wembley Stadium on cup-final day. I wondered what was going on. A pop concert on the Roodee, Chester's racecourse, perhaps? A Billy Graham rally in the castle grounds? I asked a lady with four small children in tow. 'Not a bit of it,' she said. This was a Saturday morning routine for Chester. The people were shoppers and day-trippers – more serious visitors were already installed for the weekend in the larger hotels in the centre, though City Road was lined with overnighting luxury coaches outside slightly less-favoured hotels. Chester was merely playing its part as tourist honeypot of the north-west.

Not that Chester takes its tourists for granted. In mid-1987 the Duke of Westminster, President of the Chester Marketing Bureau, was urging Chester people and especially Chester businessmen not to be complacent. In his view, the city needed all the admirers it could get, and was a long way from saturation point. Which is quite true: it is busy but not overfull. It is also an exceptionally well organized place, with more history in its little finger than half the counties in England have in their whole body.

I suggest parking in the Newgate Street multi-storey car park. The Chester Visitor Centre is close, the inner ring road takes you very near the car park entrance, and I have never known it to be full. If it is, there is another car park on the opposite side of Pepper Street.

Start at the Visitor Centre in Vicar's Lane. Built about a hundred years ago as a school, it incorporates a Tourist Information Centre. It is not only close to the oldest bits of Chester's tangible history but near one of the best starting points for a walk along Chester's unique wall. A little café on the premises does such a roaring trade that it has recently been moved and enlarged, and the room that previously housed it is now given over to souvenirs, picture-postcards, decorative tea towels, flags and personalized pens. The motif of Chester's Eastgate Clock pops up everywhere: in silver and brass, on pepper pots, ashtrays, and place mats. Upstairs, there is a reconstruction of a Victorian street scene, based on the Rows, Chester's unique arrangement of three- and four-storeyed buildings (often shops) containing galleried arcades reached by steps from the road. A tiered viewing room is adjacent, with local prints and an all-too-brief ten-minute video film of Chester and its history.

As you emerge blinking into the daylight, the church of St John the Baptist is across the road. It is *not* the cathedral but it used to be in Anglo-Saxon times. Until 1102 it was the cathedral church of the diocese of Chester, though in the 1540s it became simply a parish church. Notice the attractive Victorian almshouses of brown patterned brick on the right as you leave the Visitor Centre, walking towards Newgate.

Turn left before Newgate into the excavated Roman amphitheatre (the largest ever uncovered in Britain), which you enter by a gate in the railings. It was thought for many years that the Roman fort would have had an amphitheatre, but none was found until 1929, when part of a Roman wall was discovered. This amphitheatre probably fell into disuse in about AD 350. It had a capacity of about 7,000, and would almost certainly have seen condemned men thrown to wild animals, but probably not gladiatorial contests, as these were apparently expensive to stage in comparatively far-flung outposts of

Eastgate, where the city wall crosses the street, framed by the mainly Victorian half-timbered buildings of Eastgate Street. The Grosvenor Hotel, outstanding among city hotels in Britain, is beyond the arch on the left.

the empire. Pebbles and gravel now form the base, but remember that what is now visible is only half or less than half of the original open space, and also that the walls would have been much higher than what remains today. Plans are already on the drawing-board to transform the ancient site by the 1990s into the Deva Roman Centre, a blockbuster attraction on the lines of York's Jorvik Viking Centre. This will include a partial reconstruction of the amphitheatre as it was two thousand years ago.

Just before you reach the Newgate arch, notice across the road the remains of the foundations of the south-east angle of the Roman fortress wall, now a little garden with seats from which to watch passing lorries and the green-and-white buses. Before you walk through the arch, turn left through the gates into the Roman Garden. The Roman columns give the garden a certain elegance, and as you walk past them, with high walls (mainly Saxon) on your right, you will come to a reconstructed hypocaust, basically a system of underfloor heating in which slaves kept a supply of hot coals in position.

Through Newgate arch turn sharp left, and a few yards along on the left a flight of steps leads up onto the wall. The wall-based route continues due north over Eastgate, towards the red, black, green and gold Victorian Eastgate Clock that is a symbol of Chester. On your right, as you walk north over Newgate with the Eastgate Clock just in sight, notice Thimbleby's Tower, repaired in 1879. A couple behind me peered into it. 'Nothing down there!' In the fourteenth century it was a watchtower, but was badly damaged in the year-long Civil War siege of the city. As you come up to the Eastgate Clock, you will find a completely unexpected antiques and second-hand bookshop on your left. The clock itself, very eyecatching indeed, was presented to the city by 'Edward Evans-Lloyd, citizen and freeman' in 1897, to commemorate Queen Victoria's Diamond Jubilee.

Looking down onto Eastgate Street, you can see High Victorian black-and-white and stone buildings, lots of shoppers and strollers, and very little traffic apart from the occasional bus. If you crane your neck slightly to the left, looking towards Watergate Street, you will get a glimpse of part of the city's celebrated galleried Rows. Eastgate Street was the Romans' *Via Principalis*, and Eastgate their *Porta Principalis Sinistra*. This was a wide and elaborate gate, ceremonial as well as defensive; there is a scale model of it in the Grosvenor Museum. The present arch was built in 1769 to replace the remains of the medieval gate that followed the Roman one. The medieval gates were run as toll gates and the job of gatekeeper was usually a sinecure for favoured citizens.

Beyond Eastgate, you begin to approach the cathedral, described near the end of the route. But notice especially, on your left, the independent bell tower, erected in 1975 and opened by the Duke of Gloucester. It was the first free-standing bell tower built for an English cathedral for over four hundred years. A local sport is to watch unsuspecting tourists strolling along the wall jump suddenly when the bells sound. There are several pubs, cafés and shops at wall level, and occasionally street musicians perform here.

Two hundred yards from the bell, notice on the right – if you are sharp-eyed – something out of the ordinary in the wall. This is just before a walkway on the left leading down to the cathedral precinct. An inscription, with an anchor, has the number 692F. It is thought to have been placed here by the great engineer Isambard Kingdom Brunel, who calculated that the distance from this point to the King Charles Tower nearby measured the same length as his ironclad ship, the *Great Eastern*, which laid the first transatlantic cable. If you follow that walkway down before returning to the top of the wall, notice a door set into the wall at ground level. According to one story, the monks in the monastery that later became the cathedral petitioned the Archbishop of Canterbury for a gate to allow them access to their vegetable garden without having to pass through Eastgate and run the gauntlet of the local populace. The latter sometimes considered the monks to be a bad lot, with good reason, for they would certainly have included among their number criminals on the run. Permission was granted as long as the door was not large enough for a man on horseback to pass through and was used only up to 9 p.m. each night, for security reasons, as this was effectively breaching the city walls. To this day the curfew bell is still sounded and the gateway locked.

Continuing along the wall, you approach the King Charles Tower, also known as the Phoenix Tower, from the badge (cut in 1613) above the doorway of the Guild of Painters, Glaziers, Embroiderers and Stationers, who once used it as a meeting place. To your left are the pleasant fields called Deanery Gardens with a pretty Georgian terrace, the view beyond which is almost entirely spoiled by the top two storeys of a characterless office block in the middle distance. Cricket is played here on the green.

As I walked, a particularly heavy shower drove most people off the walls as surely as if it were a fusillade from Cromwell's troops during the siege of 1645. I was glad of the shelter provided by the King Charles Tower. Charles I – there is a portrait of him in the city's superb Grosvenor Museum – is said to have stood at this point on the walls during the siege of Chester to watch the progress of the battle of Rowton Moor, which took place on 24 September 1645. It is a romantic notion, but it should be said that, because of the distance, the best he could have seen would have been a few stragglers or deserters. One of the reasons why the King Charles Tower is so appealing is that, having absorbed the downstairs display, you can then go upstairs for a fairly private and rather cosy inspection of first-hand accounts of the Civil War and the history of Chester at that time. I thought the best part was the view from the windows and the life-sized models wearing Royalist and Cromwellian uniforms. They were apparently virtually indistinguishable except for the colours of the sashes that were tied diagonally across their uniforms.

Continue walking as far as Northgate, the best preserved of the Roman gates. I stopped for a moment, beside a couple of tiny shops, as a black and green canal longboat passed far below. Occasionally still employed for commercial haulage, these craft are now mainly used by holidaymakers. The canal here is part of the Shropshire Union system, and was created to link Shrewsbury with the River Mersey. The Chester-to-Ellesmere Port section was opened in 1795. Below, to your right, is the Bluecoat School, with the original carved statue of a Bluecoat boy and restricted and intriguing views of fine high-ceilinged rooms. Until the Second World War Bluecoat students here wore the exact uniform depicted on the statue above the school entrance, but in 1944 the school was absorbed into the state system. Just beyond the Bluecoat School, nearly opposite it, look out for a fine example of late Victoriana. This is the Bull and Stirrup Hotel.

As you pass over Northgate look very carefully to your right, on the canal side of the Bluecoat School. You will see a narrow bridge, known (as so many bridges are!) as the Bridge of Sighs. This was built in 1793 to enable condemned prisoners to cross easily from Northgate Gaol that existed below the gate to the Chapel of Little St John on the other side of the canal. About 150 yds further on, as you approach Chester's busy ring road, you can climb up to Morgan's Mount on the right. It is named after a Captain Morgan who commanded a Royalist

Part of the canal basin near Tower Wharf, from where there are waterborne excursions. On the left is a corner of the covered boatyard in which canal boats are constructed or repaired.

gun-post here during the Civil War siege. There is a tiny shelter that is handy if it rains.

The new St Martin's Gate in the city walls, which allows you to cross over the ring road, was opened by Barbara Castle, then Minister of Transport, in 1966. It won a Civic Trust commendation for its design, as it was not too much out of sympathy with the original that had to be destroyed. Walk down from the walls, especially if there is activity on the canal you can see to the right. There are several locks, demanding patience from boatmen and causing much excitement among the small dogs that seem to travel on most boats. It is all very companionable, as whenever possible boats go through two by two. The railway to North Wales also runs past here.

For a short and worthwhile detour leave the wall area close to the two water towers, called Bonewaldesthorne's Tower and, simply, Water Tower. The towers were built in the fourteenth century to protect the river; the second tower was necessary because silting-up caused the Dee to change course. In the middle distance, to your right, is a boat-yard and to the right of the canal basin is Tower Wharf, most of which was built during the nineteenth century. To the left is a dry dock dating from 1798. During the summer a horse-drawn canal barge called the Chester Packet operates from here – a welcome change of pace for most visitors. Inside the boat-yard, which is a kind of dry dock, a boat was getting an overhaul, and the smell of the generously applied glossy black paint was powerful.

Back on the wall walk a particularly striking red-brick building is the Chester Royal Infirmary, on the left. It is very pleasing to the eye, and is a rare instance of a mid-eighteenth-century hospital still in regular use. A little way past the hospital, but on the right, well below the wall, are the playing fields of the Queen's School, an independent foundation for girls. The very imposing late-Victorian main building of the school is on the left as you walk towards Watergate. It replaced a prison, which had superseded the dungeons in Northgate. Described at the time as 'gloomy looking', it was pulled down in the 1870s.

Notice as you approach Watergate, and the main racecourse entrance, the handsome and understated Georgian buildings to the left. On the left just past the City Walls Hotel, for example, is Stanley Place, with its pleasant and rather surprising, narrow green. Notice, too, the Linenhall Stables, now used during Chester race meetings, which commemorate a linen hall that in the eighteenth century processed Irish linen shipped in when Chester was still a port. Nearer the wall is Sedan House, with its rare 'sedan porch'. There are several blacked-out windows, the result of an eighteenth-century window tax. The Watergate pub, hard by the racecourse entrance, is completely unassuming but is far from dark and unwelcoming. I had a ham sandwich with mustard – and how! There was great excitement in the bar, as Wales was playing France at rugby – interesting to note that despite old enmities people were cheering Wales on.

Even when there is no racing, the emerald green tracks, the paddock, stables and racecourse paraphernalia are all worth a look. (The railway viaduct you can see in the distance was built in 1846 in the early years of the railway age, but collapsed the following year, killing four train passengers.) The Chester races, the oldest in Britain, take place on the Roodee, and are staged on the site of the former, massive Roman harbour, indicating how much the terrain has

ABOVE *The Roodee is closer to the town centre than almost any other racecourse in Britain. It is also the oldest racecourse in the country.*

OPPOSITE *The Water Tower, on a spur of the wall near the Chester Royal Infirmary. Originally one of the river defences, it now contains a museum.*

changed since the Dee silted up. The name 'Roodee' comes from the 'rood', or cross, which once stood here and 'eye', a word used to describe a meadow or piece of ground partly surrounded by water. The earliest mentioned horse race was run in 1540 and replaced an annual football match which had become too violent. And just as Chester cathedral is fairly unusual for being so close to the heart of the city, Chester racecourse is one of very few in the country that is only a stroll away from the city centre.

The controversial eight-storey police headquarters are to the left as you continue southwards – not a happy intrusion on the skyline, and not a patch on the handsome Grosvenor Bridge on your right. Notice on the left the wide boulevard that was the first incursion into the original medieval town plan. The bridge was designed by Thomas Harrison, who died before its completion in 1833. In its time it was the largest single-span bridge in the world, at 200 ft, and has stood up to the ravages of modern-day traffic very well. I recommend that you leave the wall walk via Grosvenor Road to see the castle and the Grosvenor Museum. The castle is close enough to warrant immediate attention from wall-walkers, but you get only a poor impression of it from the slightly downhill walkway with the Little Roodee to your right and the County Hall ahead of you. What you see from here is the wall of the upper ward, built of sandstone and much restored in the nineteenth century.

The castle was one of the ruins that the Georgians tampered with, and I find the much praised 'Greek Revival' buildings drab and functional. Beyond the impressive main gateway, with a little lodge on each side, lies the Cheshire Regimental Museum, the Crown Court and, to the right, the officers' mess of the Cheshire Regiment. To see what remains of the original castle, including the intriguing Agricola Tower, follow the signs at the far right corner. The Agricola Tower, also known as the Magazine Tower, has Norman foundations but is mainly medieval, and has a winding stone stairway that gives access to the roof and yet more far-ranging views.

Returning to Grosvenor Road, turn right and continue towards Grosvenor Street. The Trustee Savings Bank adjacent to the Grosvenor Museum has an air of antiquity about it, although it is, in fact, nineteenth century in the Tudor-Gothic style well-loved by the Victorians. The clock in the turret is original, and still working. Do try not to miss the museum. 'County Museum' can have a rather dull ring to it, but Chester is rightly proud of this one. You walk up and up, via a grand spiral stairway that in a stately home would be a major feature in its own right, and in the uppermost room – much less frequented than those below – there is a medium-sized and therefore not too overpowering collection of mainly local paintings and furniture. This is a lovely way to get an impression of Chester's character and development, especially during the last two hundred years. Signs ask you not to touch the furniture and I am sure you would not. If you were to, however, you would find that drawers glide as on a dream, that two-hundred-year-old walnut table tops exude a life and warmth of their own, and that hinges on bureaus are attached so perfectly that a baby's breath would move them one way or the other. An hour in the museum will also enable you to grasp the importance of the Roman origins of Chester. The high point for me was a diorama of the Roman legionnaire fortress in about AD 220, showing the tightly packed houses, the whole of the amphitheatre, and much other detail

Part of the seven-arched Old Dee Bridge is seven hundred years old. The 'jolly miller of Dee' lived by the city end of the bridge.

that explains the Roman origins of the city extremely well.

Returning to the wall walk, continue past the castle walls and cross Castle Drive. From the little green in front of the council offices, the Dee (named after a local Roman deity) is some two hundred yards wide. You will probably see fishermen on the far banks and behind them gardens, sandstone outcrops and old stone walls. This is a good point from which to admire the Old Dee Bridge, beyond which are some ugly, cheaply built, modern flats. They stand on the site of the Roman quarry. The village beyond the bridge is Handbridge. For nearly two thousand years this was the only approach to Wales, and the village of Handbridge, so clearly seen across the river, has a Welsh name, *Treboeth*, meaning 'burnt town'. It was always vulnerable when trouble was in the air, and was burned by the English whenever a Welsh incursion threatened. In the foreground look across to the place where the 'miller of Dee', immortalized in song and verse, had his mill, and where corn was ground until 1903. The Dee mills were done away with in 1910.

From here walk north-east along the river bank towards The Groves, designed by one Alderman Charles Brown in the 1880s. It is really a maritime park, very Edwardian, rather civilized and even continental in atmosphere. You could be beside a Swiss lake or at a German spa in the early years of the century, were it not for the incongruous amusement arcade, the synthetic ice creams and the hamburgers. Glossy showboats dock here after river cruises, and even ghetto blasters cannot compete with the occasional accordion concert in the pink and green ironwork bandstand. Beyond this is the white-and-grey, pedestrian suspension bridge, built more recently than you might expect, in 1923. Further along the bank are open air (and indoor) cafés. Ducks warm themselves in the sun, and if you look across the water you will see grand private houses on the far side of the river.

Return to the top of the wall via one of the flights of stone steps and walk north, being careful not to miss the Albion Inn, an Edwardian

Down by the riverside.
Half-close your eyes on a
warm summer's day and
you could be back in 1910.
The ambience is decidedly
Edwardian – despite the
odd 'ghetto blaster'.

pub famous for its real coal fire, its authentic atmosphere and its tempting pub menu. Just a few yards further on are the Nine Houses. They date from the time of the Reformation, and only six remain in a very smart terrace. Built of tile and brick, they were restored in 1969, but the originals are mentioned in the Assembly of Corporation Minutes for 19 September 1690 and are marked on a city map in 1745.

Roughly at the same point as the Nine Houses, on the opposite side of the wall, remember to look down to the right at the Roman Garden below you – a legionary's eye view this time. Unless, after perhaps the most remarkable two-mile walk in any English city, you want to lie down in the sun (assuming good weather) and award yourself a rest, carry on as far as Eastgate again and descend to street level to become acquainted with the centre of Chester. The most obvious way to do this is to follow a roughly star-shaped walk within the walls, which takes you into the medieval heart of the city.

The Grosvenor Hotel, on the left, is all carpets that 'tickle your armpits' and expensive chandeliers. It has recently undergone substantial alterations and improvements and is certainly handsome, but for a really memorable taste of Eastgate's elaborate architectural feast, walk up to the Rows on your right. (If you follow signs to the Boot Inn, once Chester's best-known brothel, you will be directly across from some traditional – though mostly Victorian – black-and-white buildings, set off nicely by nineteenth-century Gothic and earlier red-brick buildings, all of which contain Rows.) The origin of the Rows is uncertain, and Chester people seem to have given up arguing about them. They were certainly first mentioned in 1331, and much later, very graphically, in an account by a German traveller who visited the city in 1842: 'Chester is the very town for curious promenades, for it contains walks even more curious than the wall.... These are "the Rows" as they are called. They are long covered passages, running parallel with the streets through the first floors of the houses. ...' One theory, though there are several, is that after the Battle of Chester the Saxons destroyed the city, but later, as new settlers, they built wooden houses on top of the earth mounds that flanked the depressions marking the line of the old Roman roads. These mounds were developed and excavated, and the first floor arrangement above the mud and dust of street level was found to be convenient. One thing I especially appreciate about these unglazed windows on the world is not being jostled by the crowds.

Stay at first floor level and continue towards the church which you should just be able to make out ahead of you, through a closed-in and slightly eerie walkway. In fact this is sometimes known as 'Dark Row'. The church is St Peter's, heavily restored in the late nineteenth century, but still mainly fourteenth- and fifteenth-century inside. From just beside the church you can look across to an extremely intricate black-and-white building near The Cross (described later in the walk) on the corner of Bridge Street and Eastgate Street. This was built in 1888 to the design of a local architect and was reproduced on one of the stamps issued by the Post Office in 1975 to mark European Architectural Heritage Year.

Cross the main road, and with Bridge Street below on your right go up into the Rows again, walk for about 150 yds and turn into St Michael's Arcade – a mainly late twentieth-century but also partly Edwardian version of the medieval Rows – and very good too, with cafés and plenty of greenery. A pity, though, that the pot plants and the creepers appear to be fake and not real. They attend to their squeaky-clean image, too: a loudspeaker catches one shopper unawares and barks out, 'Please get that dog out of here.' From the centre of St Michael's Arcade you can reach other Rows or streets.

Four principal streets meet at The Cross: Northgate, Eastgate, Watergate and Bridgegate. Most of the original High Cross was destroyed by Cromwell in 1646.

One sign points to Newgate Row, for example, another to Newgate Street. Before you descend from the Bridge Street Rows, notice, across the road, the three arches incorporated in the Owen Owen's department store. Known simply as 'Three Old Arches', they proudly proclaim the date '1274 AD' and this is probably close, though houses that have dates on them, at least until Victorian times, are notoriously suspect. Dates were usually added later for effect. On the corner of Bridge Street and Pepper Street, notice the Chester Heritage Centre, housed in the redundant parish church of St Michael's. It began its new lease of life in 1975, as part of the European Architectural Heritage Year celebrations.

Do not be put off by the main road. Continue down Lower Bridge Street, where on the corner of Grosvenor Street you can admire the splendidly restored Falcon Inn, the town house of a former mayor, who arranged for the Rows gallery to be removed from the structure so that he could enlarge his parlour and entertain his friends. The landlord may be able to give you a private tour of the cellars, where the Rows that used to stretch the length of Bridge Street can still be seen. Even without the Rows, the street is a remarkable parade of the domestic architecture of several centuries. Gamul Terrace is a walkway open to the skies, with a Greek restaurant and a low parapet from which to enjoy Lower Bridge Street. The name Gamul com-memorates Sir Francis Gamul, who accommodated Charles I in his house on the corner of Castle Street after the Rowton Moor defeat. Lower Bridge Street leads to Bridgegate, which is easily the oldest of the river crossings. Notice, ahead of you, close to Bridgegate, the Bear and Billet pub. It was originally a town house belonging to the Earl of Shrewsbury, who was a joint custodian of Bridgegate, and was built in 1664. Do not miss pretty little Gamul Place, on your right as you go downhill, with its yellow, red and white doors in two modest terraces, its window boxes, paved courtyard, trees and shrubs – it should give heart to inner city developers all over Britain.

On the right, turn into Shipgate Street, then right again to St Mary's Hill, which, although it is steep and partly cobbled, has an iron railing to help you on your way. To the left is St Mary's Church, which has now become the St Mary's Centre and is used for educational projects. Turn right into Castle Street and then left at the bottom of the hill back into Lower Bridge Street. As you retrace your steps up Bridge Street notice Scrivener and Burgess, a good name for a bookshop, which it is, and the exterior of the palatial St Michael's Church, with three storeys extending even above the first floor Rows.

You are now returning directly to the Chester Cross, which stands at the point where Eastgate Street becomes Watergate Street. Northgate Street is just a few yards to the east. The earliest known reference to the cross was in the fifteenth century. It was destroyed during the Civil War but parts of it were preserved and it was eventually re-erected in the Roman Garden by Newgate. In 1975 it was moved to its present position. Well-connected or well-organized parties leave their coaches at the crossroads and are greeted by the Chester town crier, a full-bearded, blue-coated throwback, who is very good indeed for business.

Go up into the north-side Watergate Rows and walk on across a little footbridge. This is probably the oldest and most interesting section of all Chester's Rows, with less glossy interiors than in most of the other houses. 'Mind Your Head' warns a sign by a shop selling

Part of Watergate Rows. The Rows offer the visitor a rare opportunity both to watch the world go by below, and to admire buildings on opposite sides of the street.

expensive, chunky, handmade furniture from real wood; no veneer here. They have followed the tradition, now mostly lost, of hanging a craft sign over the street. In this case it is a cane chair. From outside this shop you can look across to Bishop Lloyd's House, named after George Lloyd, Bishop of Chester between 1605 and 1615. Heavily restored in the 1970s, it is unusual for its coloured coats of arms set among the black-and-white half-timbering, which includes intricate and well-preserved carvings. Bishop Lloyd's daughter married (her second marriage) Theophilus Eaton, founder of the New Haven, Connecticut, settlement.

Cross the road and retrace your steps briefly on the opposite side of the street to look across at Booth Mansion, for you have, perhaps unknowingly, been in this impressive Georgian house, which is actually the local premises of Sotheby's, the auctioneers. The Trinity Church, further down, is now the Guildhall of Chester City Companies. Designed by James Morrison and built in 1865–9, the church replaces a previous church of the same name. The old Customs House building in an angle of the church, is now the offices of the magazine *Cheshire Life*.

Here it is best, I think, to retrace your steps. Back near the cross, go up to the north-side Watergate Rows. Turn into a passage which is unnamed but is beside the Old Deva pub. A sign says boldly 'Passage Leading to St Peter's Churchyard'. This unexpected and attractive backwater has considerable Georgian elegance, as well as the back of a Victorian pub and of St Peter's church. Emerging from the passageway, turn left up the pedestrianized Northgate Street. (Chester has put the car into its proper place, and this is one reason for the city's great success as a tourist destination). The cathedral is on your right, but continue on for the meantime towards the Town Hall. This is a High Victorian Gothic treat, opened in 1869 by the youthful Prince of Wales. Most of its richly, almost cloyingly, decorated chambers are open to the public.

From the Town Hall square continue north towards the Pied Bull

pub, next to which is the Red Lion, and next to that the Blue Bell! A plaque on the Pied Bull identifies this as the Bull Mansion, residence of Chester's Recorder in 1533. Rebuilt in brick in 1654, it became a pub and then a coaching house in 1780. George Borrow left from here on his tour of wild Wales in 1854, referring to the Pied Bull as 'an old fashioned inn in Northgate Street, to which we had been recommended. On the whole we found ourselves very comfortable.'

Retracing your steps past the Pied Bull, turn left into Little Abbey Gateway. You are now in Abbey Square. Again on a Sunday morning, I was too late to see inside the cathedral because a service was in progress. For a few minutes I stood in Abbey Square and tried to work out the origin of a tall obelisk in its centre. The strains of hymns seeped through the rather gaunt sandstone fabric of the cathedral. I was at least able to take a look at the cloisters while waiting for the service to end. Most of what you see in the cloisters dates from the 1500s, though there is Norman arcading in the south cloister. The cloisters were part of a monastery which stood here for more than five hundred years from its foundation in 1093 and then became a cathedral. You can walk freely all the way round. The effect is of chunky, chocolaty dark stone, very solid and heavy, combined with delicate vaulting and fluting. If you peer through the modern stained glass that now encloses the cloisters you can see a half secret little garden, with flowers and a sunken lily pool. Although it was closed for a function, I peeped through the keyhole of the thirteenth-century Refectory. Appropriately, the table was laid in readiness for a feast. I could make out the windows with representations of kings and saints and episodes from their lives. These included St Werburgh, the pious daughter of King Wulfhere and Mercia, after whom the church from which the original Benedictine monastery emerged was named.

Daniel Defoe, author of *Robinson Crusoe*, visited Chester twice at the end of the seventeenth century and very early in the eighteenth. Among much else he described the cathedral – a long time, of course, before the major renovations of the nineteenth century: 'The great church here is a very magnificent building, but 'tis built of a red, sandy, ill-looking stone, which takes much from the beauty of it and

which yielding to the weather, seems to crumble, and suffer by time, which much defaces the building.'

As almost always happens when I am told a place is undistinguished and not worth a lot of time, I liked Chester cathedral immensely. For one thing, even on an early summer Sunday, it was free of those coach parties so familiar in better-known cathedrals. The heavy restoration of the cathedral in Victorian times has been widely criticized. It was, however, in such a bad state of repair when Sir Gilbert Scott was commissioned to restore it that it might not have lasted into the twentieth century. Scott described it in 1868 as 'a mere wreck, a mouldering sandstone cliff'. Over-restoration may have kept sightseers away, but they miss the exceptional fourteenth-century choir stalls – remarkable for the fanciful misericords – and the thirteenth-century chapter house.

After leaving the cathedral by the west door, go down St Werburgh Street, past the south front of the cathedral and turn right into Godshall Lane, one of four original lanes within the city walls and referred to in the fourteenth century as St Goddestall Lane. Chester has chic shops everywhere, and some of the chicest are down here. This brings you back to Eastgate Street and via St John Street to the car park.

The previous day, surrounded by Saturday afternoon shoppers in Eastgate, I had been slightly taken aback to hear so many Welsh accents, but realized when I consulted my map in my hotel room that I had not done my geographical homework. For though in the early 1970s Chester came within an ace of being officially embraced by Greater Manchester, it does not really belong to the north country and is a Welsh border town writ large. Buses trundle in over the Grosvenor Bridge with messages in Welsh on their sides and the names of Welsh trainers crop up frequently on racecards at the Roodee. I cannot claim that the countryside around Chester is spectacular, though it is soft and pleasant enough, especially to the south. If it were, this remarkable city would be accused of being just *too* well endowed. It is one thing to have 'nearly two thousand years of recorded history' and quite another to have two thousand years of history you can reach out and touch.

LINCOLN

LINCOLN

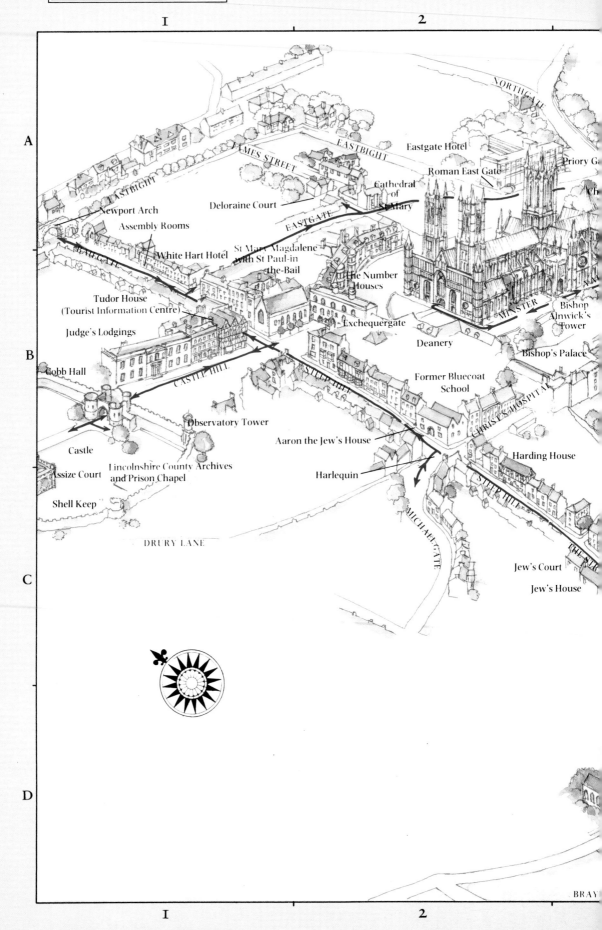

NORTHGATE

Eastgate Hotel

Priory G

Roman East Gate

Cathedral
of
St Mary

EASTBIGHT

JAMES STREET

EASTBIGHT

Newport Arch

Deloraine Court

EASTGATE

Assembly Rooms

BAILGATE

White Hart Hotel

St Mary Magdalene
with St Paul-in
-the-Bail

The Number
Houses

MINSTER

Bishop
Alnwick's
Tower

Tudor House
(Tourist Information Centre)

Exchequergate

Deanery

Bishop's Palace

Judge's Lodgings

CASTLE HILL

STEEP HILL

Former Bluecoat
School

CHRIST'S HOSPITAL

obb Hall

Castle

Observatory Tower

Aaron the Jew's House

Harding House

ssize Court

Lincolnshire County Archives
and Prison Chapel

Harlequin

STEEP HILL

THE STR

Shell Keep

DRURY LANE

MICHAELGATE

Jew's Court

Jew's House

BRAY

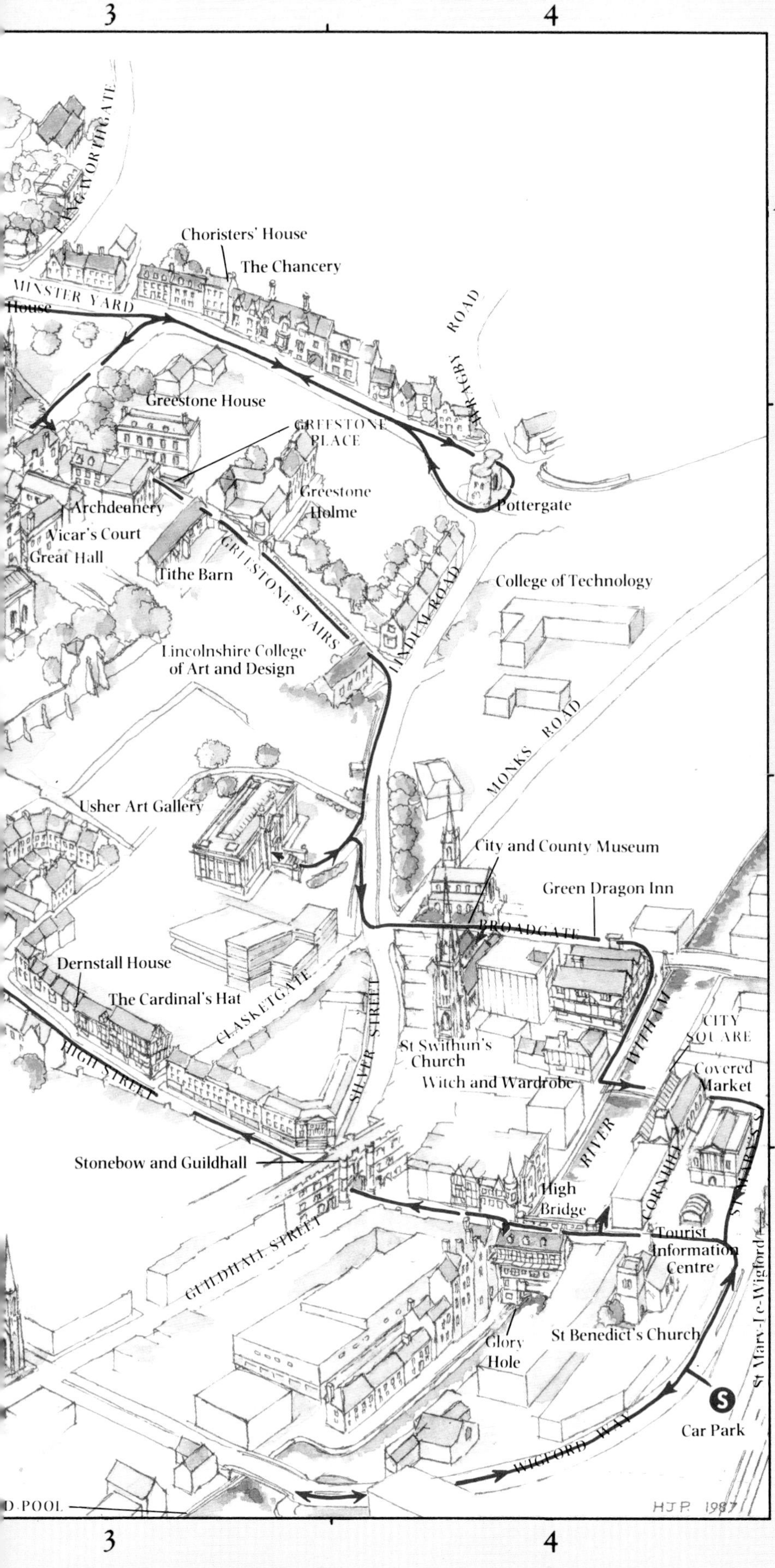

3 **4**

BUILDINGS AND
PLACES OF INTEREST

Aaron the Jew's House
  (c.1170) B2
Archdeanery B3
Assembly Rooms B1
Assize Court (1823–6) B1
Bishop Alnwick's Tower
  (1436–49) B3
Bishop's Palace (1886) B3
(Former) Bluecoat School
  (1784) B2
Castle B1
Cathedral (c.1075–1320) A2
Chancery (c14–15) A3
Chapter House A3
Choristers' House (1616) A3
City and County Museum C4
Cobb Hall (c13) B1
Covered Market C4
Deanery (c15–18) B2
Deloraine Court A2
Dernstall House C3
Eastgate Hotel A2
Exchequergate (c14) B2
Glory Hole D4
Great Hall (c13) B3
Green Dragon Inn C4
Greestone Holme B3
Greestone House (c18) B3
Harding House B2
Harlequin B2
High Bridge D4
High Street/Wigford Way Car
  Park D4
Jew's Court C3
Jew's House (c12) C3
Judge's Lodgings (1810) B1
Lincolnshire College of Art
  and Design B3
Lincolnshire County Archives
  and Prison Chapel B1
Newport Arch A1
Number Houses B2
Observatory Tower B1
Pottergate B4
Priory Gate A3
Roman East Gate A2
St Benedict's Church
  (c13) D4
St Mary Magdalene with St
  Paul-in-the-Bail
  (c.1290) B1
St Mary-Le-Wigford D4
St Swithun's Church C4
Stonebow and Guildhall
  (c15) D4
Tithe Barn (1440) B3
The Cardinal's Hat (c15) C3
Tourist Information
  Centre D4.B1
Usher Art Gallery (1927) C3
Vicar's Court B3
White Hart Hotel B1
Witch and Wardrobe C4

A

B

C

D

Map labels:

Choristers' House
The Chancery
MINSTER YARD
House
Greestone House
GREESTONE PLACE
Greestone Holme
WRAGBY ROAD
Pottergate
Archdeanery
Vicar's Court
Great Hall
Tithe Barn
GREESTONE STAIRS
LINDUM ROAD
College of Technology
Lincolnshire College
of Art and Design
MONKS ROAD
Usher Art Gallery
City and County Museum
Green Dragon Inn
BROADGATE
Dernstall House
The Cardinal's Hat
CLASKETGATE
SILVER STREET
St Swithun's Church
Witch and Wardrobe
CITY SQUARE
Covered Market
RIVER WITHAM
HIGH STREET
Stonebow and Guildhall
High Bridge
CORNHILL
Tourist Information Centre
GUILDHALL STREET
Glory Hole
St Benedict's Church
St Mary-Le-Wigford
Car Park
WIGFORD WAY
D POOL

HJP 1987

3 **4**

PAGES 84–5 *Like a
medieval vision, Lincoln
Cathedral dominates the
town. The Bishop's Palace
can also be seen sheltering
beneath its walls on the
left.*

Should you arrive in Lincoln on a rainy evening in February, with the
wind gusting roughly from the direction of Skegness and the North
Sea, and home-going traffic snarled up at the level crossing, you may
wonder whether the place is worth the candle. Traffic lights will make
more demands on your attention than the floodlit cathedral on the
hill. But visit Lincoln on an early summer day, preferably midweek
when there are fewer crowds. Stroll under the medieval arch called
Stonebow and then up Steep Hill, where birds twitter in the gardens
tucked away between cheek-by-jowl, red-brick buildings, and you
will be glad you came.

My favourite memory of the cathedral and its Minster Yard,
however, is of one January night, not when it was raining but when
six inches of virgin snow blanketed the crest of the hill and 'nothing
stirred, not even a mouse'. Yellow pools of light from the street lamps
around the cathedral precinct illuminated just a few details of this
tranquil and beautiful place and I could suddenly share the feelings of
all those who resist even the minutest change to their surroundings.

I have also climbed Steep Hill and wandered around during the
annual German-style Christmas fair, when the sound of the hurdy-
gurdy in the grounds of the castle was faintly audible, and the
pleasant whiff of *bratwurst* and *glühwein* on the afternoon air was a
reminder that medieval Lincoln would have been a smelly place, even
up here. If you go to the Christmas fair (along with Lincolnshire and
his wife), you will rub overcoats with a good part of the population of
Neustadt in West Germany, Lincoln's wine-producing twinned city.
Some guidebooks start you up here, close to heaven, but then the way
is all downhill. I prefer to follow the pilgrim's route uphill, and in any
case the area at the foot of the hill is much more interesting than it is
given credit for.

So the High Street/Wigford Way car park is the starting point of this
walk, close to the level crossing where the railway runs, most
unusually for a city, past the traffic lights and the chain stores. From
the car park walk the few yards to Brayford Pool. Slightly dark and
forbidding at times, the pool looks natural, but it actually owes its
existence to the oldest manageable canal in Britain, created nearly
two thousand years ago by the Romans to link the rivers Witham and
Trent. This was one of the reasons for Lincoln's early prosperity as a
trading centre. It is known to canal enthusiasts, but does not appeal
much to holidaymakers as it passes through flat and generally
featureless countryside. Brayford Pool, where the Fossdyke Canal
meets the River Witham, has to be negotiated with care by boatmen,
for, although it is wide, it is also shallow – apart from a dredged
channel on the north side. Among the goods Lincoln exported by
barge many hundreds of years ago was Lincoln Green, a kind of loden,
like that worn widely in Austria and Germany today, and made
famous in the chronicles of Robin Hood and his merry men. The south
side of Brayford Pool is ideal for distant photographs of the cathedral.
It was used as a vantage point by Peter de Wint, who painted several
of his canvasses from here.

Retrace your steps briefly past the multi-storey car park, then via
the underpass below the junction of Wigford Way, St Mary Street and
High Street, where you will emerge again. Look towards the Lincoln
City railway station and, closer to you, at the church of St Mary le
Wigford. A Danish settlement existed here, a trading post outside the
town. The tower of the church is Saxon. Virtually on the level

Brayford Pool brings commercial river traffic close to the heart of the city. It is shallow but has a narrow dredged channel which permits craft of a deeper draught.

crossing, very close to the signal box called High Street, and as if it were a romantic architectural flourish added to the Victorian railway is St Mary's Conduit. This was once part of a sixteenth-century system that supplied water to this corner of Lincoln from a hill to the east.

Things improve considerably as soon as you cross the road and turn northwards via the pedestrianized part of the High Street, away from the traffic fumes and with the cathedral ahead of you up on the hill. Hazy in summer, floodlit at night, this always seems further than it is. This part of the High Street, following the line of the Roman Ermine Street, is a broad, inviting, traffic-free precinct, in which stores have a little more space than usual to breathe. A pizza chain restaurant on the right has a handsome façade in white and green, newspaper vendors do not need to shout because they have a place to stand, and a small copse of direction signs stands near an area shaded by plane trees where there are seats usually occupied by tired old ladies rather than by tramps. There was once a corn market here, and now this is called Cornhill. The Tourist Information Centre (TIC) is housed in a Victorian-inspired kiosk. This is indeed a well-organized city, for while the main TIC is between the cathedral and the castle, the less touristy and more workaday 'downhill Lincoln' is not treated like a poor relation.

Unfortunately, the whiff of hot dogs and onions simmering in their pans on a mobile stall might have you holding your nose and quickening your pace. The food *inside* the covered market seems more wholesome; Lincoln after all is in the heart of some of England's most rich and productive fruit- and vegetable-growing farmland. I have been here at peak shopping time and also just minutes after the shops opened on a Monday morning, when a convention could be held in the big, two-storeyed branch of W.H.Smith. At such a time I found myself discussing the finer points of the difference between the Lincolnshire marshes and its haunting Fens with a cheese vendor from Spalding.

My disapproval of comatose hot dogs and onions did not, on one of

High Bridge from Glory Hole. Bath's Pulteney Bridge is a parvenu: Lincoln's bridge is the oldest in Britain with houses and shops on it.

the peak shopping days, prevent me from sitting down beside the River Witham, a few yards from the covered market, and polishing off a pound's worth of fish and chips, though the silently pleading swans had half the chips. The swans are so numerous here that from time to time their numbers have to be controlled by destroying the eggs. Apparently they were well-known as a delicacy at royal banquets and in 1251 Henry III ordered 125 from Lincoln and other places on the east coast. Life may indeed have been 'nasty, brutish and short', but it seems to have depended upon who you were. The swans have always been here though their numbers have been artificially boosted by ready access to chip butties, but the precinct called City Square is a recent reconstruction of a once-decrepit area. The result is not antiseptic but pleasantly human. For hundreds of years this was a busy commercial quayside, because cargo boats used to come right up as far as High Street.

Walk towards High Bridge, past the C&A department store. The steps leading from the river up to High Bridge are made to look even more functional than they are by the public lavatories on the right. Seen from along the river bank at a distance, the unusual steepness of the steps makes people on them seem to bob up and down urgently. Bath's Pulteney Bridge can eat its heart out, for High Bridge is the

ABOVE *Stuck right in the heart of commercial 'downhill Lincoln', Stonebow Arch can get overlooked. But it is an interesting structure which has stood here for hundreds of years and now contains an unusual museum.*

oldest in Britain to have houses on it. Much of the original twelfth-century structure survives, and the best of it is the entrance to the Gents. If you cross the street and go down another flight of steps on the far side of the bridge you will find yourself in the Glory Hole, an ironic local name for what must have been a dank and unwelcoming section of the river, with High Bridge and other buildings looming above.

Turn left at the top of the steps, assuming you have been into the Glory Hole, and walk as far as the Stonebow, a five-hundred-year-old archway in Tudor Gothic which in medieval times was the city's southern gate. The figures on each side of the central arch represent the Virgin Mary (patron saint of the city and the cathedral) and the Archangel Gabriel. Above the arch are the arms of James I, who visited the city in 1617. The city council meets in an imposing room at the Guildhall, above the gate, summoned by the tolling of a huge bell over six hundred years old. There is a small museum containing royal charters and civic insignia. About two hundred yards beyond here the strangely named Cardinal's Hat and Dernstall House stand side by side opposite a fancy dress shop and a café with a resident pianist, who can be seen on sunny days sitting on the traffic-free pavement in his straw hat and candy-striped jacket. This corner of Lincoln was once known as Dernstall, and the three-storeyed house called Cardinal's Hat probably refers to Thomas Wolsey, Bishop of Lincoln in 1514, who became a cardinal in 1515. It is thought to have been an inn around 1520, but after 1801 simply became a rooming house.

This is one of the shorter walks in this book, though what it lacks in distance it makes up for in gradient. With the variety of domestic architecture on the way up, the intriguing and very visitable castle, the cathedral itself, and the Usher Art Gallery discovered on the way downhill the walk is closely packed. Do not be daunted by the hill: there are railings when the ascent becomes steep to help you on your way, pubs and restaurants to stop at, and shops to browse in to save you admitting you need a breather. But best of all for morale is the fact that what awaits you is one of the most glorious hilltops in Britain.

Before reaching Steep Hill, you walk up The Strait, which approaches Steep Hill obliquely and not head on, as if to avoid deterring people from the strenuous climb. It is straight *and* narrow. Lincoln's Jewish enclave was the second largest in the country after London, and Jew's Court, on The Strait, is thought to have once been a synagogue. It stands next to Jew's House, now a restaurant – not, I think, kosher. The best recorded story of the twelfth- and thirteenth-century Jewish community concerns a certain Belasset of Wallingford. Her son's wedding, in about 1275, brought Jews to Lincoln from all over Europe. In 1290, the same year that the Jews were expelled from England, she was hanged for supposedly clipping coins. These, and other buildings on Steep Hill that have more reliable Jewish associations, have survived since the twelfth century because they were built of stone and not wood.

Does Steep Hill really get steeper as you approach the top or is it merely an impression? Certainly, people coming down can feel smug. Aching legs tend to distract one from the domestic charms of red-brick tiled houses with lichened garden walls, Regency bay windows, well-worn stone flags on the pavement, and handsome cast-iron lamp standards only recently converted to electricity. All this is a cheek-by-jowl, no-space-wasted Toytown, with some good modern in-filling and a surprising amount of greenery. This can best be seen from the roof terrace of the White Hart Hotel as well as from several points in Lincoln Castle: here a garden, there a park, here a fruit tree overhanging a brick wall, and there a manicured area of the cathedral close (Minster Yard). A lamp-post and a wooden rail across Steep Hill, with the unlikely name of the 'Mayor's Chair', are said to have been placed here to prevent the modern-day equivalent of a mid-nineteenth-century feat by one Colonel Sibthorpe, a Lincoln MP and also Lord Mayor. He is reputed to have driven down Steep Hill in a coach and four for a bet.

As you continue up Steep Hill look from the junction with Michaelgate to where the three cathedral towers soar above you. If you see it on a day when clouds are scudding past the towers, the whole structure seems to be moving. For a better view still, walk just a few paces along Michaelgate, which snakes uphill roughly parallel with Steep Hill from a little square to the side of The Strait. The tall tower at the centre of the cathedral is the tallest cathedral tower in the

country – just over 270 ft – and the bell in it is called Great Tom O'Lincoln. All three cathedral towers are out of true, though this is best seen from the Observatory Tower of the Castle. Not quite the leaning towers of Lincoln, however.

Diagonally across Steep Hill from a former inn known as the Harlequin, still with its sign, stands the highly photogenic Aaron the Jew's House, as it is popularly known, though there is some doubt as to whether it actually belonged to this particular member of the twelfth-century Jewish community. Its age is authentic, at least, though the intriguing first-floor decorative stone window has been restored and reset.

As if in a final flamboyant gesture Steep Hill gets steeper still, but the end is in sight. The last few yards are the most developed commercially, but the shops are real enough and thankfully this is no museum piece. There is also a surprisingly large number of restaurants. One of the restaurateurs created a precedent in the trade in the 1980s by being the first in Britain to produce his own credit cards. This apparently pleased his local customers and improved trade. Restaurants and wine bars seem to do well up here, and the Wig and Mitre was full of life every time I passed, but I was puzzled by the apparent paucity of antique shops.

Steep Hill was fought over by British kings – tribal chiefs, really – long before the Romans made a military base of it. *Lindum Colonia* was established roughly around the end of the first century AD, when the Ninth Legion, called *Hispana*, were in control. Later, Saxons and Danes used it to advantage.

Turn left at the top of Steep Hill towards the castle. The Assize Court, at the far end of a drive that passes through the castle precinct, is a very handsome-looking, early nineteenth-century miniature Gothic palace. One effect of this is to give the castle a municipal look, but once you are past the entrance it is a gem of its kind. The gardens alone are worth the entrance fee; I looked hard and failed to find a weed. It is recorded that 166 houses were destroyed by William the

Approaching the top of Steep Hill, with the 'uphill Lincoln' Tourist Information Centre ahead. Small wine bars and restaurants abound.

Conqueror to make room for the castle, which he built on a six-acre site at the south-west corner of the original Roman settlement; it is worth remembering that the Romans were nearly as far away in time for William as William is for us. A small exhibition illustrating the history of the castle is housed in the old prison bath-house in the grounds, behind an unlikely statue of the head and shoulders of George III, which was originally at the top of a tall column off the Sleaford-to-Lincoln road. It was removed during the war because of danger from low-flying military aircraft.

It might seem like a bad joke, if you have already negotiated Steep Hill, to say that the only way to appreciate the castle and its buildings is to keep on climbing. To get the best out of it, follow the leaflet that you are given at the pay booth on entering via the castle's eastern gateway. You will not regret the modest entrance fee. No moderately anxious child or reasonably active grandmother will feel short-changed. There are arrow slits to peer through (very secure, but with an extremely limited angle of fire), high walks to peer down from, and a good measure of gory history. It is especially worth climbing the narrow stone stairway of the Observatory Tower for impressive views over the old city and much of Lincolnshire. Only the inspection stairways and access points on the cathedral known just to the maintenance staff would take you any higher, and even those have a restricted view.

William the Conqueror did not, contrary to many people's impressions, arrive in a completely uncivilized and impoverished country, and Lincoln was a prosperous and well-organized place. He started work on the castle only about two years after the invasion, using part of the original, decayed Roman walls, covered as they were by earth banks, as a base.

Cobb Hall, closest to the entrance gate that also houses a better-than-average souvenir shop, would have been familiar to condemned prisoners from down in the well of the castle, for its roof was used for public hangings between 1817 and 1859, about twenty years before the prison was closed. Following the free and very lucid castle plan I took a sharp turn to the right alongside what used to be the prison and now houses the Lincolnshire Archive office, and made my way to the prison chapel. This is a unique survivor in England, and on a quiet, sun-dappled afternoon I had the strange, sinister but rather touching place to myself. Steeply racked rows of miniature wooden cells are just large enough for one man, with openings at the front so that when standing the prisoners could see, and their faces be seen from, the pulpit. Condemned men sat or stood at the back, debtors (many of whom were probably safer inside than out) sat at the front and women in the wings, to the clergyman's right. If walls could speak. . . .

Returning from the castle, you come back into Castle Hill, also known locally as Castle Square, where there are several very impressive buildings. The upper city Tourist Information Centre is housed in one of those imposing black-and-white, half-timbered buildings that add just a dash of picture-postcard 'olde worlde' to the predominantly red-brick or yellow-stone fabric of the old city. It stands on the corner of Bailgate and Castle Hill and is an interesting building in its own right, dating from about 1543, when it was probably occupied by a wealthy merchant. It seems to lie exactly over the Roman's *Via Principalis*, which ran from the settlement that spread over much of the top of the hill down towards Brayford Pool.

Exchequergate is at a pivotal point of 'uphill Lincoln'. This view is taken from the approach to the castle, with Bailgate to the left and Steep Hill off to the right.

To the left of this building as you face it is an impressive town house, a little more than a century older. To the left of that is the Judge's Lodgings of about 1810. On a quiet afternoon, through a half-open door, I glimpsed white-jacketed waiters with trays of drinks and heard a low murmur of voices on their best behaviour. It was a reception of some kind, but the house is used mainly by visiting judges when the Assize Court is in session.

Admire Exchequergate, which leads into Minster Yard, but do not, if keeping to this route, go through it. Instead, turn left into Bailgate and walk north past the White Hart Hotel, noticing the old-fashioned covered garage on the left. This is both an asset and a charmer. As you park your car, you half expect to find a grey-uniformed, peek-capped chauffeur removing specks of dust invisible to the normal human eye from an open-topped Bentley.

If you are staying in the White Hart Hotel phone in advance to see if you can get a room overlooking the cathedral. It makes all the difference, like being at a seaside hotel and having a view of the sea. What's more, the cathedral is regularly and spectacularly floodlit except during Lent. Looking up at its intricate west front during the night is fascinating. (In the half-light, a pigeon sweeps down from a parapet – or is it a piece of waste paper? And surely one of those seven-hundred-year-old carved figures actually moves every now and again?)

I stood and sheltered from a short, sharp shower in the entrance to the White Hart car park, and only then noticed a modest church tucked into the walls that I had previously missed. This is the parish church of St Mary Magdalene with St Paul-in-the-Bail. The original foundation was in 1290, but it was all but rebuilt in 1882. The White Hart is very old, but the extremely elegant façade belongs to the 1840s (the name, by the way, may derive from a visit to the city by Richard II, since the white hart was his personal emblem). This is one of those deep-carpeted city hotels with many stairs, ticking clocks and polished mahogany. It is said that in one room, the Yarborough Room, the idea

Bailgate and the White Hart Hotel, looking towards Steep Hill. The White Hart Hotel has an original 1840s facade and upper rooms with a spectacular view of the cathedral.

for the military tank was first expounded on 2 August 1915. The high-ceilinged dining-room, in the bowels of the building, is superb.

Continue up Bailgate, noticing on the right the Assembly Rooms and, ahead, the Newport Arch. Impressively intact and the only Roman arch in the country still spanning a main road, this looks lower than it was originally because the road level has gradually risen over almost two thousand years.

Here, retrace your steps to the White Hart Hotel and turn left along Eastgate. It is underrated but promises well. I browsed among the antique shops which, though surprisingly thin on the ground in Steep Hill, are more in evidence here. However, prices were high; a moth-eaten Victorian 'spoonback' chair was £600, spindly Georgian tea tables, 'as found', were more, and a walnut bureau ran into several thousands. As I browsed in one shop, a pert young female RAF officer breezed in to ask about repairing a musical box. I should not have been too surprised, because Lincolnshire is ankle-deep in RAF stations. Do not ignore James Street, opposite this. It was once known as Vinegar Street, which is thought to be a corruption of Vineyard Street. Notice a house called Deloraine Court, which has a Norman cellar. The Lady Deloraine who once lived here was famous for throwing bricks at Cromwellian soldiers when they came to desecrate the cathedral. To the left along Eastgate is the Bishop's House, opposite the Cathedral School, and then the modern Eastgate Hotel, out of place now but perhaps in twenty or thirty years' time. . . . The ruins on the left in the grounds of the hotel are thought to have been the foundations of the north tower of the Romans' East Gate, the double gate leading archaeologists to suppose this was the main gate of *Lindum Colonia*. The conquering Romans arrived in Lincoln in about AD 60, and they had a military base here for more than twenty-five years. By the third century AD the conqueror had endorsed a further fifty acres of the upper town, and Stonebow stands at the southern entrance of this.

With the hotel behind you cross the road, observed as you might be

ABOVE *Tennyson's statue, in Minster Yard, is a favourite point for tourists to sit and investigate their sandwiches. Tennyson was 'Lincoln's poet'.*

LEFT *The old Bishop's Palace, hard by the cathedral, is the evocative ruin of one of the finest ecclesiastical buildings of the thirteenth century.*

by window-seat diners in the hotel's first floor restaurant, and walk towards the statue of Tennyson. Near it are seats on which to eat your sandwiches or get your bearings. Tennyson was Lincolnshire's poet, as Peter de Wint was its painter. He lived in a spacious rectory, down a shady lane at Somersby, among the Lincolnshire Wolds.

Walk across the green to Pottergate, turn right and continue south-east along it. Pottergate itself marked the fourteenth-century boundary of the property owned by the Dean and Chapter of the cathedral. It now stands uncomfortably close to a main road down which, as if down a nightmarish helter-skelter, traffic thunders towards the new city centre. But it is intact and very photographable. Notice at No. 10, as you walk towards it, a Choristers' House dating from 1616 and, beside it, a fourteenth- and fifteenth-century chancery; this is the house with the unusual oriel windows. Just beyond this was the Academy established in 1840 by George Boole, the man who devised modern algebra. As you walk back up Pottergate, turn left along the southern part of Minster Yard towards Exchequergate and the west entrance of the cathedral. The word 'yard' for the cathedral close, by the way, is of Saxon origin. There has been a wall round it since 1285, and some of this original wall, usually incorporated into houses or gates, still exists. Notice on the north-west side of Minster Yard the impressive houses, which are a ready-made pageant of the best domestic architecture as it developed over several centuries. The properties were once known as the 'Number Houses', simply because they were the first in the city to have numbers.

Before entering the cathedral one sunny weekday morning, I stopped to admire the scaffolding covering a good half of the west front. For without scaffolding no English cathedral would seem complete. The Clerk of the Works was gazing upwards too. I muttered something trite about him probably not being able to get craftsmen the way they used to in the old days. He was forthright about this: 'It's not the craftsmen – we've got twenty of them, from stonemasons to plumbers. They're much easier to find than people think. They could certainly recreate the cathedral from scratch.' He sighed. 'No, it's the scale of everything. The weight of stone, for example. A twelve-inch block of the original cathedral stone weighs nearly as much as an average-sized person, and it's giving us big structural problems.' It transpired that the original roof timbers were cut from single trees and are getting on for 50 ft long. The lead covering the roof weighs altogether nearly four hundred tons.

The cathedral is huge, and its hilltop position makes it seem more so. It was conceived by Hugh of Avalon, a Carthusian monk whom Henry II appointed to the bishopric towards the end of the twelfth century. A fabulous undertaking now, but then – well, the mind boggles. As you walk round Minster Yard you will be assailed by massive flying buttresses, and there is an intricate polygonal Chapter House (so called because meetings were preceded by the reading of a chapter from the Bible). Inside, it seems vast: more than two thousand people can be accommodated in the nave. But it has intimate moments, too. I stopped to admire an exhibition for blind people, with a sound commentary. Elaborate carved figures, pieces of original masonry now replaced and sheets of lead from the roof were some of the items to handle.

Late at night the Minster Yard is noticeably quiet. Once, at midnight, I braced myself for an earth-shattering peal but nothing happened. It turned out that no bells toll between 11 p.m. and 7 a.m. unlike the medieval period when the bells were silent only between 1 a.m. and 5 a.m. There was much more ringing then than now, and altogether it was a noisier world than we usually imagine (carts in the street, salesmen shouting their wares, night watchmen calling out the hours, cattle thundering through on their way to market . . .). I once walked almost as late along Bailgate, Eastgate and Minster Yard. I peeped into the remains of the thirteenth-century Bishop's Palace and then strolled on down Steep Hill window-shopping for second-hand books.

My unorthodox glimpse of the ruined Bishop's Palace on the south side of Minster Yard was so intriguing that I found myself there at opening time the next day. The energetic Bishop Hugh, not satisfied with creating the greatest cathedral in Europe, set out to build a residential palace worthy of the cathedral itself. The main feature, the shell of which remains, was a huge aisled ceremonial hall. Hugh died in 1220, shortly before the building was completed. It was used until the sixteenth century, but suffered in the Civil War. By the eighteenth century it was the ruin that can be visited today. It is possible to tire easily of a certain type of ruin, but the Bishop's Palace has atmosphere, and it is well worth making the short detour to the site for the exceptional worm's eye view of the cathedral towering (literally) high above.

Greestone Stairs, with the Lincolnshire College of Art and Design on the left. At the top of the steps are the peaceful surroundings of the cathedral precincts.

Between the entrance to the Bishop's Palace and Pottergate lies unobtrusive Greestone Place, and the walk continues down here. It is a rather secret little lane that opens up wide views ahead and a healthy portion of architectural detail to left and right. It gives way to Greestone Stairs – a flight of stone steps – and thus back to the twentieth century with a jolt, arriving in busy Lindum Road. Notice on the right as you reach the road, among trees, the ornate nineteenth-century, red-brick and tiled building that is the Lincoln-shire College of Art and Design. A few yards further down the hill, as it curves to the left, is the Usher Art Gallery, set in gardens on the right. I went to see its Peter de Wint collection. For quite irrational reasons I had expected municipal cream and green, dimly lit galleries and a smell of paint. I found one of the handsomest and most intimate, local museum-galleries I have found anywhere, with grandfather clocks at the foot of a grand staircase, smiling custodians, lots of space, high ceilings, no crowds and inexpensive postcards and prints. I also noticed a portrait of Colonel Sibthorpe, and a note that he so greatly annoyed Queen Victoria by refusing to vote in favour of an increase in Prince Albert's Civil List payment that she refused ever again to visit the city while he remained its MP.

De Wint's special relationship with Lincoln, to which he came as a stranger in 1806, arose from his affection for the young sister of a fellow painter, William Hilton, who lived in Lincoln. Many a city would envy Lincoln's good luck, and there is a whole series of imposing watercolours of the city and especially the cathedral. Painted when cattle grazed within a hassock's throw of the cathedral's doors, and when muddy or dry and rutted tracks – depending on the time of year – would take a saddle-sore tourist's mind off the beauty of the west front, these are a unique record of the city's development. De Wint married the sister, Harriet, when she was nineteen and they lived in a house near the south-west corner of the castle. Although they travelled extensively they kept their Lincoln house as a base. An elaborate monument to De Wint (and Hilton), with carved angels and expensive flourishes, was erected by Harriet in the cathedral after her husband's death.

From the Usher Art Gallery turn right down Lindum Road, and, ignoring Clasketgate and Silver Street on your right, continue down Broadgate. Take the next lane on the right for access to the small City and County Museum housed in a Norman guildhall, restored by the Lincoln Civic Trust. Turn right again on Broadgate and you are back at the river. Immediately to the right is a fourteenth-century house called the Green Dragon, now a restaurant, and further along to the right is the Witch and the Wardrobe pub, about a century older (modernized and complete with jukeboxes inside, however). Cross the little footbridge over the water and you are back on City Square, having completed not so much a full circle as up the hill and back again.

If you drive away from Lincoln and it is dark but not raining, park your car in a lay-by and look back at the floodlit cathedral. (The A607 Grantham road is best, because it gives you a hill from which to look back.) It will be shining on its hill like a medieval vision, an incomparable sight that seems to transcend the workaday irritations of the twentieth century. That it is possible to approach it on foot up Steep Hill, along a route that gets better and better by every ancient yard, is one of eastern England's greatest joys.

NORWICH

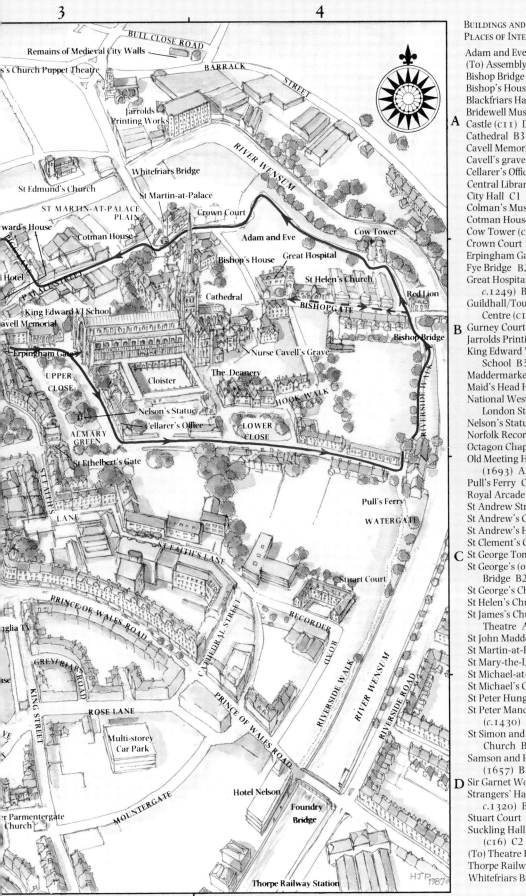

BUILDINGS AND
PLACES OF INTEREST

Adam and Eve pub A4
(To) Assembly House D1
Bishop Bridge B4
Bishop's House B4
Blackfriars Hall B2
Bridewell Museum C2
Castle (C11) D2
Cathedral B3
Cavell Memorial B3
Cavell's grave B4
Cellarer's Office (1370) B3
Central Library D1
City Hall C1
Colman's Mustard Shop C2
Cotman House A3
Cow Tower (C13–14) A4
Crown Court A4
Erpingham Gate (1420) B3
Fye Bridge B2
Great Hospital (from
  c.1249) B4
Guildhall/Tourist Information
  Centre (C15) C1
Gurney Court B3
Jarrolds Printing Works A3
King Edward VI Grammar
  School B3
Maddermarket Theatre C1
Maid's Head Hotel B3
National Westminster Bank,
  London Street C2
Nelson's Statue B3
Norfolk Record Office D1
Octagon Chapel A2
Old Meeting House
  (1693) A2
Pull's Ferry C4
Royal Arcade D2
St Andrew Street Car Park B2
St Andrew's Church C2
St Andrew's Hall (C15) B2
St Clement's Church A2
St George Tombland B3
St George's (or Blackfriars)
  Bridge B2
St George's Church A1
St Helen's Church B4
St James's Church Puppet
  Theatre A3
St John Maddermarket C1
St Martin-at-Palace A3
St Mary-the-Less B3
St Michael-at-Plea B2
St Michael's Church A1
St Peter Hungate B2
St Peter Mancroft
  (c.1430) D1
St Simon and St Jude
  Church B3
Samson and Hercules House
  (1657) B3
Sir Garnet Wolseley Pub D1
Strangers' Hall Museum (from
  c.1320) B1
Stuart Court C4
Suckling Hall/Cinema City
  (C16) C2
(To) Theatre Royal D1
Thorpe Railway Station D4
Whitefriars Bridge A3

It is a travel writer's cliché that the best towns are out on a limb. You only visit them if you have to, and do not come across them by accident. This comparative isolation has helped Norwich, a self-contained and prosperous city for hundreds of years, to survive intact.

Football fans probably know more about Norwich than Mr and Mrs Average, for both the green-and-yellow strip and the nickname ('The Canaries') of the Norwich team derive from the pet canaries traditionally kept by the Huguenot immigrants who helped to make this an exceptional weaving centre in the sixteenth century. The team should perhaps have been called 'the mustard pots', for although Colman's are now part of a large conglomerate, the company still retains its identity as a city institution. No coach party worth the salt on its fish and chips fails to include on its itinerary the reconstructed mustard shop in the medieval heart of the city.

Visitors might end the day at the Theatre Royal, run by a highly successful partnership that against all odds has made this provincial theatre into a gold-mine. But if they have a real sense of *local* history they might do better to take in a performance at the Maddermarket Theatre, home of the Norwich Players since 1921 and right in the heart of the ancient city centre. Apart from anything else, they might be glad to sit down in either the Theatre Royal or the Maddermarket, for Norwich's labyrinth of hilly back streets ('*not* very flat, Norfolk', to rephrase Noel Coward) taxes the visitor who aims to see the city properly. Because the areas that are of interest to visitors are so compact, and because its suburbs are not sprawling and oppressive, Norwich belies its size. Its population is about 120,000, and it is fair to call it the unofficial capital of East Anglia. It wears its history well, and is not precious or self-conscious.

The huge car park below the castle, occupying the site of the original Cattle Market, is impressive as these things go, but for many it is too close to the heart of the city, and this makes it harder to get orientated. Better, I think, to find your way to the St Andrew's Street multi-storey car park. One should not complain too much about the appearance of this and other concrete multi-storey car parks in the town: in the 1920s, when Norwich had so much of its medieval past intact, development threatened its character, but thankfully, it took the course of preservation and pedestrianization, and functional buildings have on the whole been kept away from the ancient heart.

Strangers' Hall, as you cross the road and turn just a few yards to your right, was, unusually, turned into a museum early this century, becoming the first folk museum in Britain. It was once a prosperous merchant's house, and dates from about 1320. The name probably derives from the fact that a succession of immigrant weavers lived there, since at the time the city was encouraging the settlement of foreign weavers to help re-establish its supremacy in cloth manufacturing. It is a medieval town house with later additions, a rhapsody in wood, and a tribute to beeswax. Traffic sounds fade as soon as you enter the courtyard, but the creaking and groaning of ancient, polished, uncarpeted floors can be slightly alarming. It is a no-nonsense sort of place, and the uniformed custodian is brisk and businesslike. As I hesitated in the Great Hall of the house, he said, 'Please start *up*stairs, sir.' Do not miss the cellar rooms, or confuse them with the way out. Especially touching is the garden seat on which Joseph Fry proposed prior to his marriage to Elizabeth Gurney. Elizabeth Fry (1780–1845) was to become famous as a prison

St John's Alley, looking towards St Andrew's Street, with the Maddermarket Theatre on the left and the ancient cemetery on the right. The design of the theatre is based on that of Elizabethan theatres.

reformer. Notice also the collection of original street signs. Some of these – like the barber's pole – are familiar, others – like the beautifully crafted Chinese figure, denoting a tea merchant's – are less so.

From Strangers' Hall turn right, but remember that the museum's Georgian Room is designed to be seen from the street – a clever idea, for who does not like to peer into the interior of other people's houses if they do not have net curtains? Turn right again into St John Maddermarket, whose name comes from the red vegetable dye made from madder, the root of a herbaceous climbing plant that was once sold here. Then fork immediately right up St John's Alley, and on your left you will see one of Norwich's ancient cemeteries now converted into gardens; 10,000 citizens are said to lie buried here. To your right after a few paces is the inviting yard of the Maddermarket Theatre, set well back from the lane.

I only went to the theatre to see what was on but somebody in the spacious foyer, where there was an exhibition of local painters, thought I was there to audition for *Cowardy Custard*, a compilation of Noel Coward's songs and sketches (including no doubt 'very flat, Norfolk' from *Private Lives*). The Maddermarket Theatre was created by the Shropshire-born Nugent Monck in 1921, in what had originally been built as a Roman Catholic Church in 1794. Monck was the first person in modern times to revert to the Elizabethan idea of an open stage, and before he retired in 1952 he had personally produced nearly 280 plays, including all of Shakespeare's.

Turn right if you have been into the Maddermarket Theatre, or continue up St John's Alley if you have not, and walk through the arch of the tower of what was St John Maddermarket but is now a Greek Orthodox Church – one of Norwich's redundant churches that has had a new lease of life. Norwich has over thirty parish churches, mostly in the perpendicular style, and three-quarters of them are now redundant. In most cases they owe their existence to highly prosperous wool merchants hoping to assure themselves of a place in heaven. They are generally faced with flint, and this can look

The church of St Peter Mancroft is sometimes mistaken – on account of its size and its magnificent interior – for Norwich cathedral. It broods over the market place.

particularly good in wet weather, which is a consolation if you have chosen a bad day to visit the city. The first written comment on these flint churches seems to have come from Celia Fiennes, the inexhaustible traveller and diarist who explored much of England in the last years of the seventeenth century. She said they were 'built of flints well headed or cut which makes them look blackish and shining'. The flints she referred to had been 'knapped' – that is, cut and worked, with the shiny parts exposed.

Turn right into Pottergate, a busy little street during shopping hours and also an archaeologist's delight. For this street, once part of Norwich's medieval network of back-alleys, was as the name suggests occupied in part by potters, whose artefacts have always been good survivors. Turn left into Lower Goat Lane, walk up a slight incline, and you begin to approach the market place and City Hall. Lower Goat Lane is good for window shopping: expensive fabrics, a record and tape shop and a small baker's.

Cross Guildhall Hill, turn left, with the red-and-white, green-and-white and blue-and-white stripes of the open-air market awnings ahead of you, and allow yourself a few minutes in the Tourist Information Centre, which could hardly be more impressively housed than here in the fifteenth-century Guildhall. It is much more spacious than most, and has the great advantage of having the whole of the county of Norfolk to promote – an unknown quantity to most travellers who award themselves a pat on the back for even finding Norwich. The Guildhall was begun in 1407, and its builders were organized on a very simple basis: they were forced! The Guildhall was the seat of city administration until 1938, when it was superseded by the new City Hall that many Norwich people love to hate.

If you have not spent too long in the Strangers' Hall, and time is on your side, continue down Guildhall Hill, noticing the elegant old library set back from the lane, and turn left into the pedestrian precinct. Here there is a National Trust shop, a couple of pubs and a betting shop, which can be handy if you find yourself here on Derby Day, as I did once. Turn left again into Pottergate and into Lower Goat Lane once more. Despite modernization, it is a way to appreciate what the medieval streets might have been like.

Walk through the market, under the multi-coloured awnings, towards the church of St Peter Mancroft, which is one of the thirty-six original parish churches in Norwich, and the most distinguished, and has watched over the activities of the market for several hundred years. It dates from about 1430 and is sometimes mistaken for the cathedral. There is some superb fifteenth-century stained glass in the east window. Try to see it against a winter afternoon sky, when Norfolk, one of England's larger counties, seems particularly eerie and vast, and Norwich feels like a city on the edge of the world, with a raw-edged beauty that is often rather muted on a balmy summer day. Several Norwich characters are commemorated or buried within its walls, notably Sir Thomas Browne, physician, philosopher and author, who lived in Norwich from 1643 to 1682.

The predecessors of the well-upholstered market gardeners and the trinket and spice sellers you see today in the open-air market would have heard St Peter Mancroft's bells peeling to celebrate the defeat of the Spanish Armada in 1588. Norfolk dialect still survives in the market and beyond. I overheard an example of this as I strolled among the stalls: 'Who that? She know we but we don't know she.'

City Hall, with the market below, would not hold a candle to the church or the Guildhall, but it has a good reputation among architects for its hand-made, multi-coloured bricks. There is also much affection for the clock picked out in gold and topped by a green pinnacle. Parts of the interior, including the council chamber, are usually open for inspection by arrangement. On a bright day the clock catches the sunlight, and is unconsciously complemented by the unmistakable Whitbread cockerel perched outside the Sir Garnet Wolseley pub on your right as you look towards the market. It was named after a local soldier who arrived at the Battle of Khartoum too late to save General Gordon. Also to your right you can just make out – partially obscured – the castle keep upon Castle Hill.

From here it is worth a detour via the library towards Theatre Street to see the Theatre Royal and the Assembly House. In what is now the music room of the latter, four hundred guests danced on one occasion to celebrate Nelson's triumph at the Battle of Trafalgar. In Rampant Horse Street, at the eastern end of Theatre Street, horses were sold, as well as fish, most of which was imported from Scandinavia.

From St Peter Mancroft, turn right out of the iron gates parallel with Pudding Lane, and walk towards Gentleman's Walk (on some maps, simply called The Walk), which flanks the east side of the market. This is a popular rendezvous, with the chance to dodge into Royal Arcade if it rains while you are waiting. An evocative picture of Norwich market, painted by John Sell Cotman in 1806 and now in the Castle Museum, shows Gentleman's Walk as well as many other fascinating details. The Royal Arcade was created in 1899 by George Skipper, a local architect whose work on this and other late Victorian and Edwardian buildings did not disgrace the city's rich medieval style and character. It is well liked by buskers, as they don't get rained on. At the end of the arcade cross over the road into Arcade Street, which leads up to Castle Meadow. Here turn right and left, following the hill round to reach the road which brings you to the castle.

In 1075, about fifty years after it was built, the castle became the county gaol, and this was its main function for over seven centuries. It is one thing to see the dungeons today, among parties of excited schoolchildren, another to have been confined in them. It is said that in 1692 over thirty prisoners were held for nearly two months in conditions so cramped that they were unable to lie down. In 1887 a new prison was built to the north-west, on Mousehold Heath, and in 1894 the castle became a civic museum.

What you see of the eleventh-century castle today is not exactly a fake, though it has been restored over the centuries and all the exterior fabric was skilfully resurfaced with Bath stone between 1834 and 1839. The interior is not what it was, either, but the result is to everyone's advantage: a prize-winning museum, mainly of local archaeology and paintings of the Norwich school. The dioramas of primitive life (anxious looking three-dimensional scale figures squatting among flints, red-bearded village elders, and small elephants in the distance) put the much more famous dioramas in London's Science Museum in the shade. The most spectacular areas of the museum, however, are the cool, high-ceilinged galleries in the Rotunda, opened in 1969 and devoted to John Sell Cotman, John Crome and other painters of the evocative and popular Norwich school. The Dutch influence on Norfolk was not confined to weaving and domestic architecture: their tradition of landscape painting

The Royal Arcade, which leads off the market. Buskers like it here, as they can keep out of the rain, and apparently the acoustics are good.

Norwich Castle, which was restored by the Victorians in a fairly faithful reconstruction of the original. The Castle Museum is probably best known for its collection of paintings by the Norwich School.

translated well to this part of the country, which is remarkable for its huge skies, slow-moving rivers and slightly undulating landscape dotted with church towers. The skill with which the Norwich school captured the essence of this rural Norfolk influenced the whole of English painting.

To move from the Norwich school galleries back in time into the keep is dramatic. Traces of Norman rooms are visible, and the most exciting thing for many small visitors is the original well, seen through a metal grille and over 100 ft deep. Notice at the main entrance to the castle, along with panoramic views of the city, the inscribed memorial to Robert Kett, leader of the Norfolk Revolt of 1549, hanged for his pains after the failure of the rebellion.

After the castle return to Castle Meadow, cross the road, turn right and negotiate the knots of people waiting for buses travelling towards Thorpe Road and Carrow Road, the direction of Colman's mustard works. In summer the high bank below the castle is a mass of tall grasses and wild flowers, left unharmed by passers-by. Turn left down Opie Street, known a couple of centuries ago as Devil's Lane. At the bottom of the street, next to a jeweller's shop, a plaque marks the spot where a sedan chair used to stand for hire. By all means admire the National Westminster Bank ahead of you as you turn into the pedestrianized London Street, but note that for all its classical lines it dates not from the 1760s or thereabouts but from 1924. Past here (forking to the right of the bank) turn second right into Bridewell Alley for a real treat even by Norwich standards. Almost immediately on the right is the Mustard Shop, the very effective public face of Colman's, selling variations on the mustard theme, and with a little museum too. I was impressed to read that the original factory hooter at the factory in Carrow Road could be heard from 13 miles away.

On the same side of Bridewell Alley is the Bridewell Museum. I arrived in the peaceful little courtyard that it flanks rather late in the afternoon and the custodian looked doubtfully at his watch. 'You've got only half an hour,' he said. 'I'm sure that'll do,' I replied, but how wrong I was. For this museum bursts at the seams with the most compelling artefacts of all – those that are just within living memory. (It is the kind of place where you hear people say, 'Oh, my grandmother had one of those. I threw it out just after she died.') As so often in this type of museum, the most poignant exhibits are old photographs. A row of shopboys, from about 1910, gazes slightly suspiciously at the camera outside the butcher's: how many of them, I wonder, survived the First World War? In photographs of houses around the old market, before it was pulled down, a handsome man in a wing collar strolls by, oblivious of the photographer. If you have children with you, make sure they are in the clock room at twelve noon, when the cacophony of a score of Norwich striking clocks at their finest hour is quite an event.

This is roughly the mid-point of the walk, and by chance you are only a couple of hundred yards from the multi-storey car park. At the bottom of Bridewell Alley, turn right into St Andrew's Street. From St Andrew's Church you can see a substantial building across the street which looks like another church but is actually something else. Here, you are at St Andrew's Plain – 'Plain' being a local name for an irregularly shaped town square derived from the Dutch *plein* and just one of several reminders of Norwich's early Huguenot associations. St Andrew's Plain is mentioned in a contemporary account of the Kett rebellion, when the Earl of Warwick's troops were met by 'a mighty force of arrows as flakes of snow in a tempest'. The large building you see is St Andrew's Hall, the great nave of a Dominican friary whose original cloisters form part of the adjacent Blackfriars Hall. These two unusual city-centre buildings were bought by the town after the Reformation and used for civic occasions. The famous physician Thomas Browne was knighted here in 1671 by Charles II, and a local poet wrote of the event: 'Then the King knighted the so famous Browne whose worth and learning to the world are known.'

As you cross St Andrew's Street look to your right at Cinema City. The Tourist Information Centre in the Guildhall is impressive, but to go to the pictures in Suckling Hall, a fourteenth-century merchant's house with Tudor and Georgian extensions, is a memorable event. I walked through St Andrew's Hall and Blackfriars Hall on a Saturday morning making for the exit to Elm Hill. I could have had coffee in the crypt, bought home-made fudge or crochet-work at a craft market, or been a fly on the wall at a junior dancing class. If the two halls are not open, turn right in front of them along Princes Street, then left before St Peter Hungate Church into Elm Hill. St Peter's is redundant, but it has been reincarnated as a church museum and brass-rubbing centre. Notice, in particular, the full-sized, rather contented-looking skeleton in its open 'coffin'.

Near the top of Elm Hill, a few yards from St Andrew's Hall, I looked into a small café called the Briton's Arms, getting in just before it closed. There I found a log fire (actually a gas imitation, but not bad all the same), home-made apple pie and cream, and a smiling pro-prietress. This handsome, tall, thatched building was originally a pub, but was given to the city by the brewers. The survival of the thatch is a small miracle, as a series of disastrous fires in the sixteenth century eventually led to a ban on thatched roofs in Norwich.

Turn right out of here, walk just a few yards, and pause in front of a descendant of the elm tree from which Elm Hill gets its name. This one appears to have survived the ravages of the Dutch elm disease of the

ABOVE *Wensum Street, with part of the Maid's Head Hotel on the right and the redundant church of St Simon and Jude, which stands on the corner of Elm Hill, on the left.*

Princes Street, displaying a happy juxtaposition of the domestic architecture of different periods. Such back streets tend to be quiet even when the city is busy.

1970s and is located in a part of the street called The Plain (another Huguenot reminder, as explained earlier). Notice on the house almost opposite the Briton's Arms the plaque to one Father Ignatius, who attempted between 1864 and 1866 to establish a Benedictine Monastery here (the street running from the top of Elm Hill in the direction of the river is called Monastery Street). A little further down Elm Hill is the Stranger's Club (open by prior application), from one of whose windows Elizabeth I watched a pageant in her honour. She was moved by the affection shown to her by the people and always retained a fondness for the city.

It is not surprising that the small handful of antique shops here do so well, for it is a natural reaction of visitors to want to take a little bit of the past back with them. Hardly a house in the street is less than three hundred years old and several are period pieces in their own right. But happily none puts the others into the shade. Eight mayors of Norwich have lived here, which is an indication of the street's importance, but a hundred years ago it was almost derelict and was saved shortly after the First World War by the city council. They intended at first to demolish the ancient houses and develop the valuable site, but finally decided to preserve it, and it stands today as a rare early example of environmental protection.

As you walk downhill, be sure to turn left into the Elm Hill Riverside Gardens, to one side of which there is extremely central car parking (for lucky or tenacious motorists). The gardens are ideal for picnicking, getting orientated, taking a riverboat cruise for a mallard's eye view of the city's backyard or just gazing at the River Wensum. On a Saturday morning I looked into a jumble sale in St Simon and Jude Church, on the corner of Elm Hill and Wensum Street. A triumph of hope over experience, perhaps, but there was some Georgian silver among the junk and battered Dinky cars in a glass case – only veteran Rolls Royces can have appreciated so well in value, pound for pound.

Turn right into Wensum Street. On the opposite side of the street is the Maid's Head Hotel, which is one of the county's most celebrated

Augustine Steward's House, on Tombland Alley, was the headquarters of the royal army sent to crush the Norfolk Revolt in 1549.

old coaching inns. It is now a three-star hotel whose comfortable antiquity is somewhat disguised under Edwardian black-and-white half-timbering, and whose old coaching yard has been glassed in to create a buttery-cum-wine bar. H.V.Morton, the travel writer whose books about Britain in the 1920s and 1930s ran into dozens of reprints, spoke admiringly of 'a fourteenth-century hotel which has hot and cold water laid on to the bedrooms' and this was presumably the Maid's Head. That was in about 1926 or 1927, and though things have improved since, the Maid's Head is still *the* hotel in Norwich. The Maid's Head has figured in enough accounts of visits to Norwich and life in the city to fill a book in themselves. These include those of Parson Woodforde, bon viveur, Norfolk-based clergyman and author of *The Diary of a Country Parson*, who dined here with a niece on 11 October 1786 at a cost of 4 shillings. The hotel figures in L.P.Hartley's *The Go-Between*, whose main character, young Leo, is taken to lunch by the daughter of the family with whom he is staying in the country. 'We lunched at the Maid's Head in Wensum Street, and this was a great occasion for me.' Immediately in front of the Maid's Head's main entrance is a statue of Edith Cavell, a nurse, whose grave is in the cathedral. Born in the Norfolk village of Swardeston, she was executed by the Germans during the First World War for helping Allied prisoners to escape.

Tombland, looking towards St George's Church. The name 'Tombland' has nothing to do with graveyards, and in fact derives from a Saxon word for open space.

From the bookshop in Wensum Street, opposite the hotel, walk along Tombland, as far as the curiously decorated house on your right, set well back from the road. This is Augustine Steward's House, built *c.* 1530 and used as the headquarters of the royal armies sent to crush the Norfolk Revolt in 1549. Steward was sheriff in 1526, and mayor three times, in 1534, 1546 and 1556. Turn right past the house (it is anyway best seen from the side) into Tombland Alley, with the church of St George's Tombland on your left. Then turn left into Princes Street – though a detour to the right of a hundred yards brings you to the Princes Inn Restaurant, said to have been Robert Kett's headquarters – and left again back into Tombland with the Erpingham Gate into the cathedral close across the road to your left. The pub on the corner of Princes Street and Tombland is The Edith Cavell. This was formerly the Army and Navy, after a home for soldiers and sailors that used to be nearby.

I have, sad to say, overheard a tour-bus guide (not a 'blue-badge' guide officially registered by the English Tourist Board) tell his party that Tombland was so called because it covers the site of former graveyards. This is wrong, but perhaps an understandable mistake, for the heart of Norwich is peppered with old churches and many of their burial grounds are covered over. In fact 'Tombland' derives from the Saxon word *tom*, meaning open space. This was originally a

market place until the present site near St Peter Mancroft took precedence.

If you enter the cathedral close through the Erpingham Gate, built in 1420 by Sir Thomas Erpingham, you will see to your left some of the earliest buildings of the King Edward VI School, where Cotman, Crome, the traveller and writer George Borrow, and Nelson were all pupils. The cathedral's west front is not the most handsome in Britain. The great spire peeps out from behind it like something that belongs to another church altogether; some people think this was because an original plan to build a west tower had to be abandoned. Inside, however, virtually everything is harmonious.

I once had a good opportunity to appreciate the special beauty of the nave while attending a University of East Anglia performance of Handel's *Messiah* a few days before Christmas. The acoustics, alas, did not enhance their efforts, but the exceptionally long, predominantly Norman nave was a pleasure to gaze at. I have also seen it at dusk, when more light than you might expect from the twelfth-century nave had begun to die, and shadowy figures moved like friendly ghosts. Above the Norman columns, however, the roof is fifteenth-century, built after a fire, caused by lightning, destroyed the original wooden Norman roof.

In 1362 the wooden spire collapsed in a gale and a hundred years

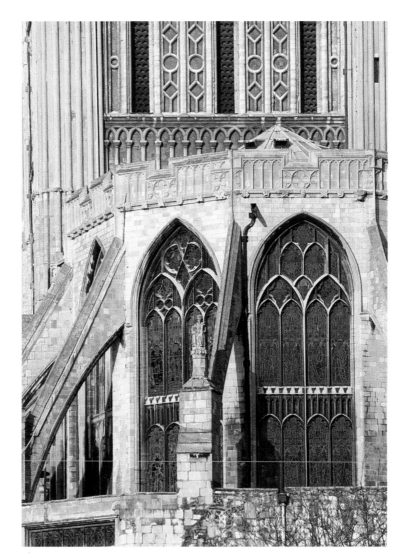

ABOVE LEFT *The cathedral close with pupils of the King Edward VI school in bright blue blazers. The cathedral spire is the second highest in Britain after Salisbury.*

ABOVE RIGHT *A detail of the cathedral, including some of the continental-looking flying buttresses. The cathedral has been heavily but very sympathetically restored.*

later this was replaced with the beautiful spire you see today, the highest in England after Salisbury's. Cathedrals and wood were not, it seemed, made for each other. But it was to support the new roof that the cathedral acquired the distinctive flying buttresses that give it a continental appearance.

From the cathedral close walk eastwards to the river and Pull's Ferry. The arched gateway, which was the original site of the ferry, was built in the fifteenth century to guard the approach to the cathedral and the priory, and spanned the narrow canal that led from the River Wensum to the cathedral close. The canal was dug before work started on the cathedral in the twelfth century, and was used to transport the stone from Normandy, iron from Sweden and timber from the shores of the Baltic, all of which arrived in Norwich via the North Sea, Great Yarmouth, and the rivers Yare and Wensum. The waterway would also have been used to deliver peat from the fens to the priory kitchens. Not long after the priory was closed down during the Reformation, the Ferry House was built and was also used as an inn. The first ferryman, at the time of Elizabeth I, was called Sandling, but the man from which Pull's Ferry gets its name lived and worked here at the beginning of the nineteenth century.

Follow the river walk northwards towards the Red Lion pub. It is worth taking a short detour up Bishopgate to see the Great Hospital.

Pull's Ferry is named after a one-time ferryman. The gravelled path under the arch was once a waterway leading towards the cathedral.

To do so, turn left just before the pub, and walk towards the city centre, away from the river. The bridge you leave behind is Bishop Bridge, which is the route John Kett took into Norwich in 1549. The Great Hospital was founded exactly three hundred years before John Kett's incursion, to house thirty 'poor and decrepit chaplains' and to provide hot midday meals and warmth in winter for thirteen paupers.

From the Red Lion, follow the river again towards the intriguing and unmistakable Cow Tower ahead of you. They say that a shot from Kett's gunner grazed the top of the tower, which must have been very good for morale but would not have had much strategic importance. Cow Tower was ancient even then, having been part of the fourteenth century city's defences at a strategic bend in the River Wensum. Keep walking along the towpath amid rural-seeming and usually quite deserted pastureland to where you have to turn sharply left, and then, with the Adam and Eve pub in sight, go into the pub yard, with a car park on your right. A pub of this name has stood here for over seven hundred years and parts of the present building are six hundred years old. The striking sign, depicting Adam and Eve as naked children, was mentioned in a 1720 reference to 'the garden called Adam and Eve's garden from the sign of an alehouse there'.

Walk straight on from the Adam and Eve, with the new Norwich Crown Court on your right, towards Palace Plain – 'Plain' again, but in reality rather decorative, with the north gate of the cathedral opposite, and bright-blue blazered boys of King Edward VI School playing French cricket as I passed by. The Georgian house next to the Wig and Pen pub was the home of John Sell Cotman, who lived from 1782 to 1842. Walk past the car showrooms and, immediately before you reach the Maid's Head car park, turn right into Pigg Lane. At the end of Pigg Lane, where you reach Quayside, you are once again by the River Wensum, roughly in front of a huge antiques and bric-à-brac warehouse. On the opposite bank of the river, well to your right, is Jarrold's printing works. This was built on the site of the Whitefriars monastery, which is commemorated by Whitefriars Bridge to the east of the Blackfriars Bridge, or St George's Bridge, that we will cross very near the end of the walk.

Turn left and, with the river on your right, walk along Quayside, then cross the bridge. Turn first left by the Church of St Clement's, Colegate. This is probably the oldest church in Norwich, and its light and simple interior is pleasantly unpretentious. It is also one of only seven Norwich churches that still function as parish churches. Colegate, where prosperous wool merchants once lived, is a quiet backwater worth exploring for its interesting mixture of medieval and Georgian buildings. Here, you are 'over the water' in a corner of Norwich many visitors miss entirely. Even on a weekday afternoon, when rush hour traffic is snarled up in the city centre, Colegate – so near and yet so far from the heart of Norwich – has a sleepy Sunday afternoon atmosphere. As you walk west along the street, look out for an opening on the right leading to the Old Meeting House of 1693. A few yards further on is the Octagon Chapel, in the process of being spruced up in blue and white when I called. John Wesley called it 'the most elegant meeting house in Europe', and asked 'How can it be thought that the old coarse gospel should find admission here?'

John Crome is buried in St George's Colegate, the rather low-roofed church on the opposite corner as you turn left up St George's Street. Along this street you pass a clutch of fashionable, new shops, a patio with seats outside and a brand new shopping precinct, before you return via St George's Bridge to St Andrew's Hall, where there is a low-ceilinged pub – another Red Lion – on the corner of St Andrew's Street. Here, you are just a few yards from the St Andrew's Street car park, which lies to the right.

For all its flinty character, Norwich is relaxed and welcoming. It does not have the air of complacency some places seem to have, though visitors who respond to, say, the extremely warm and outgoing character of the citizens of York may find East Anglians rather reserved and cautious. They have a laconic, dry sense of humour, as a snippet from the local Eastern Daily Press indicates: an elderly farmworker, it seems, had been confined to bed for weeks, and under strict doctor's orders had been denied any food for days. During his last visit the doctor told the man's wife that death was only hours away, and that she could give him anything he wanted to eat. After the doctor had left she called up the stairs, 'The doctor he say you can hev anything you like to eat now!' This was very good news indeed for the old man. He called down, 'Blast if I wouldn't love some o' that ham you've got cooking down there.' 'You can't have none o' that,' his wife shouted up, 'that's for the funeral.'

OXFORD

OXFORD

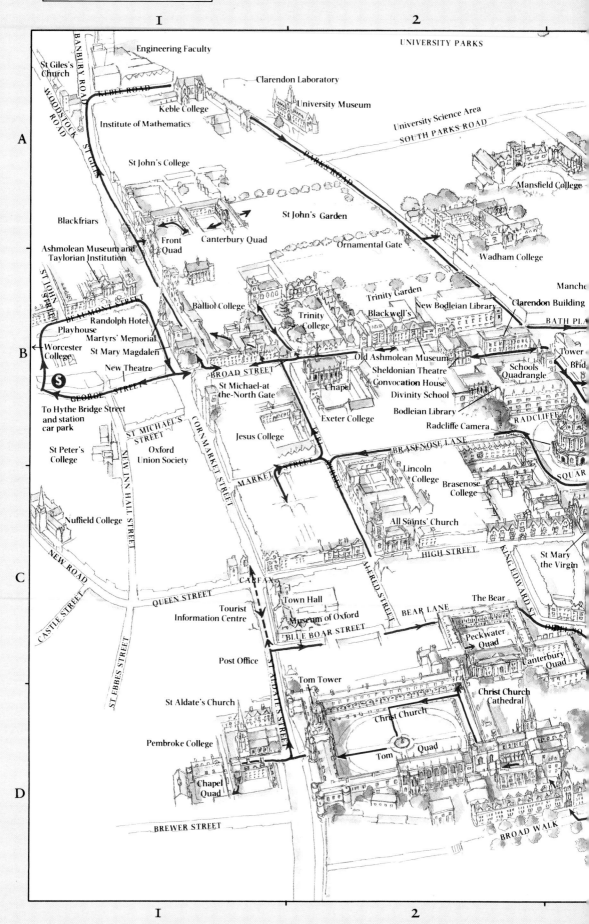

1 **2**

UNIVERSITY PARKS

St Giles's Church

Engineering Faculty

Clarendon Laboratory

University Museum

Keble College

University Science Area

SOUTH PARKS ROAD

WOODSTOCK ROAD

BANBURY ROAD

KEBLE ROAD

Institute of Mathematics

A

ST GILES

St John's College

Mansfield College

PARKS ROAD

St John's Garden

Blackfriars

Front Quad

Canterbury Quad

Ornamental Gate

Wadham College

Ashmolean Museum and Taylorian Institution

ST JOHN

BEAUMONT STREET

Balliol College

Trinity Garden

New Bodleian Library

Clarendon Building

Manche

Randolph Hotel

Trinity College

Blackwell's

BATH PLA

Playhouse

Martyrs' Memorial

B

Worcester College

St Mary Magdalen

Old Ashmolean Museum

Schools Quadrangle

Tower Brid

New Theatre

BROAD STREET

Sheldonian Theatre

Ⓢ

St Michael-at-the-North Gate

Chapel

Convocation House

Divinity School

GEORGE STREET

Bodleian Library

RADCLIFFE

To Hythe Bridge Street and station car park

Exeter College

Radcliffe Camera

ST MICHAEL'S STREET

Jesus College

BRASENOSE LANE

SQUAR

St Peter's College

Oxford Union Society

Lincoln College

Brasenose College

NEW INN HALL STREET

CORNMARKET STREET

MARKET STREET

All Saints' Church

HIGH STREET

St Mary the Virgin

Nuffield College

KING EDWARD ST

C

NEW ROAD

QUEEN STREET

CARFAX

Tourist Information Centre

Town Hall

Museum of Oxford

BEAR LANE

The Bear

CASTLE STREET

ST EBBES STREET

BLUE BOAR STREET

Peckwater Quad

Canterbury Quad

Post Office

ST ALDATE'S STREET

ALFRED STREET

Tom Tower

Christ Church Cathedral

St Aldate's Church

Christ Church

Pembroke College

Tom Quad

Chapel Quad

D

BREWER STREET

BROAD WALK

1 **2**

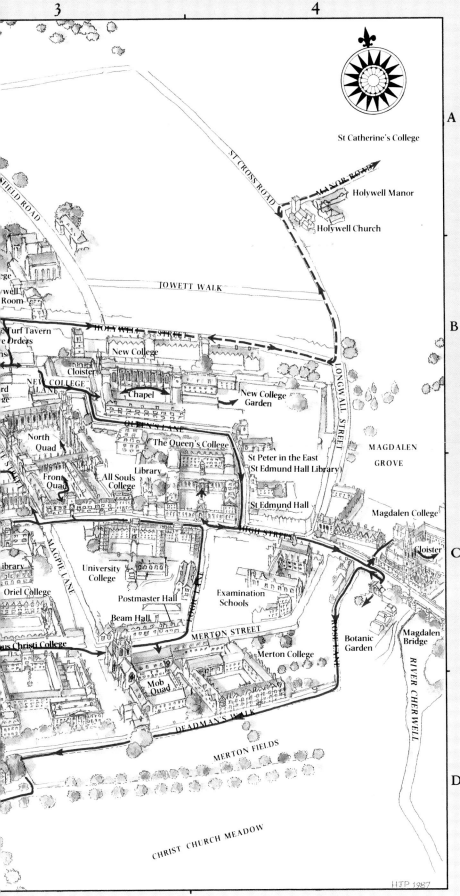

Grid references: 3, 4

BUILDINGS AND
PLACES OF INTEREST

All Saints' Church C2
All Souls College (f.1437) C3
Ashmolean Museum B1
Balliol College (f.1262) B1
Beam Hall C3
Blackwell's Bookshop B2
Bodleian Library
   (1613–19) B2
Botanic Garden (1621) C4
Brasenose College
   (f.1509) C2
Bridge of Sighs (1913–14) B3
Christ Church (f.1532) D2
Clarendon Laboratory A1
Corpus Christi College
   (f.1516) D3
Divinity School (begun
   c.1420) B2
Examination Schools
   (1877–82) C4
Exeter College (f.1314) B2
Hertford College (f.1874) B3
Holywell Music Room
   (1748) B3
Institute of Mathematics A1
Jesus College (f.1571) B1
Keble College (f.1870) A1
Lincoln College (f.1427) C2
Magdalen Bridge (1778) C4
Magdalen College
   (f.1458) C4
Manchester College
   (f.1889) B3
Mansfield College
   (f.1886) A2
Martyrs' Memorial B1
Merton College (f.1264) C4
Museum of Oxford C2
New Bodleian Library
   (1939) B2
New College (f.1379) B3
Nuffield College (f.1949) C1
Old Ashmolean Museum B2
Oriel College (f.1326) C3
Pembroke College
   (f.1624) D1
Playhouse B1
Queen's College (f.1340) C3
Radcliffe Camera
   (1737–49) B3
Randolph Hotel B1
St Aldate's Church D1
St Catherine's College
   (f.1960) A4
St Edmund Hall (f.1269) C4
St John's College (f.1555) A1
St Peter's College (f.1929) B1
Schools Quadrangle B2
Sheldonian Theatre
   (1663–9) B2
Tom Tower (1682) D2
Trinity College (f.1554) B2
Trinity Garden B2
University College
   (f.1249) C3
University Museum
   (1855) A2
Wadham College (f.1612) A2
Worcester College
   (f.1714) B1

HJP 1987

PAGES 120–21 *Merton
Street runs roughly
parallel with the High, but
it seems a world away.
Bicycles are carelessly
propped against a wall, and
cars are a rarity.*

On a late spring day in Oxford, the local radio station is prattling on
about the unaccustomed hot spell ('never since records began …').
The famous fallow deer at Magdalen, a far cry from Landseer's *Stag at
Bay*, are grazing half-heartedly, and the clunk-click of croquet played
in T-shirts and shorts on the adjacent lawn attracts nearly as much
attention from assembled tourists. Magdalen is certainly one of the
two or three most popular colleges among visitors, but perhaps it is
just a little overrated.

The severe Victorian architecture of the main quad at Keble (which
is *under*rated) is somewhat relieved in the early afternoon by knots of
students sitting cross-legged on the grass. They are relaxed and
cheerful: exams are close, but not that close. In the background the
clatter of knives and forks from the dining hall drowns out the
birdsong.

The porters at the impressive St Aldate's entrance to Christ Church.
Tom Quad behind them, are bouncing on the balls of their feet, not
betraying the uncomfortable stuffiness of their dark suits, balefully
eyeing the tourists as they approach the hallowed portals. For visitors
to the college must sidle in by a different entrance beside Christ
Church Meadow, on the south side of the college.

The city does seem to need good weather. Cambridge is more
melancholy, on the edge of the flat and lugubrious fen country, and
seems able to shrug off drizzle. Oxford warms to the sun, and the
Headington stone of which so many colleges are built glows in it.

The place is no joke for motorists, which is why Oxford runs a
successful 'park and ride' scheme, ferrying people into the city by bus
from outlying car parks. Happily it remains just right for strollers,
though anyone attempting to see all the university's forty colleges
may start to feel some affinity with one Pastor Moritz, who in 1782,
intending to see the whole university, found himself walking wearily
along the High after crossing Europe on foot. He got into conversation
with an English clergyman who described it as 'one of the finest,
longest, and most beautiful streets, not only in a city but in England,
and if I may safely add, in all Europe'. A difficulty is that Oxford is so
jam-packed with both exquisite corners and more formal and
imposing sights that it can be a frustrating experience. No sooner do
you tell an acquaintance that you absolutely loved the gardens at
New College than he says, 'Ah, but did you see Cloister Quad?' If you
mention how impressed you were with the music emanating into
Merton Street from Merton College chapel he will then say, 'Mm,
though if you haven't heard the choir at Magdalen you haven't lived.'

If this walk were designed as a twenty-minute stroll with a glimpse
of the best of Oxford I would say start in the High Street, walk round
Radcliffe Square, and up towards Broad Street. Or call it the Broad:
except for New College most Oxford names, colleges and streets carry
some sort of abbreviation. But for a more serious walk, I suggest
taking as your starting point the railway station car park, which has
easy access and a large capacity.

From the station car park walk to Worcester Street via Hythe Bridge
Street. Worcester College is on the left as you walk north along
Worcester Street. Behind its imposing front, which was designed in
1720 to close off Beaumont Street visually, lies one of Oxford's most
remarkable gardens. It also has the only lake among the college
gardens and one that is substantial, peaceful and rural-seeming too. I
walked here on a midsummer evening, when there was still enough

sun to flatter flowerbeds pretty as a seed-packet picture, set around the lawn of the mid-eighteenth century quad.

From Worcester bear right into Beaumont Street, noticing Walton Street on your left as you turn. Beaumont Palace, birthplace of Richard I, once stood here. Not much frequented by visitors, Walton Street is probably best known for its cinema, two Indian restaurants at the last count, and a wide variety of student 'digs'. It also contains the offices of the Oxford University Press. Beaumont Street is a little gem, worth dawdling along, even if it were not for the Ashmolean Museum on the left at the end, which stands opposite the Randolph Hotel – High Victorian juxtaposed with Greek Revival. Do not, however, miss the charming, low-key St John Street, on the left before you reach the Ashmolean. It has scarcely a hair out of place, with modest two- and three-storeyed, terraced stone houses, the whole scene little changed since the early nineteenth century. Notice too, on the right, the discreet exterior of the Oxford Playhouse, which at the time of writing was closed, though it seemed inconceivable that a fairy godmother would not come to its rescue, especially as several of its best undergraduate productions have gone straight to the West End.

The Ashmolean grew out of the original endowment in Broad Street, opposite Blackwell's bookshop, to house Elias Ashmole's 'closet of rarities'. The Old Ashmolean Museum was built in 1678–83, but the collection outgrew its original home, which is now the Museum of the History of Science, and in 1841–5 the present Ashmolean was created. Its riches are impossible to detail here, for it is one of the greatest treasure-houses of fine art in Britain.

The exterior of the mid-Victorian Randolph Hotel, built in 1864 of yellow brick, was recently cleaned, thus doing justice to one of the

The Ashmolean Museum, from St Giles. Opened in 1683, it was the first public museum in Britain.

Balliol College, in the heart of the city, wears its impressive academic mantle lightly, and is one of the most welcoming of all the colleges to visitors.

best-looking city hotels in the country, an almost perfect example of its period, standing with justifiable pride at the important road junction of St Giles and Beaumont Street. If you sit here and linger over breakfast during term-time, you can sit back and watch Oxford hurry by on its bike.

Immediately opposite the hotel are telephones and public lavatories, which make a useful rendezvous for tourists. And human nature being what it is, these might assume more importance in people's minds than the death agonies of the three clerics commemorated by the Victorian-Gothic Martyrs' Memorial which is St Giles's most famous landmark. However, the exact spot at which Latimer and Ridley were burnt at the stake in 1555 for preaching their Protestant beliefs, followed a few months later by Archbishop Cranmer, is just around the corner in the Broad – marked by a metal cross in the road opposite Balliol.

Balliol College stands on the corner here and, apart from being one of the most academically distinguished in the university, with a great many luminaries to its credit, it is one of the most welcoming colleges to visitors. When it is open, walk through the first rather sombre, high-sided, High Victorian quad towards the north-west gate and thus into the tree-shaded Garden Quad, in which recent residential buildings are not at all unattractive. It is interesting to note that two out of three well-known public figures who were serious contenders for the chancellorship of Oxford in 1987 were Balliol men. The successful candidate, Roy Jenkins, was one of these. Another of Balliol's claims to distinction is that it is one of the three oldest Oxford colleges – the others being Merton and University College (or 'Univ'). This aspect of the university's history is a complex matter, needing more than three or four pints in the Turf Tavern or any other Oxford hostelry to resolve, but, briefly, Balliol was in existence in 1263, University's original legacy dates back to 1249, and Merton, whose statute was approved in 1264, is 'the oldest foundation to have *collegiate* form and stature'.

Canterbury Quad, St John's College, is a blend of styles from slightly different periods, but is extremely harmonious. You pass through it en route for the garden.

From Balliol, turn right along the Broad – with the metal cross commemorating Cranmer and the other 'heretics' on your left – then right again in front of St Mary Magdalen Church. I suspect only a minority of visitors walk north up St Giles, away from the main body of the city. All the more reason, however, to appreciate the extra wide road that leads to north Oxford and its substantial Victorian villas, built when regulations forbidding university Fellows to marry were lifted in the late nineteenth century. Opposite St John's, on the corner of St Giles and Beaumont Street, and adjacent to the Ashmolean Museum, is the Taylorian Institution, founded in 1788 for the teaching of modern languages.

As you walk north up St Giles you might have the impression that these famous colleges only have inconsequential back or side entrances. First there is Balliol's entrance, which tourists are not encouraged to use, and then Trinity's, which appears to be a well-kept secret even from some Oxford people. But the main entrance to St John's, is on St Giles. In every college high walls dramatically reduce the noise of traffic – in most cases to an acceptable low rumble like distant thunder. This is true of St John's, whose Front Quad dates from the fifteenth century and is part of the original Cistercian College of St Bernard. From this first quad you enter Canterbury Quad, designed in the 1630s, and via this you reach the gardens. True to Oxford's tradition of architectural surprises, the exterior of the dining hall in Front Quad is pure fifteenth century while the interior is a perfect example of early eighteenth-century architecture. Adjacent to the dining hall is the chapel, where according to one seventeenth-century report, after a period of unrest and indiscipline, some drunken undergraduates vomited into their hats. St John's, incidentally, was one of the last colleges to allow its Fellows to marry. It had no married Fellow until 1898, twenty years after the university had approved the change from enforced celibacy.

St John's Garden is exceptional even in Oxford terms. The Dutch elm disease that caused some long famous college elms to be felled has

On coming out of Hertford cross Catte Street. If Radcliffe Square, the Clarendon Building, the Sheldonian Theatre, the Old Ashmolean, the Schools Quadrangle and the Divinity School, along with the adjacent Convocation House, are all you see in Oxford, your journey will not have been in vain. This is picture-postcard stuff, perhaps a little formal, austere and repetitive despite the individuality of the buildings. It is the heart of the university that Cambridge lacks, and goes part of the way to answering the age-old bemused tourist's question asked of passing undergraduates: 'Where exactly *is* the university?' ... 'Well, you could try Radcliffe Square.'

The Bodleian Library, opposite Hertford, incorporates the Schools Quadrangle. Built in 1613–19, it was the first home of several university faculties and was where examinations were held until the Examination Schools were built in 1882 close to University College. Facing the Broad is the Sheldonian Theatre, built by Sir Christopher Wren between 1663 and 1669 to provide a setting for great ceremonial occasions. Next to this is the Old Ashmolean Museum. Opposite the entrance to the Sheldonian is the door to the Divinity School, dating from the mid-fifteenth century. This was the scene of the trial of Cranmer, Ridley and Latimer in 1555. At the end is Convocation House, where in theory trials of wayward undergraduates can be held with the full sanction of the law. A recent case involved arson, for which, however, an undergraduate was merely sent down. It was also the scene of Charles II's last parliament in 1681. The Clarendon Building, alongside the Sheldonian, housed the Oxford University Press for over a century after 1715, but now it contains the University Registry and the Proctor's offices. The Radcliffe Camera, star of hundreds of pictorial calendars, is also part of the Bodleian. It has recently been opened to the public, but only by means of official guided tours. It will be seen from the most advantageous angle later on in this route.

From Catte Street retrace your steps down New College Lane and under the Bridge of Sighs once more. The lane, whose high walls are actually part of three college boundaries, has been called 'a grim ravine' by its detractors, but I find myself making excuses to walk along it. I like the way the entrance to New College lies as if at the end of a small spur where New College Lane proper veers sharply to the right, emphasizing the independence and slight isolation of this exceptionally beautiful college. New College, incidentally, was the first Oxford college to propose the admission of women.

The remarkable gardens must be something of a mixed blessing, especially for undergraduates. How can the approaching exams be reconciled with all this beauty? Do the examiners make special allowances for New College students on account of the temptations of the garden and the harmonious honey coloured buildings, some of which are set off (depending on the time of year) by scarlet geraniums in white window boxes? And even the most irreligious New College student must find himself moved by the Chapel, whose structure is original fourteenth century ('New' College dates from 1379) but whose interior is Victorian, or by its exceptional music, especially at evensong. And as if New College did not already have more than its fair share of beauty, its Cloister Quad is perhaps the most sublime corner of Oxford I have yet discovered. The college was founded by William of Wykeham, who also founded Winchester College at about the same time and as part of the same educational idea.

Turn left out of New College by the same gate by which you entered, and follow New College Lane. On the right, over the wall, is All Souls and further on the back of The Queen's College. Near where the lane (now Queen's Lane) turns sharply right I paused by the church of St Peter's in the East, and marvelled that such a rural-looking church-yard had survived in the heart of the city. But I had misunderstood the Oxford way of doing things, and it turned out to be no longer a church but the library of the adjacent St Edmund Hall (Teddy Hall to local and university people alike). For, of all the Oxford colleges that are short of space, none is so circumscribed as Teddy Hall. It is a miniature survivor against all the odds – the last Hall, one of those medieval student residences that existed prior to the appearance of the residential colleges that now characterize Oxford and Cambridge.

It could hardly contrast more sharply with The Queen's College, on the corner of Queen's Lane and the High. To see Queen's, detour briefly by turning right into the High and the entrance is a few yards along on the right. Queen's is an architectural *tour de force*, and it enhances an already elegant street. It was founded a generation before New College but was entirely rebuilt between about 1675 and 1775, and these 'original' buildings survive most elegantly, even dauntingly. The college library, incidentally, has been called 'the most beautiful room in Oxford', all rococo plasterwork and ornate bookcases – a far cry from the makeshift arrangements made by other colleges (not just Teddy Hall), which have a redundant church to hand.

Turn left back along the High, where window-shopping may slow you down between Queen's and Magdalen. Longwall Street, between the two colleges on the left, leads to a fairly workaday, untouristy arrangement of extra-mural colleges, college extensions, faculty libraries and college sport fields. It also leads towards, but not directly to, St Catherine's. Magdalen, just a few yards further along the High on the left, lies out on an eastern limb, but it justifies the extra effort to walk to it, and the Botanic Garden immediately opposite is a bonus. Magdalen's popularity rests largely on its deer park, where the herd of fallow deer do have an agreeable tendency to graze close to where tourists can see them. Its choir is even more talked about than New College's, and traffic in the High still stops at 6 o'clock every May Day morning for the traditional hymn sung by the choir up in Magdalen Tower. After walking through Cloister Quad, then round in front of the New Buildings and its croquet lawn, I crossed the River Cherwell – rather dark, narrow and muddy here, it has to be said – and paused to watch beginners taking out punts below Magdalen Bridge: an unromantic business, with much shrieking and not a lot of help from the boatmen, who have, of course, seen it all before.

The Botanic Garden was originally known as the Physic Gardens, in which herbs for early medicaments were produced under the auspices of the Faculty of Medicine. Created in 1621 at a cost of £5,000, the Physic Gardens occupied the site of what had been the medieval Jewish cemetery, and by 1648 there was a collection of over 1500 different plants and species. It is interesting to note that the chair of the Professor of Botany is made from the wood of the pear

Looking towards Magdalen Tower from the Botanic Garden, originally known as the Physic Garden. Even in winter it is much visited.

trees grown by the founder Henry Danvers, later Earl of Danby, and also that over a hundred years ago people were charged a shilling – expensive then – to see the giant waterlily. Now it is all free.

Do not return to the High Street, but leave the Botanic Garden by the iron gate opposite Magdalen and walk – parallel with the High – to Rose Lane. Turn left into Rose Lane until you come to another gateway. Fork right past this, and you will be at the northern edge of Christ Church Meadow or, more correctly at this point, Merton Fields. Follow the northern path, adjoining the walls of Merton College's extensive grounds. This is called Deadman's Walk, and while most such colloquial names seem to refer to condemned men's last outings, on their way to the gallows, this is said to mark the route taken by Jewish funerals many hundreds of years ago. There is believed to have been a synagogue in the thirteenth century on the site of what is now one of Oxford's most famous landmarks, Tom Tower, at the St Aldate's gate to Christ Church.

On summer days distant cricketers add perspective to Christ Church Meadow. This is no manicured greensward, more a case of farmland daring to encroach on the city; you half expect to find college servants with allotments (a little home-grown asparagus for High Table, perhaps). Almost unbelievably, there were plans in the 1950s and 1960s to drive a road across Christ Church Meadow, a few hundred yards from Merton, south of Broad Walk. Christ Church Meadow is huge and flat, but I have never been able to see for any great distance across it, because of heat haze or winter mists off the Cherwell, which keep it rather intimate and mysterious.

If you only have time for, say, two Oxford colleges, make these New College and Christ Church, for they embody respectively the splendour of medieval Christendom and the glory of the English Renaissance. Known in Oxford shorthand as 'The House' (from *Aedes Christi* meaning 'House of Christ') Christ Church is also pure Oxford in that, while it is the richest and grandest of all the colleges, it is the only one apart from St Edmund Hall that never uses the appendage 'college'. It has, incidentally, nurtured no fewer than twelve undergraduates who were later to become Prime Ministers. Two quads are very impressive indeed: the Great Quadrangle, also known as Tom Quad, is bigger than any other in Oxford or Cambridge, except for Cambridge's Trinity College Great Court; and Peckwater Quad, to the north east, is a quite perfect example of early eighteenth-century Palladian architecture. The library which makes up the fourth side of the latter quad is a superb example of Italian Renaissance, built between 1717 and 1738. It is also a model of restoration, having been refaced in the early 1960s. Christ Church's chapel, much older than the college and originally known as St Frideswide's Church, became Oxford Cathedral. When Christ Church's founder, Cardinal Wolsey, died (for a while it was known as Cardinal College) Henry VIII turned the college chapel into a cathedral served by the college canons. For all the marvels of this college, Tom Tower, whose great bell strikes 101 times every night to call the original complement of students home, is the most famous landmark. To get the best impression of it, walk along Pembroke Street towards Pembroke College and look back.

If you cannot actually go to Oxford, you could settle for reading Samuel Johnson on the university. It might also be useful if you want to get an impression of Pembroke College, where Johnson was a student from 1728 to 1729. He was extremely poor and lived on a

ABOVE *The Bear, Bear Street, coming as it does a little past the mid-way point of the walk, may prove tempting. The pub is best known for its extraordinary collection of neckties.*

OPPOSITE *Christ Church Cathedral was originally the college chapel. Christ Church is the largest college in Oxford, with about 365 undergraduates.*

LEFT *Oriel is a fine example of seventeenth-century Gothic architecture. Sir Walter Raleigh and Cecil Rhodes are among the famous graduates of this college.*

BELOW *Picture-postcard stuff: the Radcliffe Camera from St Mary's Church, with the North Quad of All Souls College on the right and part of Brasenose College on the left.*

prison diet in the confines of his own room. He even remained in college during the holidays, when everyone else had gone home, simply because he could not afford the stagecoach fare back home to Lichfield, in Staffordshire. In December 1729 he gave up and left, never to complete his formal studies.

I watched croquet players in the Chapel Quad of Pembroke, festooned with ivy and full of afternoon shadows. After tea ('only by the pot, love') and caramel-and-chocolate cakes in an unlikely tea room close to St Aldate's Church, I turned left up St Aldate's, crossed the road, and just before the Town Hall (the impressive Museum of Oxford is also here, by the way) turned right down Blue Boar Street and Bear Lane towards Oriel Square.

It is worth a detour, though, to the Oxford Information Centre on the left further up St Aldate's, to the crossroads at Carfax and, beyond that, Cornmarket (Oxford's principal shopping complex is to the left of Carfax, and major chain stores are to be found in Cornmarket). The great divide between town and gown is never so sharp as the point at Carfax where Cornmarket runs northwards and embraces – as if to get them out of the way – the essential chain stores and their uncompromising facias. 'Carfax' is derived from Carrefour, or crossroads. Here I was jostled by people queuing for cash card machines. You would hardly believe that this was the way, past Carfax Tower and along the High, that cattle used to be driven in the last century from farms north of Oxford to the watermeadows beyond Magdalen Bridge.

Bear Lane is not quite 'town', not quite 'gown'. The Bear is a rare case of a pub that has a town, tourist and student following. It is also famous for its collection of neckties, but it is not yet the case, as far as I know, that the presentation of a tie they have not previously had is worth a free pint. Continue along Bear Lane, which leads into Oriel Square. This is something of a backwater, which belies its closeness to traffic-packed streets. Amid more formal surroundings, with Oriel College ahead of you and the Canterbury Gateway to Christ Church down to the right, the pastel green and pink houses seem unexpectedly light-hearted, as if a town planner had said, 'This is all getting too sombre – let's have a bit of colour.' Oriel is charmingly labyrinthine and most interestingly incorporates an original medieval Hall, St Mary's. The library by James Wyatt is one of Oxford's best.

Bear right through Oriel Square and turn left into Merton Street, passing Corpus Christi on your right. This is a small college, famous for its sundial, and part of its buildings overlook Christ Church Meadow. But save your more thorough perambulations for cobbled Merton Street, where cars do not really belong and where very few filter through. Several of the unassuming domestic buildings, most attractively varied in style and period, belong to the adjacent colleges. Beam Hall – No. 3 – is an original medieval Hall. If you dawdle outside Merton College you have a good chance of hearing organ music through the walls of the chapel, well known for its recitals. This was also a parish church until 1891, but it was no run-of-the-mill church and is no run-of-the-mill college chapel either. It is a most impressive Gothic structure, with some original thirteenth-century stained glass in the chapel. But Merton is full of superlatives: it is the oldest college site foundation, and some of the original buildings remain, including Mob Quad (*c.* 1300) and the oldest library in England, dating from about 1370. It is also marvellously situated, overlooking Christ Church Meadow at the back.

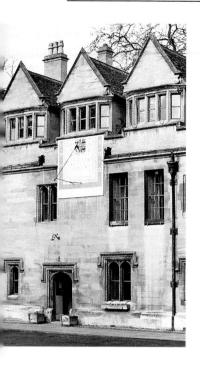

A sundial, dated 1719, in the Old Quad of Brasenose College. Founded in 1509, the college was named after a previous Hall on the site and probably after the brazen nose of its door-knocker.

Notice Magpie Lane on your left, but continue down the street as far as Logic Lane. Surely only Oxford could possess a street with such a name? It runs past the eastern flank of University College and brings you back into the High again, where your sense of the past, which has perhaps been sharpened by the quiet backwaters, may be under-mined. Build in extra time to climb the tower of St Mary's, the university church – one of those things that on the whole tourists rather than university people get round to.

Before walking north into Radcliffe Square, double back into the High to see All Souls, whose North, or Codrington Quad, is, for all its size and grandeur, actually one of the quietest in Oxford. This is because most people fail to find it, having stopped short at Front Quad, said 'Ah, very nice I suppose' and turned tail. Others, perhaps, are daunted by the idea of All Souls, for the college is composed only of Fellows and has a formidable academic reputation, with dons who, against the trend, tend to spend their weekends *in* college after commuting to Oxford's drab station or driving via the impressive M40 from London.

Radcliffe Square is dominated by the Radcliffe Camera, without a large picture of which no Oxford photographic album is ever complete. It came about after a Dr Radcliffe left £40,000 in the early eighteenth century for a new library, and this was begun in 1737 and finished in 1749. It was designed by James Gibbs, but Nicholas Hawksmoor had also been asked to submit a design (it is said anyway that Gibbs had been inspired by an earlier Hawksmoor design). By a nice coincidence, the Camera is seen very effectively from the North Quad of All Souls, above Hawksmoor's cloister screen and cupola.

Turn left along Brasenose Lane, skirting Brasenose College on your left ('BNC' in the vernacular). The name comes from the brazen nose of the original thirteenth-century knocker that used to adorn the front door, but now resides in the dining-hall. Notice the chestnut tree that leans across from Exeter College on the right. It is said that in any year in which it touches BNC Exeter will defeat Brasenose at rowing. As you walk along Brasenose Lane, the walls of BNC on the left give way to Lincoln College (where John Wesley was a Fellow). To see this rare example of a virtually intact fourteenth-century college turn left in Turl Street – 'the Turl'. Lincoln is another college, with little room to expand, that has taken over a redundant church for its library. It did well, for All Saints, on the corner of the High and the Turl, is exquisite. The Mitre, on the opposite corner, was originally one of Oxford's most frequented coaching inns, and although it has become an equally democratic steak and wine bar it still manages to look the part.

Retrace your steps up Turl Street, and turn left into Market Street for access to Oxford's famous covered market. Your nostrils will be assailed by a heady combination of aromas: sawdust, fresh meat, seeds and cereals, earthy potatoes from the greengrocer's stall, fish, peat from the flower stand and steam from the urn in the tea bar which seems to be full from opening till closing time. Butchers boys' delivery bikes are propped up against Victorian shop fronts, and barrows with herring boxes stand, incongruously, next to a bright-red pillar box. The surprisingly elegant iron girders that support the roof are reminiscent of a small railway station.

The smell of bacon frying in a small hotel where I was staying once had me up and about early, and I was inside Exeter's chapel even before the cleaner had finished his morning's mopping. The college is near the north end of Turl Street. I stepped apologetically over the puddles, but he was far from cross. 'Burne-Jones is it?' he asked, assuming I had come to see the tapestry of the Adoration of the Magi, done with William Morris. The two pre-Raphaelite painters formed a life-long friendship when they were students at Exeter.

Jesus College is directly across Turl Street from Exeter. It has always had strong Welsh connections, and on St David's Day the chapel service is conducted in Welsh. At this point you are just a few paces from Broad Street, across which is Trinity College. The Old Ashmolean is to the right on the Broad, and roughly opposite that is Blackwell's bookshop. An innocent visitor might easily be persuaded that Blackwell's bookshop is part of the university. And, indeed, its remarkable Norrington Room, the biggest room devoted to the sale of books in Europe, is constructed under the main quad of Trinity College (a very subterranean place, Oxford).

Undeterred by what goes on under its nose in Blackwell's, Trinity occupies a large site, and butts on to St Giles, Parks Road and the Broad. Happily and harmoniously, the wrought-iron gates on the Broad are an exact copy of those through which curious passers-by peer into the gardens opposite Wadham. The Parks Road gates date from 1713, the others 1737. After Trinity, turn right down the Broad. Ahead is George Street, with the shops of Cornmarket to the left. Beyond George Street is Hythe Bridge Street and the station car park.

If a college porter seems a little abrupt towards you and a good deal more deferential to a member of his college, remember that the colleges and their staff look after their own: outsiders are welcome to step inside and admire, but 'inner sanctum' is everything. It is what has enabled Oxford, as well as Cambridge, to survive. Oxford's souvenir shops have not yet found a way to put history and romance in a bottle, as Londoners once claimed to do with fog, but ten minutes in a five-hundred-year-old quad or a sneaky look inside an aromatic, officially out-of-bounds Fellows Garden can go a long way to help.

ABOVE *Blackwell's Bookshop is an integral part of most tourist itineraries. Its subterranean room is the biggest of its kind in the world.*

BELOW *Trinity College, seen across Trinity Gardens, looks a little like a country house. One famous undergraduate here was the explorer, Richard Burton, who was sent down for trying to arrange a duel.*

SALISBURY

SALISBURY

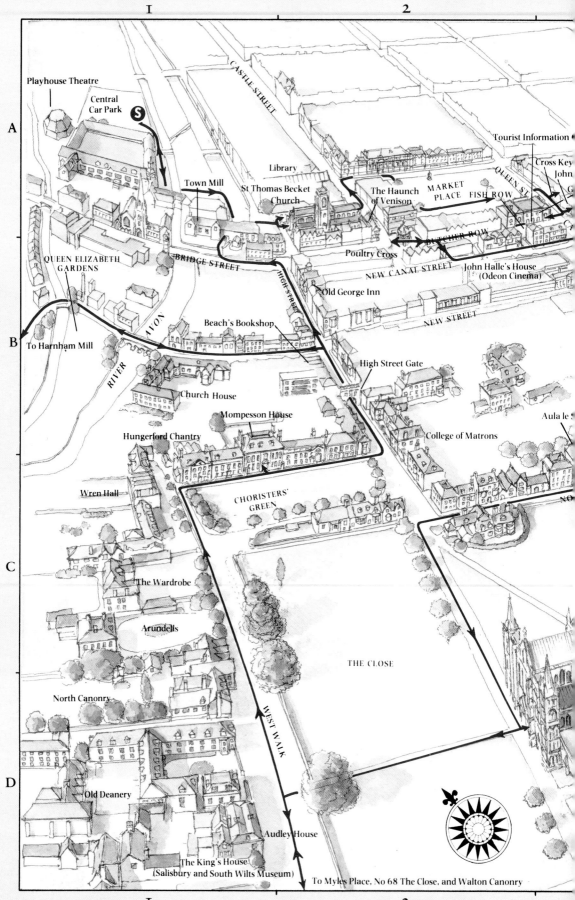

Playhouse Theatre

Central
Car Park

S

Town Mill

CASTLE STREET

Library

St Thomas Becket
Church

The Haunch
of Venison

MARKET
PLACE   FISH ROW

Tourist Information

Cross Key
John

QUEEN ST.

QUEEN ELIZABETH
GARDENS

BRIDGE STREET

HIGH STREET

Poultry Cross

BUTCHER ROW

NEW CANAL STREET

John Halle's House
(Odeon Cinema)

Old George Inn

To Harnham Mill

RIVER AVON

Beach's Bookshop

High Street Gate

NEW STREET

Church House

Mompesson House

College of Matrons

Aula le

Hungerford Chantry

Wren Hall

CHORISTERS'
GREEN

NO

The Wardrobe

Arundells

THE CLOSE

North Canonry

WEST WALK

Old Deanery

Audley House

The King's House
(Salisbury and South Wilts Museum)

To Myles Place, No 68 The Close, and Walton Canonry

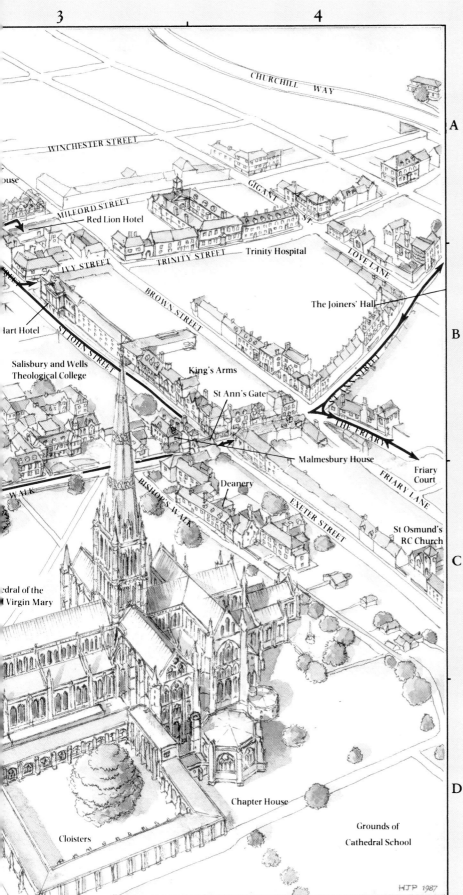

3   4

CHURCHILL WAY

WINCHESTER STREET

MILFORD STREET

Red Lion Hotel

GIGANT ST.

IVY STREET

TRINITY STREET   Trinity Hospital

BROWN STREET

LOVE LANE

The Joiners' Hall

Hart Hotel

ST JOHN STREET

Salisbury and Wells
Theological College

King's Arms

St Ann's Gate

ST ANN STREET

THE FRIARY

Malmesbury House

Friary
Court

FRIARY LANE

WALK

BISHOPS WALK

Deanery

EXETER STREET

St Osmund's
RC Church

edral of the
Virgin Mary

Chapter House

Cloisters

Chapter House

Grounds of
Cathedral School

HJP 1987

3   4

BUILDINGS AND
PLACES OF INTEREST

Arundells (1749) C1
Audley House D1
Aula le Stage C3
Beach's Bookshop (c14) B2
Cathedral (1220–66) C3
Central Car Park A1
Chapter House
   (1263–84) D4
Church House (c15) B1
Cloisters (1263–84) D3
The Close C2
College of Matrons (1682) B2
Cross Keys Chequer A3
Deanery C4
Friary Court (c17) B4
Guildhall (c.1795) A3
The Haunch of Venison A2
Hungerford Chantry B1
John A'Port House
   (c.1435–50) A3
John Halle's House
   (1470–83) B2
Joiners' Hall (c16) B4
King's Arms B4
The King's House (Salisbury
   and South Wilts
   Museum) D1
Library A2
Malmesbury House
   (1749) B3
Mompesson House (1701) B1
North Canonry D1
Old Deanery (c13) D1
Old George Inn B2
Playhouse Theatre A1
Poultry Cross (c15) B2
Red Lion Hotel
   (1820–23) A3
St Ann's Gate (1338) B4
St Osmund's RC Church
   (1847–8) C4
St Thomas Becket Church A2
Salisbury and Wells
   Theological College B3
Tourist Information
   Centre A2
Trinity Hospital (1702) A4
White Hart Hotel B3
Wren Hall (1714) C1

A

B

C

D

PAGES 140–41 *Georgian houses on the eastern side of the cathedral close. This is one of the most prestigious postal addresses in Britain, with a long waiting list for any houses that come onto the market.*

It seemed churlish to intervene when I overheard somebody telling a first-time visitor to Salisbury that this was the same River Avon that flows through Shakespeare's Stratford, as they both leaned over the bridge beside the County Hotel to watch cygnets bobbing around their mother. It is in fact a different river, the 'Salisbury Avon', which rises in the Vale of Pewsey, north of Salisbury Plain, then runs close to Stonehenge, and finally reaches the sea in Christchurch Harbour, close to Bournemouth. It does not dominate the city, as, say, York's Ouse does, and you could probably enjoy Salisbury without seeing it at all, but John Constable painted the cathedral most memorably from its banks and nowadays it greatly enhances a shopping precinct in the town centre. The name 'Avon' comes from the Celtic and simply means 'water'.

Each new visitor has his or her own overriding first impression of a city. Local residents may scoff, but my first impression of Salisbury was of late afternoon sunlight on perfectly pointed red brickwork, which reaches its apotheosis as a building material in the close, and of a town layout that is symmetrical almost in an American way, having changed little in its development since medieval times. I very much like the way Salisbury has coped with its historical associations, for the result is not contrived: people sit with pushchairs and hamburgers under the Poultry Cross, ignore a rumbling brewer's dray from the Anchor brewery as it passes W.H.Smith's, or go to the pictures in a partly fourteenth-century, timbered merchant's house.

The Maltings, looking back towards Salisbury's principal car park – a harmonious and sympathetic commercial development. The river is a tributary of the 'Salisbury Avon'.

If it seems odd to enthuse about a car park, it is because Salisbury's Central Car Park really is superior to most. It has a substantial part under cover, which is handy not only when it rains but in hot weather too. The covered section, in modern red brick and tile, blends easily with Sainsbury's new store; and as you walk from the car park towards the shopping precinct adjoining Sainsbury's, a large part of the cathedral spire can be seen rising ahead of you, and ducks potter

about on a rather grubby stretch of river, a tributary of the Avon. This is a very superior new development indeed, proving that at last we have really emerged from the architectural blandness of the 1960s.

The new precinct partly embraces the original old Town Mill, which will be seen at a later stage. Bear left as you reach a row of small shops, then right, with the main body of the river to your left. Follow the path round to the left through The Maltings precinct and across the river. You will reach the church of St Thomas Becket, the parish church of Salisbury and ancient 'chapel of ease' to the cathedral. On a bright summer morning the door of this church was open. I had not planned to, but I went in, looking up immediately to the high five-hundred-year-old carved and panelled roof. Even more impressive is a still colourful painting of *Doom*, thought to have been given to the church hundreds of years ago by a parishioner who made a pilgrimage to Canterbury. A few examples of the original stained glass remain, and an organ that was presented to the cathedral by George III in 1792 found a home here nearly a century later. A lady bringing flowers in through the porch identified me as a stranger. 'You know that parts of the church are older than the cathedral, don't you?' she said, as she swept by at speed.

Turn right out of the church – or left if you haven't entered it – past a baker's and confectioners. The smells of baking bread and freshly roasted coffee carried on the morning breeze will add to your appreciation of St Thomas's Square, a little enclave in a busy city. Here, birdsong is louder than delivery vans and lorries, and it is a good place if you like reading the inscriptions on ancient headstones.

Follow the little passageway, also called St Thomas's Square, and you will emerge into the market place. Notice the impressive public library entrance on your left, the site of the 'Cheese Cross', where milk and cheese were sold in the fifteenth and sixteenth centuries, and where today charity collectors like to position themselves. This was one of several crosses where produce was sold, but only Poultry Cross, a couple of hundred yards away, remains. The clock above the library was presented by Salisbury Rotary Club in honour of the Queen's Silver Jubilee in 1977. I wonder if in time this will look as quaint and somewhat out of place as some of those memorials to Queen Victoria's Diamond Jubilee of 1897. Before the building became a library it had an entirely different function as a Market House, with an unlikely broad-gauge railway connection to what is now Salisbury station.

The library steps make a good point from which to take in the market square. As I watched the market day comings and goings, I was reminded of the actor Ralph Richardson, who played the Duke of Buckingham in the Laurence Olivier film version of Shakespeare's *Richard III*. Buckingham was beheaded in Salisbury's market place in 1483. He had been a supporter of Richard's claim to the throne, but only a few months after the coronation the king had turned against him, accusing him of treason. It is said he was given away when a farm labourer noticed an unusual amount of food being delivered to his hiding place. There have been markets on this site since the granting of a city charter in 1227. Originally this permitted a weekly Tuesday market which grew into nothing less than a daily market. However, objections from neighbouring towns, including nearby Wilton, resulted in a cutback; now, markets are held on Tuesdays and Saturdays, and a three-day funfair is held here every October.

I walked among the market stalls, down the suitably named *Meat*

Row, past pot plants, sweets, a cold chicken stall, and a barker selling meat from a lorry. Under the shade of one of the market square's many trees, a painter sitting in shorts and T-shirt at his easel was not, curiously, painting the scene in front of him, but one that was only similar. Perhaps he was looking for background detail.

The Guildhall also serves as a Magistrates' Court, and until 1971 Assize Courts of the Western Circuit were held here. There are probably worse places to be if you are in trouble with the law, for it has a fine staircase, and an interesting collection of mayoral paintings in oils. The Guildhall was built in the last years of the eighteenth century from plans by Sir Robert Taylor, the wealthy architect who founded the Taylorian Institute in Oxford, devoted mainly to the teaching of modern languages. The bronze statue on the north side of the square is of Henry Fawcett, a Postmaster-General born in nearby Queen Street. He was blinded in a shooting accident in 1858 but despite this became a local Member of Parliament. The market place is still remembered for the success of the open-air public feast held here to celebrate Queen Victoria's Golden Jubilee in 1887. Fifteen years later, to celebrate Edward VII's coronation, four thousand guests sat down to a meal of roast beef and dessert, and later in the day four thousand more people – perhaps some of the same who had sat down to lunch – consumed a ton of cake and fifty pounds of tea.

Walk across Queen Street into the new shopping precinct of Cross Keys Chequer, originally a fourteenth-century development and now a well organized arrangement of shops, including a good bookshop and several restaurants. The name 'chequer' originates from the grid system laid down by the distinguished Bishop Poore, in about 1225. He specified a rectangular grid of five streets running parallel from north to south and six from east to west, which made up twenty squares or chequers. Happily Salisbury's present-day pattern closely resembles the medieval layout that in so many old cities has become adulterated. The use of practical and sympathetic infilling rather than unthinking expansion, in the cathedral close as well as in the city as a whole, has kept Salisbury intact.

Turn left out of Cross Keys Chequer and walk along Queen Street to John A'Port House, a china and glass emporium on several levels where browsing is encouraged, even for people only wanting to see the deliberately exposed wattle-and-daub wall construction and the 'before and after' photographs of the restoration. The house was built in about 1425 by a six-times Mayor of Salisbury. If you cross Queen Street again you will come to Fish Row, where the Tourist Information Centre is on your right. Fish Row becomes Butcher Row which leads to the Poultry Cross. This is a copy of Chichester's Cross, and is largely fourteenth century. It provided shelter and a base for country people in town to sell their home-grown produce, and sermons were preached here by itinerant preachers. In the half-timbered Haunch of Venison pub opposite, the details of its exterior picked out in gold to make a very effective impression, I did not eat venison, but – high up in a cosy panelled bar – I had a better-than-average ploughman's lunch. This being 'finger food', I was reminded of the gruesome tale of the Haunch of Venison's severed hand. The inn possesses a mummi-fied, severed hand holding playing cards, which was discovered in 1905. It is presumed to commemorate an incident in which a card player was caught cheating.

Retrace your steps to Poultry Cross, then turn right down a little

Poultry Cross, looking towards Butcher Row. It still provides shelter for the occasional tradesman, and makes a handy rendezvous.

unnamed alleyway, between Dunns the outfitters and Ratners the jewellers, and across New Canal Street to the left is the Odeon Cinema – better known in the guide books as John Halle's House. Despite its mock Tudor exterior it is actually an elaborately timbered fifteenth-century building, and belonged to a wealthy wool merchant called John Halle, who was mayor of Salisbury four times and also an MP. The house was built for him between 1470 and 1483 and later became an inn. It was restored by Pugin in 1834.

Continue along New Canal Street, and cross over the road junction into Milford Street, where the Red Lion Hotel is situated, opposite the Cathedral Hotel. The most striking feature of the Red Lion is the entrance, with its high coaching arch, iron gates, distinctive red lion that children climb on to be photographed, and a rare variety of creeper that is spectacular with the sun behind it. There are very few known examples of this creeper in Europe, one of the best being at Worcester Cathedral. Bearing the botanical name of *Vitis coignetiae*, it originated in Japan and is unusual in that it is shunned by insects and flies. It grows extremely fast – 10–12 ft a year – and needs constant pruning. During the great coaching age the inn was the starting point at 10 o'clock every night for the 'Salisbury Flying Machine', bound for London.

The Red Lion is also famous for its unusual clocks. One of these is the 'skeleton organ clock' which incorporates carvings said to be the work of Spanish prisoners held in the original Dartmoor prison following the defeat of the Spanish Armada in 1588. Three mechanical skeletons can be activated on the clock's face, and in addition it has a built-in barrel organ. Another clock, in the oak-panelled Victoria Lounge, makes the average station clock look very modest indeed. It is an 'Act of Parliament clock', so-called because it was built in the late eighteenth century when a severe tax (fairly soon repealed) on clocks and watches meant that far fewer people bought them for their personal use. So it was a popular publican who could be relied upon to have a big clock on his premises.

The house of John Halle, who was a notoriously irascible fifteenth-century mayor of Salisbury. One wonders what he would have said about his elegant half-timbered house becoming part of a cinema.

Turn left out of the Red Lion into Milford Street, and then left again down Catherine Street, *en route* for another famous Salisbury hotel, the White Hart. Ahead, on the left, but actually in St John Street, the White Hart Hotel has a statue of a white hart on its roof. The Greek Revival façade dates from about 1800, while the handsome *porte-cochère* projecting over the pavement, and the Ionic pillars above this, are later, from about 1820. The effigy of the hart was erected in 1827 to undermine a similar three-dimensional sign put up by a rival hostelry that did not survive. On 9 October 1780, in the aftermath of the American War of Independence, Henry Laurens, a former President of the American Congress, was captured at sea and brought to the White Hart before being taken to London and incarcerated in the Tower.

Just before you reach the White Hart look down Ivy Street, named after one John Ivie. In 1627, as mayor, he attempted to bring a degree of order to the chaotic situation during a plague which claimed more than a tenth of the population of Salisbury. Just a few yards past the White Hart, the King's Arms appropriately incorporates an antique shop and a picture gallery. It is a treat, a beautifully maintained building, with a coaching entrance, hanging baskets, and a pristine black-and-white exterior. It is said to be the place in which supporters of Charles ΙΙ planned his escape to France after the Battle of Worcester.

Turn left into St Ann Street. It might be worth coming to Salisbury for this street alone, which rivals even the cathedral close. If you wanted to recreate a street in which all the charms of English architecture over several hundred years are paraded, you could hardly do better. Here, you will find Georgian red brick, Victorian stucco, slate roofs, tiles, shutters and an abundance of ivy. I wanted to go into the Post Office-cum-sweetshop, but it was closed for lunch, and I was intrigued to see that, of all places, the shop had no street number. On the exterior of the Joiners' Hall, notice the wooden carved figures and ornamental brackets beneath the oriel windows. These were probably carved by Humphrey Beckham, who might also have been responsible for part of the elaborate carving on the house of John A'Port. It is said that these figures were meant to represent the city council as a group of old women, for the Joiners' Company suffered constant friction with the Mayor and Corporation. Such companies grew out of the medieval guilds and were, roughly, forerunners of the modern unions. The joiners were amalgamated with rope-makers, painters and millwrights. The timbered house next to the Joiners' Hall was the home of Christopher Batt, who was Mayor of Salisbury in 1659.

Walk back down St Ann Street the way you came, but before the end turn left down The Friary to Friary Court. A notice says that around 1225 Franciscan Friars established a religious house near this place, and that the land was originally granted by the enlightened Bishop Poore. The Franciscans were frequently penniless, and lived off barley loaves and poor quality beer that had to be diluted to make it palatable. The foundation was dissolved, however, in 1538 as part of Henry VIII's drive against the monasteries.

Carry on to the end of St Ann Street and cross St John Street. With St Ann's Gate on the other side of the road prepare yourself for a treat. This is one of three ways into the cathedral close, and it is my favourite – not least because the approach to the cathedral is perfect. The High Street Gate, by which most people approach the cathedral, is very fine but is much more touristy and more often crowded. St Ann's Gate was built in 1333, when the close was created, partly by using stones from Old Sarum, the hilltop settlement two miles away that was effectively the first Salisbury. Some of the gate's stones still carry traces of Norman carving. Nearly four hundred years after the gate was erected, the young George Frederick Handel gave his first public concert in England in a room above the gate. Immediately to your left, at No. 14, is the house in which Henry Fielding wrote *Tom Jones*, but his neighbours were not impressed by the rowdiness of the household, feeling (as they certainly would today) that it was not in keeping with the peaceful character of the close. On the opposite side of the lane is Malmesbury House, very noticeable on account of its sparkling blue and gold sundial, dated 1749. Again on the opposite side, a few yards further along, is Bishop Wordsworth's School. The classrooms stand right on the road and it is hard not to peer in for a sense of instant nostalgia.

It soon becomes apparent that the present shape and character of the cathedral close was established in the eighteenth century. Already, Salisbury's status as a cathedral city and county town was attracting well-to-do residents, and these were the kind of people who

The cathedral nave, lined with columns made of Purbeck marble. The cathedral's many windows prevent it becoming dark and gloomy.

would want to preserve its character. Physically it is a happy marriage of grey stone and red brick. There was no room or inclination to expand, which partly accounts for the sense of harmony, but also the houses have in time blended into their environment. This applied to Salisbury at large, where, until 1800 at the earliest, there were no real changes made to the medieval street plan.

The distant spire of Salisbury Cathedral, the tallest in the country, is such a familiar sight in paintings, on chocolate boxes and jigsaw puzzles that to approach it at close quarters is a little disconcerting. An element of anticlimax is inevitable, you might think, but this is not the case. The surroundings are so impressive, the greensward around the cathedral so pristine and the Wiltshire sky so wide and clean that there can be no serious challenge to Salisbury's claim that this is the handsomest cathedral setting in Britain. I had intended to complete my exploration of the close before starting on the cathedral, but was daunted by the sudden appearance of at least two hundred schoolchildren on my right, spilling through High Street Gate. They were clearly bent on an invasion of the church, so I decided to change my plan.

Despite the clean lines of the cathedral's exterior I had expected gloom and doom inside, so I was surprised to find that it is light and airy. Happily, the public entrance was by the west door, close to the cloisters, which always enhances the atmosphere, although in this case I think it is a temporary arrangement. On a warm day everything was pleasantly cool. I remarked to one of the guides – who do not impose themselves and do not offer guided tours, but are on hand to answer questions at length – that I supposed this meant it was freezing in winter. He replied, 'It used to be, and people used to bring blankets and hot water bottles to the carol services, but that all changed when we got central heating.' It was, however, hard to imagine the cathedral in unpleasantly cold weather. The few people strolling through the nave, peering at the better-than-average collection of

RIGHT An appropriate picture of Choristers' Green, which is adjacent to the close. The principal building here is Mompesson House.

tombs and effigies, were in shirt sleeves or summer dresses, gazing up unhurriedly and not just dutifully at the remarkable fan vaulting. Those thirteenth- and fourteenth-century craftsmen were not to know that we would also use magnifying mirrors to look in detail from the ground at their intricate work. All the more credit to them for the perfection of their art. I was struck by two things especially: the graceful Purbeck stone columns lining the nave and the fact that the whole edifice stands on foundations no more than 6 ft deep.

The west and south sides of the close seem to belong more to the country than to the town, and I left the cathedral, walking due west, to be greeted by the scent of newly mown hay. If you turn left in West Walk ahead of you and walk for a few hundred yards, you will reach Myles Place, a palatial example of early eighteenth-century architecture that in any other setting might dwarf the surrounding houses. Until his death in 1985 it was occupied by Sir Arthur Bryant, the historian, whose ashes are in the cathedral. Walk back along West Walk, which brings you to the Salisbury and South Wiltshire Museum in the King's House and, further on, the Wardrobe, which contains the Museum of the Berkshire and Wiltshire Regiment. In the former, I was especially impressed by a reconstructed doctor's surgery that is effectively a memorial to a local GP, Dr Philip Neighbour, who worked in nearby Amesbury. A tableau with three-dimensional wax figures depicts his surgery as it would have been in the 1940s, and as far as possible original furniture and medicines have been used in the display. The museum is touching and evocative even for an outsider, but it can hardly compare with Mompesson House, a National Trust property on the north side of the close. If you only have time to see one of the close properties (four or five, including the museums, are open either regularly or occasionally) make this the one. It is a fine eighteenth-century house which certainly feels 'lived-in'. I was torn between admiring every piece of furniture and painting, or strolling to the front windows to enjoy the view of the cathedral and the close.

ABOVE *The cathedral cloisters date mainly from the late thirteenth century. Even when the cathedral is thronging with tourists the cloisters seem to exude calm.*

Leave the close by the High Street Gate, noticing the College of Matrons on the right just before you reach the gate. It was built in 1682 to house twelve poor widows, and it still does, although the notorious means test that used to apply in its early days has been dropped. As you pass through the gate it is worth recalling that it used to have a portcullis. The conflict between the townspeople and the privileged clergy was once so severe that Edward III allowed 'an embattled wall of stone' to be built around the cathedral.

Walk up the High Street for a few yards as far as Beach's bookshop, a second-hand and antiquarian bookshop of department-store dimensions. On the day I went in, twelve or thirteen browsers made little impact on the space. Turn left here, into Crane Street, and walk along

High Street Gate, looking towards the High Street. Although the twentieth century impinges on this part of the town, restoration is generally sympathetic.

ABOVE *Though the terrain has changed slightly during the last two hundred years, John Constable would certainly recognize this classic view of the cathedral spire from the water meadows.*

until you reach Queen Elizabeth Gardens. Cross a second bridge and take the footpath on the left, marked 'Town Path', to Harnham Mill. Of course, I should have realized that the trees would have grown since John Constable sat among the watermeadows to the left of the path and painted the cathedral. So, if you do take the half-mile path towards Harnham Mill, dodging the cyclists as you go, you will never quite be able to recreate Constable's paintings. He must, by the way, have felt quite at home among these willowy watermeadows, reminiscent as they are of his home at East Bergholt on the Essex/Suffolk border.

Cross a bridge over the river, on which the presence of anglers denotes ample supplies of fish, walk past an unkempt cottage or two, and continue to the mill. This is now a small hotel, tearoom and restaurant, and could be forgiven for being complacent about its history. Dating from about 1135, it was used to store church artefacts even while the cathedral was being moved from Old Sarum to New Sarum, or Salisbury. It later became a nuns' hostel and a leper hospital. There is also a pub in the village, and don't forget to bring food for the ducks or the swans.

Return to Crane Street, and walk up the High Street. On the right you will see The Old George, which used to be an inn, where Samuel Pepys stayed in 1668. He enjoyed 'a silken bed' and good though expensive food. At the top of the High Street turn left into Bridge Street, and then cross the road at the County Hotel to return towards the Central Car Park via the Town Mill and the millstream. This was one of four Salisbury mills mentioned in the Domesday Book, and clever landscaping has turned it into an attraction in its own right.

I became confused trying to find the right road out of Salisbury, with the result that I kept seeing the spire of the cathedral from different angles. It looked much further away than it actually was, but now I knew that just five minutes' walk from almost any part of Salisbury brings one right up to its ancient stones.

SHREWSBURY

SHREWSBURY

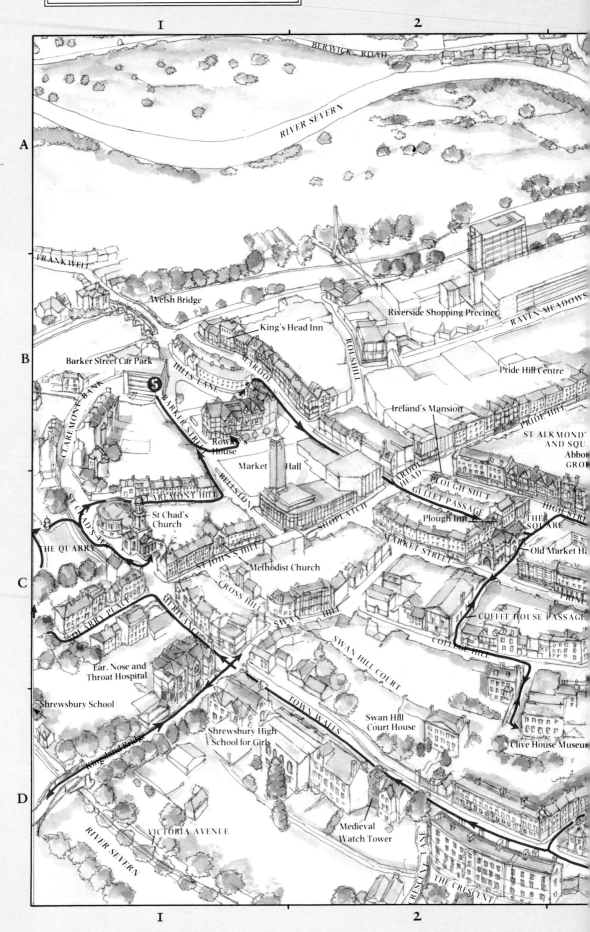

1   2

A

BERWICK ROAD

RIVER SEVERN

FRANKWELL

Welsh Bridge

King's Head Inn

Riverside Shopping Precinct

RAVEN MEADOWS

B

Barker Street Car Park

MARDOL

ROUSHILL

Pride Hill Centre

HILLS LANE

S

BARKER STREET

CLAREMONT BANK

Ireland's Mansion

Rowley's House

ST ALKMOND'S
AND SQU
Abbo
GRO

PRIDE HILL

Market Hall

CLAREMONT HILL

HILLSTONE

MARDOL
HEAD

PLOUGH SHUT

GULLET PASSAGE

HIGH STRE

THE
SQUARE

ST CHAD'S TER

St Chad's
Church

SHOPLATCH

Plough Inn

THE QUARRY

Methodist Church

ST JOHN'S HILL

MARKET STREET

Old Market Ha

C

QUARRY PLACE

CROSS HILL

SWAN HILL

COFFEE HOUSE PASSAGE

PRIN

MURIVANCE

COLLEGE HILL

Ear, Nose and
Throat Hospital

SWAN HILL COURT

Shrewsbury School

TOWN WALLS

Shrewsbury High
School for Girls

Swan Hill
Court House

Clive House Museu

KINGSLAND BRIDGE

RIVER SEVERN

VICTORIA AVENUE

Medieval
Watch Tower

CRESCENT LANE

THE CRESCENT

D

1   2

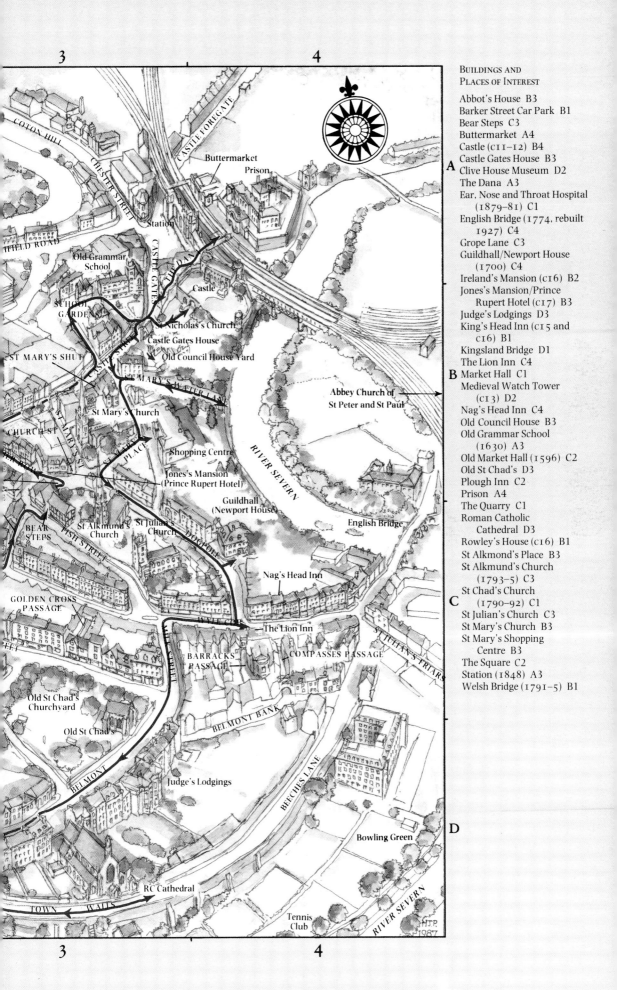

3   4

COTON HILL

CHESTER STREET

CASTLE FOREGATE

Buttermarket

Prison

IFIELD ROAD

Station

Old Grammar School

THE DANA

CASTLE GATES

Castle

SCHOOL GARDENS

St Nicholas's Church

Castle Gates House

Old Council House Yard

ST MARY'S SHUT

ST MARY'S WATER LANE

St Mary's Church

ST MARY'S ST

CHURCH ST

ST MARY'S PLACE

Shopping Centre

Jones's Mansion (Prince Rupert Hotel)

Guildhall (Newport House)

RIVER SEVERN

Abbey Church of St Peter and St Paul

English Bridge

BEAR STEPS

FISH STREET

St Alkmund's Church

St Julian's Church

DOGPOLE

Nag's Head Inn

GOLDEN CROSS PASSAGE

WYLE COP

The Lion Inn

ST JULIAN'S FRIARS

FEET

MILL GREEN

BARRACKS PASSAGE

COMPASSES PASSAGE

Old St Chad's Churchyard

Old St Chad's

BELMONT BANK

BEECHES LANE

BELMONT

Judge's Lodgings

RIVER SEVERN

Bowling Green

RC Cathedral

TOWN WALLS

Tennis Club

H.J.P. 1987

3   4

Buildings and Places of Interest

Abbot's House B3
Barker Street Car Park B1
Bear Steps C3
Buttermarket A4
Castle (c11–12) B4
Castle Gates House B3
Clive House Museum D2
The Dana A3
Ear, Nose and Throat Hospital (1879–81) C1
English Bridge (1774, rebuilt 1927) C4
Grope Lane C3
Guildhall/Newport House (1700) C4
Ireland's Mansion (c16) B2
Jones's Mansion/Prince Rupert Hotel (c17) B3
Judge's Lodgings D3
King's Head Inn (c15 and c16) B1
Kingsland Bridge D1
The Lion Inn C4
Market Hall C1
Medieval Watch Tower (c13) D2
Nag's Head Inn C4
Old Council House B3
Old Grammar School (1630) A3
Old Market Hall (1596) C2
Old St Chad's D3
Plough Inn C2
The Quarry C1
Roman Catholic Cathedral D3
Rowley's House (c16) B1
St Alkmund's Place B3
St Alkmund's Church (1793–5) C3
St Chad's Church (1790–92) C1
St Julian's Church C3
St Mary's Church B3
St Mary's Shopping Centre B3
The Square C2
Station (1848) A3
Welsh Bridge (1791–5) B1

A

B

C

D

PAGES 154–5 *The English Bridge over the Severn. A footpath, roughly a mile long and following an impressive bend in the river, links this with the Welsh Bridge.*

RIGHT *A view from the Welsh Bridge, with the churches of St Alkmund's (left) and St Chad's on the horizon. The red-brick Georgian and Victorian buildings belie the amount of black and white half-timbering in the town.*

I had been to Shrewsbury twice before I realized that it is not simply 'on the Severn' but tucked inside a horseshoe curve of the river that was a godsend to the original settlers. It encloses the town on three sides, roughly in a loose noose shape, and, of course, there is a castle where the knot should go. I missed the river almost completely because Shrewsbury is so self-contained. A lot of traffic arrives in the town over the Welsh or the English Bridge, the names of which have no obscure origin, but simply derive from the fact that the Welsh Bridge is convenient for travellers from the Welsh Marches, and the English version handy for incomers from the east. And neither bridge affords vehicles especially good views of the river. This self-containment helps to underline Shrewsbury's strong sense of identity. At its best it feels like a fortress, and the higher you climb within it the more unusual and invigorating it becomes. Which is all the more reason why Shrewsbury people get cross if you pigeonhole the town wrongly. It is neither North Country nor Midlands, but belongs to the Welsh borders. Wales is, after all, only 12 miles away.

Appropriately for a town that, like Bath, is a past winner of the 'Britain in Bloom' contest, the name probably comes from the Saxon *Scrobbesburig*, meaning town of shrubs. It was an important Saxon settlement: St Alkmund's Church, situated in a delightful leafy enclave high in the heart of the town, was founded in about AD 900 by Ethelfleda, daughter of Alfred the Great. Shrewsbury is lucky not to have an Anglican cathedral. If that sounds strange, consider how a cathedral dominates a place. Everything is subordinate to it. But not here, where each one of a handful of quite exceptional parish churches, including St Alkmund's, is worth a visit in its own right, and not just as a point of comparison with any big sister.

The town is famous for its black-and-white timbered houses. But everybody who has ever been rude about red brick should spend some time in Shrewsbury, ideally early on a summer evening when the narrow and mostly hilly streets are nearly deserted and when one can look up to take in the complete individual buildings, terraces and streets without the risk of being run down by drivers. Yet it is modest about its achievements. Nowhere in any of the voluminous material put out by the local tourist office did I find anything about 'the most remarkable this', or 'the most impressive that'. The town merely gets on with the job. But on a good day, when the wind does not whistle too keenly up Castle Gates or down Belmont, Shrewsbury can meet Chester's harmonious 'magpie' buildings and Ludlow's exquisite and delicate red-brick Georgian architecture on equal terms.

It is not really Shrewsbury's fault that there is apparently no such thing as an attractive multi-storey car park. The Barker Street car park is as visually obtrusive as any, but it is extremely convenient, and just a matter of yards from a Shrewsbury landmark and museum that gets one in the mood to appreciate the town. There is a short term car park at street level, next to the bus station, though there are dire penalties for exceeding your welcome. Cross the bus station, taking care not to get run over by a mini-bus or something more substantial on its way out to rural Shropshire, and walk round the building to the main entrance to Rowley's House and Mansion. It is all rather low-key and informal. I wandered in and had to be reminded, but ever so politely, about my entrance fee. Inside, I noticed particularly the engraved Roman headstones from the excavated town of nearby Wroxeter; touching mementos of the losing (Royalist) side in the Civil

Rowley's House Museum, which considerably enhances Shrewsbury's bus station and a multi-storey car park, is unstuffy, informal and remarkable for its Roman remains.

War, in which Shrewsbury largely supported Charles I; and a complete wall given over to photographs of individual town buildings, which is not surprising, for, though Shrewsbury is not so much all-of-a-piece as some historic towns, it is packed with individual stars. The Wroxeter connection is important: the settlers who moved there in the fifth century AD, after the departure of the Romans, and then to Shrewsbury found in the town a safer settlement than they had previously known.

Rowley's Mansion, next to his house, was the first brick-built house in Shrewsbury, an indication of how prosperous draper and brewer William Rowley, who had it built in 1618, had become. The adjoining half-timbered house was part of the original structure. From Rowley's House walk diagonally towards little Hill's Lane (there is a particularly good map shop on the left). Hill's Lane was originally Knockin Street, but was renamed in 1689 after a Mayor of Shrewsbury, John Hill, who lived at the time in Rowley's Mansion. Turn right into Mardol, called 'Mardeval' and 'Mardefole' in the Middle Ages, or detour briefly towards the end of the street to see the mainly fifteenth-century King's Head pub. There are several other well-preserved timber-framed buildings. At the top of Mardol, where there is a convenient direction sign and a bench from which old men like to keep an eye on what is going on, cross Shoplatch – a continuation of Pride Hill, which is to the left – and notice one of Shrewsbury's 'shuts'. A shortened form of 'short-cut', shuts are little passageways usually connecting focal points of the town. The first you will notice is Plough Shut but this is a let-down (not even worth the short detour) as it is a cul-de-sac. So turn left immediately past the National Westminster Bank down Gullet Passage, which like Plough Shut may have taken its name from the pub that once stood here. Now the Hole in the Wall inn and restaurant is the dominant building. These shuts were thought to have been locked after dark in medieval times, and gatehinges and bolt holes where Gullet Passage joins The Square support this idea.

LEFT *Ireland's Mansion, in the High Street, was built in about 1575 by Robert Ireland, a merchant who made a fortune out of wool.*

ABOVE *The statue commemorating Clive of India faces away from The Square. The Old Market Hall, dating from the very end of the sixteenth century, is in the background.*

This is the best approach to The Square, which is full of interest, but before seeing it from the best vantage point, make a very worthwhile detour towards a delightful small museum named after Clive of India, a Shrewsbury idol who turned out to have feet of clay. Bear right, cross Market Street and enter another shut, Coffee House Passage, at whose entrance there was an eighteenth-century coffee house. At the end of Coffee House Passage turn left into College Hill, and then right – it is clearly signed – for the Clive House Museum, which stands at the end of a cul-de-sac and is separated from an inviting garden by a wrought-iron gate. I stood here and nothing moved except a bee buzzing around a hanging flower basket. It is a charming spot and if it had been a small hotel, which at first sight it could have been, I might have booked in there and then. You open the front door to the private house which it was when used by Clive of India, who was Mayor of Shrewsbury in 1762 and the town's MP. There is a watercolour gallery and an outstanding collection of Coalport and Caughley pottery. Clive's association with Shrewsbury came after he had masterminded the recapture of Calcutta from the rebels responsible for the infamous Black Hole. To run for office back home (he was born in Shropshire but not in Shrewsbury), he had to own property in the

town and it was this house he bought. His career later took him to Ireland, but allegations of corruption there pursued him to the end of his life.

This is a quiet, little-frequented corner of the town, in some contrast to The Square. Retrace your steps here. The Square is a good point from which to get orientated. The Old Market Hall there (1596) must be very familiar to Shrewsbury people as several seats face it. The statue set into the building below the clock was saved from the original Welsh Bridge before that was demolished. Facing away from the Old Market Hall is a statue of Lord Clive and to one side of The Square is the Plough Inn, a sixteenth-century timbered building. Plough Shut connects it at the back with Shoplatch.

From The Square cross the High Street, and look immediately to the left along here for tiny Grope Lane. Though it is meat and drink to local people, this is just the sort of shut that outsiders will rarely find without guidance. It increases the impression that there are two Shrewsburys, and that the better of the two is behind the scenes, down back alleys, up hidden stairways, and round inconsequential corners, slicing quickly and excitingly at a stroke through hundreds of years of history. Grope Lane is a classic case. (The name is thought simply to have arisen from a dark and narrow passageway through which one groped one's way.) And it makes a useful link to one of the two or three most charming corners of Shrewsbury.

From Grope Lane cross Fish Street (fish markets were once held here) obliquely to Bear Steps (named after an inn that stood here between 1780 and 1910). Via these dozen or so steps you pass under a late-fourteenth-century complex of buildings recently restored by the Shrewsbury Civic Society, whose office is here too, and into a tree-shaded breathing space called St Alkmond's Place. This completely belies its situation in the heart of a closely packed ancient town where some streets are so narrow, with every square inch put to use, that houses on opposite sides can shake hands with each other. In the mid-1960s Shrewsbury was in danger of seeing its most interesting ancient buildings succumb to developers' bulldozers, and Bear Steps was the first of several imaginative projects to restore the town's best timber-framed buildings to their original form. Plaster, tar and several generations of paint were removed. But here a word of warning, for as with Chester several black-and-white timbered buildings that look as if people could have waved to Elizabeth I from their upper storeys are actually a Victorian tribute to medieval architects. The High Victorian style is rare: two of the best examples are the Halifax Building Society in The Square, and the railway station.

Only cars needing access, like taxis delivering guests to the front door of the Prince Rupert Hotel, use the narrow road that roughly encircles St Alkmond's Place (colloquially known as Church Green), and the most penetrating sounds are those of heels click-clacking across the paved paths or office girls chattering on their way to and from work. Businessmen staying in the hotel take the air after breakfast, before re-entering its dark and plush recesses. Unfortunately trees, a huge chestnut among them, all but obscure one of Shrewsbury's most handsome churches, St Alkmund's (note a slight difference in the spelling). If you only had ten minutes to experience just one corner of Shrewsbury, St Alkmond's Place would be it. For it is a very pretty encapsulation of much of the best of the town, almost

Butcher Row, with part of the Prince Rupert Hotel on the right and St Alkmund's Church in the background. The Tudor half-timbering is a Shrewsbury characteristic.

as if one of northern England's more attractive villages had been dropped wholesale onto one of Shrewsbury's highest points.

At the Rupert Hotel end of Butcher Row is the Abbot's House. It is thought that this and other houses in the lane were owned by Lillieshall Abbey and that the Abbot himself used this as a town house. Whatever the ecclesiastical associations this is a very impressive group of buildings and certainly pre-1500. Notice especially the wide sills of the windows on the ground floor, identifying this part as an original row of shops. Walk to the bottom of Butcher Row and turn left into Pride Hill for a brief detour to admire the exterior of Boots the Chemist – a delightful if fanciful example of Edwardian pargeting, or decorative plasterwork. Running the gauntlet of builders' labourers pushing barrows I discovered that a huge site adjacent to Boots was being developed as the Pride Hill Centre, to link with car parks and another shopping centre on the banks of the river some distance below. This part of Shrewsbury was always important commercially. In the Middle Ages this end of the street was part of Corvisors Row, which derived from the old French *corveiser*, meaning a worker in the Spanish leather introduced into England before the Norman conquest. In 1324 the Cordwainer's Guild was granted a Royal Charter to tan all kinds of leather except horse's. Because of this association this

is probably where medieval shoemakers were based. The name Pride
Hill comes from a local family who owned shops and a house here
during the reign of Henry III, and by Victorian times this part of
Shrewsbury had the most prestigious shops in the town. At the top of
Pride Hill – not too steep but just hilly enough to let you know you've
made the effort – you are just a few yards from (on the left) a range of
chain stores without which no self-respecting provincial town of city
would be complete.

Continue down Castle Street, noticing Halford's the motor acces-
sory shop, which stands on a building in which according to a plaque
'Shrewsbury cakes' were first made in 1760. A contemporary
chronicle mentions them: 'Oh! Palin. Prince of cake compounders.
The mouth liquifies at the very name.' But, alas, I was unable to find
anybody even in a nearby baker's shop who knew what they were.
Immediately past here and between Halfords and W.H.Smith turn left
into School Gardens. Very effectively several Shrewsbury street signs
incorporate a list of shops, and the School Gardens sign is one of these.
Again free of cars, this unassuming back lane, so close to a main road
but retaining lots of character, runs down a slight incline towards the
Old Grammar School. After extensive restoration in 1983 this became
a library. The school was built between about 1590 and 1630, and
among its famous pupils were the courtier and soldier Philip Sidney,
the notorious Judge Jeffreys, and Charles Darwin. In 1882 it moved
lock, stock and barrel across the river (good views later in the walk) to
high-lying, handsome red-brick buildings, more in keeping with a
major public school of the modern age.

Walk past Darwin's statue standing amid more of the carefully
tended municipal gardens that seem to set Shrewsbury apart from the
ordinary run of county towns. Cross the road in the direction of the
tall and extremely attractive Romanesque St Nicholas Church, which
was being extensively renovated during my most recent visit, then
turn left up the approach to the castle. Don't expect a Windsor or a
Warwick, but do appreciate yet more manicured flower beds and a
superbly maintained, cosmetically battlemented, sandstone fortification, which looks on balance more like a private house than a
fortress. This is what it became when Thomas Telford renovated it in
1787 as a private home for Sir William Pulteney, Shrewsbury's MP
between 1776 and 1805. It was a civilized and peaceful end,
effectively, to a dramatic past. Shrewsbury Castle figured prominently
in the wars against the Welsh, and was captured by Llewellyn the
Great in 1212. It was lost in 1286, on which occasion Llewellyn's
brother, David, was executed at the top of Pride Hill. It also changed
hands during the Civil War, and thus enjoys the status of one of the
castles that English history has knocked about a bit.

The main building contains the Shropshire Regimental Museum,
which I entered half-heartedly, as much to enquire about the identity
of the distinctive black-and-white house on the castle approach as to
be regaled with regimental regalia and what I imagined would be
irrelevant and long-forgotten tales of derring-do. Once again I was
very wrong indeed: this is a most moving and touchingly cared-for
treasure house of the regiment's medals, insignia and ceremonial
plate, and the recorded military music which accompanies you
throughout did not seem at all obtrusive or 'martial' but much more of
a moving memorial. I paused for a few thoughtful minutes in front of a
display that contained among others the Victoria Cross awarded to

*Statue of Charles Darwin,
a Shrewsbury native. He
was a pupil at the Old
Grammar School, the
building behind the statue,
which now houses the
public library and art
gallery.*

Shrewsbury Castle now incorporates the council chamber and an unusually emotive regimental museum. Founded in 1070, the castle was modernized in 1787 by the engineer Telford.

one Sergeant Eardley near the end of the Second World War in Holland. Presented with Britain's highest military award for gallantry, by Field Marshal Montgomery, Eardley added to his achievements by looking embarrassed and bemused in a photograph taken during his moment of glory. If you linger in the gardens, notice by the main entrance to the castle complex an unexpected memorial to Shrewsbury's almost-forgotten cabmen. This is a wood and stained glass gazebo-style shelter which once stood in The Square.

The house which I had wanted to enquire about and which I looked at more closely and a little more knowledgeably as I returned to the main street is Castle Gates House. It is an early seventeenth-century picture-postcard building that used to stand on busy, winding, narrow Dogpole, in the heart of the old town. I wondered if I had heard right when the smartly blazered custodian at the Regimental Museum – regimental tie and stiff collar present and correct – told me that the house had been moved up the hill in 1696. I had thought that was a late-twentieth-century habit, but apparently not exclusively so.

Turn right from here down Castle Street, which as the road steepens becomes Castle Gates, and look on your right for a stairway and passageway called The Dana, which skirts the north-west edge of the castle and looks down onto Shrewsbury station and, just beyond the station, Shrewsbury's distinctive prison. This too is colloquially called The Dana. It figures in A.E.Housman's poetry and, also designed by Telford, is not in the least unattractive – at least from the outside! Naturally it rarely figures in tourist board literature, but at least it crops up in one of their find-out-all-about-it quizzes. 'How many chimney pots has the prison got?' is one of the questions, and clearly the only way to find out is by taking this small and worthwhile detour. A less obvious but still intriguing building seen from the Dana is the newspaper distribution office of Surridge Dawson Ltd, which looked as if Heath Robinson and a slightly eccentric Victorian architect had got together after a few drinks at the Plough Inn. It has railings on the roof, and as if to cock a snook, these (at the time of my visit) were painted bright pink.

Retrace your steps up Castle Gates/Castle Street, this time with the library and Darwin on your right, and climb up towards the town centre, but then turn left past Castle Gates House and immediately past the church into the Old Council House yard. The Old Council House has a convenient seat in a porch, where I took the opportunity to get out my local maps and get orientated. It dates from 1501 and consists of two hall houses at right angles to each other. This was the headquarters of the Council of the Welsh Marches, an immensely powerful body in the sixteenth and seventeenth centuries in an unruly corner of the kingdom. Meetings of the Council in Shrewsbury were often the occasion for expensive receptions. Sir Henry Sidney, whose famous son Philip attended the school across the road, was a president of the Council.

Charles I lodged here when he moved to Shrewsbury at the beginning of the Civil War in 1642 and when recruits to his cause were being sought in Wales and the West Midlands. All through the war Shrewsbury was in the thick of the action. It was from here that a Royalist army marched to Chester to attempt to lift the Cromwellian siege, and the Parliamentary forces took advantage of this on the night of 21/22 March 1645 and captured the town. Part of this operation involved breaching palisades across the Severn and scrambling up Water Lane, which is a steep and very pleasant route to the river. To reach it turn off left into St Mary's Place and left again. The river is wide and usually fast-flowing. From the walkway, look left towards the railway bridge, over which trains from London enter Shrewsbury station, and right, several hundred yards away, towards the English Bridge, which dates from 1927. If it looks rather handsome for this period this is probably because it is virtually a reconstruction, stone by stone, of a bridge opened in 1774 and dismantled in 1925 because it had become too narrow for the traffic using it.

Retrace your steps up Water Lane and then turn left in St Mary's Place, the eastern side of which is dominated by a huge Georgian mansion that now incorporates the low-key and seldom uncomfortably crowded Parade Shopping Centre. This is on two levels, and it is best to turn down to your left towards the terrace overlooking the Severn and, beyond it, Shrewsbury's abbey – follow signs for the Chinese restaurant. The view is worth the short detour even if you are not in the mood for boutiques and knick-knacks, or even Chinese food. The present abbey was built around the remains of the Benedictine Abbey of St Peter and St Paul. Because of its location beyond the river it is perhaps the least visited of all Shrewsbury's churches. In any event, enter the lower shopping level if it is open and take the stairway to the first floor. Emerge again into St Mary's Place, with St Mary's Church ahead of you. The church is one of the oldest in the county, with Saxon foundations and an especially notable Norman doorway. Turn left out of St Mary's Place into St Mary's Street, noticing on your right Church Street, which leads to St Alkmund's and passes the half-timbered side entrance of the Prince Rupert Hotel. St Mary's Street runs into one of Shrewsbury's best-known streets, called Dogpole, which in turn approaches the distinctive Wyle Cop at right angles.

Near the top of Dogpole, on the left, a gardener was putting the finishing touches to the garden in front of the office of the Chief

An alley off Wyle Cop. This is one of Shrewsbury's 'shuts' – a name unique to the town – that were traditionally 'short cuts'. Some have, however, become cul-de-sacs.

Executive of the Shrewsbury and Atcham Borough Council. No glass and concrete excrescence this but a neat and handsome red-brick house of about 1700, which in its commanding position adds much to the street. I admired the pocket-handkerchief lawn and the red-and-white flower borders. 'It's the Britain in Bloom contest coming up,' the gardener explained. As a frequent winner of this, Shrewsbury was clearly on its best horticultural behaviour.

Within a few yards, you are in sight of Shrewsbury's most celebrated inn, and very imposing it is, taking up the equivalent of a terrace of substantial houses, for it has expanded over the years. The Lion has been an inn since at least 1618, and possibly a long time before that. It enjoyed its greatest prestige in the eighteenth century, when it was the place to be seen for anybody who considered themselves anybody. Occasionally, when I am allocated a hotel room that is more spacious and luxurious than I have expected, or, on arriving late at night and finding all the other rooms gone, bargain for the empty bridal suite when there is clearly not going to be a chance arrival, I am reminded of one guest who was allowed to sleep in the ballroom at the Lion: 'A sumptuous room was allotted to me .... It was a ballroom of noble proportions lighted by three gorgeous chandeliers.' The hotel acquired a different kind of prestige in about 1750, when some of the fastest and, by the standards of the time, most comfortable stage-coaches ran between the Lion and London, but that was only the beginning of a transport revolution; in the 1750s the journey took five days, in the 1820s it was down to sixteen breakneck hours.

Speed was everything, and sometimes coaches cleared street corners by inches rather than feet, which is worth remembering as you turn right along narrow Wyle Cop and then sharp left into Milk Street – another name indicating its commercial past – and thus enter a part of Shrewsbury with a distinctive character. These individual and distinctive corners of Shrewsbury add up to more than the sum of the parts, and Belmont – which continues from Milk Street beyond College Green – contributes more than most. The shady and slightly misshapen green is set slightly higher than Princess Street, which in turn leads down towards Market Street and The Square (an excellent bookshop and a mainly subterranean antiques centre *en route*, by the way).

Continue along Belmont, and admire the harmonious arrangement of Georgian buildings that most towns or cities would give their Royal Charter to possess. Notice an unusual covered porch and front patio at No. 8 and further on a good example of false windows; these were sometimes blacked out to avoid an eighteenth-century window tax but more usually included in a façade for the sake of symmetry. The road is rarely busy, and anyway double yellow lines keep nosey parkers at bay. At the bottom of Belmont detour briefly left along Town Walls as far as the mid-Victorian Roman Catholic cathedral. If you stand across the road from the cathedral, where you can look down onto a charming arrangement of tennis courts and bowling greens, you are actually on part of the original town walls.

Retrace your steps past the bottom of Belmont and continue westwards past the Ear, Nose and Throat Hospital. Look right up attractive Swan Hill, which leads to Market Street on The Square, and left down towards Kingsland Bridge. This is worth a detour (the halfpenny toll for pedestrians was phased out a few years ago) for the

Part of The Quarry, one of the finest public parks to be found in any English town or city. It has the river on one side and, among other attractions, a spectacular sunken garden.

view over the Severn, the wide boulevard of Victoria Avenue alongside it and the all-dominant red brick buildings of the Shrewsbury School, built in 1882. Cattle were grazing on the banks leading down from the school. I rather envied the people strolling below the bridge beside the river, but failed to find a footpath down from it.

Return to Town Walls, turn left past the hospital and then after a couple of hundred yards left again into Quarry Place, by which one enters The Quarry, as Shrewsbury's exceptional public park is known. This has good access to the river and also contains the sunken formal gardens called the Dingle, which was created by the late Percy Thrower, perhaps England's best-known gardener after Capability Brown. Percy Thrower was appointed parks superintendent in Shrewsbury (the youngest ever) in 1946 and stayed until retirement in 1974. I came across the Dingle quite innocently, not realizing that preparations were under way for the Shrewsbury Flower Show, which Shrewsbury takes very seriously indeed. The Elizabethan knot gardeners, who created England's first formal gardens, would probably have applauded this display, for not a leaf was out of place.

Walk past the war memorial and leave The Quarry via the iron gates in St Chad's terrace, dominated by St Chad's Church. For some visitors seeing the interiors of parish churches can be more a duty than a pleasure. Do not, however, miss going into St Chad's, whose unusual circular nave is well lit by very large windows, and whose Victorian stained glass – though inevitably rather unpopular – is to my mind very impressive. Turn right and right again out of the church, with The Quarry behind you. You will catch a glimpse of the churchyard, which was used as a location during a television film of Dickens's *Christmas Carol*. Continue along the pretty and welcoming Claremont Hill, going just slightly downhill (it seems every street in Shrewsbury has some gradient) towards Barker Street and, to the left, Rowley's Mansion and the multi-storey car park.

Late afternoon sun on Shrewsbury's red-brick houses brings out the best in this much-maligned building material, especially when age and weathering have given it a deeper shade. At the same time of day deepening shadows in St Alkmond's Place, The Quarry, and the School Gardens that set off Darwin's statue so effectively enrich the greenery and flower borders. Add to this the black-and-white half-timbering, and this comes over as a colourful town. I found it much more congenial in summer than winter, although in winter those snug bars tucked away in the far corners of age-old low-ceilinged pubs, several with real log or coal fires, come into their own.

YORK

ST. WILLIAM'S
COLLEGE
Restaurant
Brass Rubbing
Centre

YORK

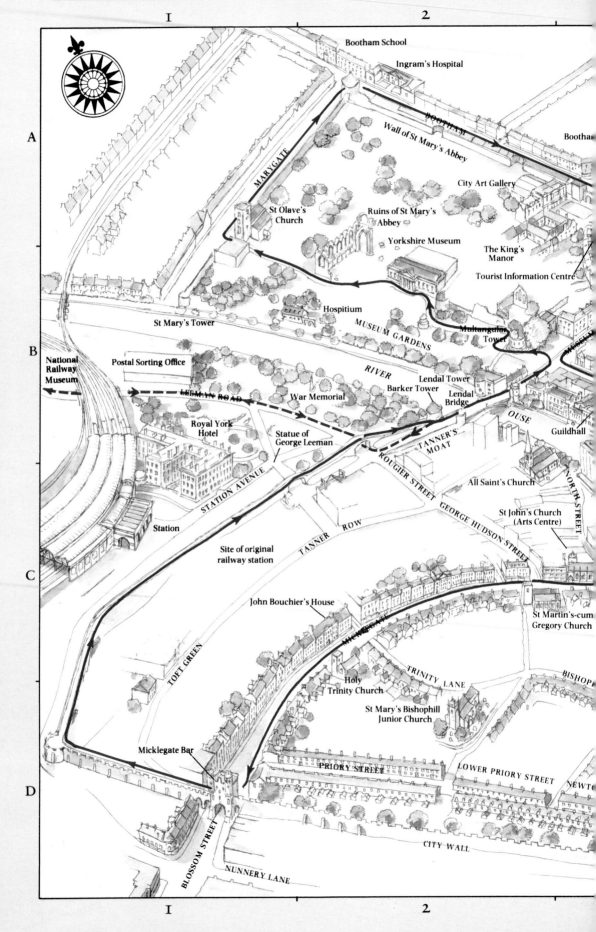

Bootham School

Ingram's Hospital

BOOTHAM

Bootha

A

MARYGATE

Wall of St Mary's Abbey

City Art Gallery

St Olave's Church

Ruins of St Mary's Abbey

Yorkshire Museum

The King's Manor

Tourist Information Centre

Hospitium

MUSEUM GARDENS

Multangular Tower

St Mary's Tower

RIVER

Lendal Tower

NESSGA

B

National Railway Museum

Postal Sorting Office

LEEMAN ROAD

War Memorial

Barker Tower

Lendal Bridge

Guildhall

OUSE

Royal York Hotel

Statue of George Leeman

TANNER'S MOAT

All Saint's Church

NORTH STREET

STATION AVENUE

ROUGIER STREET

GEORGE HUDSON STREET

St John's Church (Arts Centre)

Station

TANNER ROW

Site of original railway station

C

John Bouchier's House

MICKLEGATE

St Martin's-cum Gregory Church

TOFT GREEN

TRINITY LANE

BISHOP

Holy Trinity Church

St Mary's Bishophill Junior Church

Micklegate Bar

PRIORY STREET

LOWER PRIORY STREET

NEWTO

D

BLOSSOM STREET

NUNNERY LANE

CITY WALL

3 **4**

To Heworth Green Car Park →

LORD MAYOR'S WALK

GILLYGATE

Deanery

Minster Library

Treasurer's House

MONKGATE

Monk Bar **S**

A

OGLEFORTH

Minster Church of St Peter

St William's College

CHAPTER HOUSE STREET

Merchant Taylor's Hall

COLLEGE STREET

Bedern Hall

Our Lady's Row

The Old Residence

Unitarian Chapel

PETERGATE

DUNCOMBE PLACE

re Royal

St Wilfrid's RC Church

St Michael's Church

Old Starre Inn

MINSTER YARD

DEANGATE

LOW PETERGATE

Holy Trinity Church

ly as dging

BLAKE STREET

GRAPE LANE

SWINEGATE

KING'S SQUARE

Centenary Methodist Church

B

St Helen's Church

St Sampson's Church

CHURCH ST

COLLIERGATE

ST SAVIOURGATE

St Saviour Church

DAVYGATE

ST HELEN'S SQUARE

House of Margaret Clitherow

SHAMBLES

Stonebow

WHIP-MA-WHOP-MA GATE

Mansion House

NEW ST

DAVYGATE

PARLIAMENT ST

MARKET

All Saints Church

LADY PECKETT'S YARD

FOSSGATE

g

St Martin's Church

SPURRIERGATE

MARKETGATE

PARLIAMENT ST

COPPERGATE

PICCADILLY

Merchant Adventurer's Hall

HIGH OUSEGATE

St Mary's Heritage Centre

Jorvik Viking Centre

Coppergate Shopping Precinct

OUSEGATE

Ouse Bridge

KING'S STAITH

CLIFFORD STREET

CASTLEGATE

Fairfax House

Clifford's Tower

C

STREET

The King's Arms (formerly Cumberland House)

SOUTH ESPLANADE

TOWER STREET

Castle Museum

SKELDERGATE

CROMWELL ROAD

Assize Court

RIVER FOSS

Skeldergate Bridge

D

BISHOPGATE STREET

TERRY AVENUE

HJP 1987

3 **4**

BUILDINGS AND PLACES OF INTEREST

Assembly Rooms (1731) B3
Assize Court (1773–7) D4
Bootham Bar A3
Bootham School
(1796–1800) A2
John Bouchier's House
(1753) C2
Castle Museum (1705) C4
Centenary Methodist Church
(1840) B4
City Art Gallery A2
Clifford's Tower
(1250–75) C4
Margaret Clitherow's
House B4
Coppergate Shopping
Precinct C4
Deanery A4
Fairfax House (1750–55) C4
Guildhall (1449–59) B3
To Heworth Green Car Park A4
Holy Trinity Church C2
Hospitium B2
Ingram's Hospital (1640) A2
Jorvik Viking Centre C4
Judge's Lodging
(1718–25) B3
The King's Arms (c.1710) C3
The King's Manor (begun
1483) B2
Leeman Statue B1
Lendal Bridge (1861–3) B2
Mansion House (1725–7) B3
Merchant Adventurers' Hall
(c15) C4
Merchant Taylors' Hall
(interior c.1400) A4
Micklegate Bar D1
Minster (c.1230–1430) A3
Minster Library A3
Monk Bar (c13–14) A4
Multangular Tower (c4) B2
National Railway
Museum B1
The Old Residence
(c.1740) B4
Old Starre Inn B3
Our Lady's Row (c.1315) B4
Ouse Bridge C3
Royal York Hotel
(1877–8) B1
St Helen's Church B3
St Mary's Abbey Ruins
(c13) A2
St Mary's Heritage Centre C4
St Olave's Church A1
St Wilfrid's RC Church
(1862–4) B3
St William's College (c15) A4
The Shambles B4
Skeldergate Bridge
(1878–81) D4
Station (1877) C1
Stonegate B3
Theatre Royal (1877–9) B3
Tourist Information
Centre B3
Viking Hotel C3
Yorkshire Museum B2

PAGES 170–71 *Once a residence for cathedral clergy, St William's College lies in the shadow of the east end of York Minster.*

OPPOSITE Monk Bar, a medieval gateway guarding Goodramgate and the north-eastern entrance to the town, has a working portcullis and the original arrow-slits.

One of the questions curious visitors to York are likely to ask themselves is 'Do people having afternoon tea in their back gardens mind being peered at by tourists walking the walls?' For the low-flying bird's eye view of hollyhocks, white-aluminium garden furniture and well-mulched flower beds is one of the bonuses that will come your way if you enter any of the unassuming gateways set in York's city gates, pause as you surely will at busy times to let others come down first, and then ascend to enjoy the kind of panorama rare (though not unique) in Britain. You can see quite a lot too from one of York's open-topped sightseeing buses, though in the height of the season you might have to wait for a seat on the upper deck and miss out on some of the sights mentioned by the guide unless you crane your neck. But York is not, on the whole, a place you look down on, except perhaps from Clifford's Tower, which is all that remains of York Castle. Originally a wooden tower which was replaced by a stone one in about 1250, it tops a man-made mound that has a twin (without the very photogenic fortification) on the other side of the River Ouse it once helped to protect.

York's street pattern has evolved from the Roman occupation through the Viking and Saxon periods up to medieval times and has not dramatically changed since – hence its immediate appeal to visitors who are delighted by so many tangible reminders of York's antiquity. The city is unashamedly geared to the needs of its tourists and has been called a glorified museum by some of its mainly local detractors. Even so, on a busy summer Saturday I found myself virtually alone on several occasions: in Fairfax House, an eighteenth-century gem recently restored to almost incomparable beauty, in the cavernous fourteenth- and fifteenth-century Merchant Adventurers' Hall, and in the rambling, very evocative Treasurer's House, which stands quietly in the lee of York Minster.

Sometimes it seems that the majority of visitors do not stray more than a quarter of a mile from the railway station, which in itself attracts carriage-loads of youths in khaki shorts waving copies of the Railway Magazine. This is not meant to be disparaging, for within those four-hundred-odd yards they can take part in an orgy of nostalgia at the National Railway Museum, spread themselves over lunch in one of the finest railway age hotels in the country, have a good look at the River Ouse and sample the pleasures of York's partly Roman but largely medieval walls. In fact, the most photographed section of York's walls is conveniently across the road from the station. If and when these instant charms fade, another half mile or so will encompass what is now recognized to be one of the most impressive cities in Europe. It is, of course, most easily enjoyed on foot.

Even if it were advisable to park within the walls of the old city (it is possible but very inconvenient) I would opt to do so outside them. For this way you get a better sense of perspective. There is ample parking at or near the Heworth Green car park, on the north-east side of the city, from where it is a five-minute walk along Monkgate to Monk Bar. Notice on the left hand side of Monkgate – the suffix 'gate', from the Norse, simply denotes a street – a plaque at No. 44 commemorating the 'railway king' George Hudson. He was a reasonably successful local draper who foresaw the likely importance of railways to York on account of its geographical situation, and became manager of the North Midland Railway Company. He was also Lord Mayor three times, though, as I was to discover later, he was no saint.

On the corner of Lord Mayor's Walk and Monkgate, just to the right of Monk Bar, is a junk and bric-à-brac shop that might just yield the souvenir that more conventional shops do not. Monk Bar, at over 60 ft, is the tallest of all York's few surviving medieval gateways. It used to be thought that the gateway, built in the thirteenth century on Roman foundations and enlarged two centuries later, came to be named after a General Monk, but it probably refers to a monastery that once stood nearby. Monk Bar was a mini-fortress, each storey defensible in its own right, and, better still, the portcullis, its teeth just visible, is in full working order.

Walk under Monk Bar and along Goodramgate, which derives from Guthrun, a Danish forename. But for a worthwhile detour if time permits, turn left down Aldwark – meaning 'old fortifications' – to the Merchant Taylors' Hall, a fifteenth-century livery hall. This is, incidentally, probably as nice an example of late twentieth-century redevelopment and infilling as you will find in northern England. Returning to Goodramgate, continue along it as it bears left, with the east end of the Minster ahead and the half-timbered and stone St William's College set back on the right. The oldest existing houses in York are about 100 yds further along on the right. Called Our Lady's Row, they were built in Holy Trinity churchyard in about 1315 and, looked at with half closed eyes, are exactly as they were six and a half centuries ago. The church is now redundant, though lovingly cared for still – which is just as well, because among other things it contains a double-decker pulpit and rare box pews, asymmetrically arranged.

A few yards past here, bear left into King's Square, but as you do so look right up Low Petergate for another view of the Minster – to be seen in detail later. Look ahead, too, into Church Street, once Girdlergate, so-called because of the belts that used to be made here. More than 1300 years before that this was the south-east gate of the Roman fortress. A typical aspect of York's charm is the way you

The Shambles, with the house of Margaret Clitherow on the left. She was canonized in this century for her adherence under torture to the Catholic faith in the sixteenth century.

suddenly emerge into an open space out of closely ordered streets and then plunge again into what was a medieval stew but is now prettified. The reference to 'stew' is appropriate, because The Shambles, York's most famous street, whose entrance is at the top right of King's Square as you face away from Petergate and the Minster, used to be the butchers' street. Mentioned in the Domesday book, the name Shambles probably comes from 'hamells' or 'flesham-ells', denoting the stalls or benches on which meat was displayed. Even as recently as 1830, when York was not yet accessible by train, there were twenty-five butchers in The Shambles.

As you walk, or at certain times fight your way, down The Shambles you may notice on your right, glimpsed through narrow alleyways (locally called snickets), York's open air market. Also on the right is the house of Margaret Clitherow (1556–86), who was canonized as recently as 1970. The house is a Roman Catholic shrine, and as my eyes gradually became accustomed to the dark interior I was caught inside by the sudden arrival of a coach party of at least thirty strong. So this is clearly on the tourist beat. A butcher's wife, Margaret Clitherow was brought before the Council of the North, who were charged with stamping out Catholicism, and condemned to *peine forte et dure* for maintaining a hiding place for persecuted priests and refusing to renounce her faith. Her bizarre and convoluted 'punish-ment' involved being pressed to death under a heavily weighted door, with a sharp stone in the small of the back.

As you approach the end of The Shambles, having run the gauntlet of sweetshops, boutiques and souvenir shops, do not miss, on the left, St Crux Passage. The church from which it gets its name was demolished a hundred years ago and the remaining parish room incorporates some of the artefacts that were saved. This leads to York's second most famous but certainly shortest street, called Whip-ma-whop-ma-gate, the origin of whose name is not really known but

The medieval Merchant Adventurers' Hall was the prestigious headquarters of the Merchant Adventurers' guild, and included a hospital and a chapel.

has given rise to several imaginative explanations. The most enduring of these is that a whipping post and pillory were once close by.

Turn right into Pavement, cross the road and look closely for a very low-key passageway called Lady Peckett's Yard. This was renamed after the widow of John Peckett, who was Lord Mayor of York from 1702 to 1703; traditionally wives of Lord Mayors became 'Lady', even though their husbands did not receive any permanent title. Originally, as early as 1312, records show this as Bacusgail or Bakehouse Lane. Pavement, too, had an earlier name. In Domesday it shows up as Marketshire but became Pavement in 1329 probably because it was the city's first paved street. Turn left into Piccadilly for a brief detour to the Merchant Adventurers' Hall, set below the road on the left about two hundred yards from the junction and thus easily overlooked. By no means one of York's most vaunted historical properties it is nevertheless something of a showpiece. The prowess of York's fourteenth- and fifteenth-century entrepreneurs was vital to the wealth and prestige of the city, and the Hall was the headquarters of the guild. So important was it that it even included a hospital and a chapel. The great hall is massive: in 1358 one hundred trees were felled for its construction.

Retrace your steps to the junction of Pavement, Piccadilly and Coppergate, and turn left into Coppergate with the recently cleaned, very elegant church of All Saints on your right. Its tall, octagonal open lantern tower is a landmark of this corner of the city, and the new Coppergate shopping precinct has been arranged partly so that it can be seen at the northern end. A light is kept on during the night to commemorate the dead of both world wars. The name Coppergate, from the Danish word 'koopen', meaning 'to bargain', recalls the Viking invaders and seems to refer to the commercial activity that went on here. Turn left after a few yards into the pedestrianized shopping precinct that, down a slight incline, emerges into St Mary's Square, with the Jorvik Viking Centre on the right and the modern shops ahead. When I arrived tourists were massaging their feet under the shade of a chestnut tree and pulling off sweaters as the sun warmed up. A wide passageway just past the Jorvik Centre leads up to the redundant St Mary's Church, now a 'Heritage Centre', in which the social history and architectural growth of the city is traced by means of tapestries, dioramas, scale models and an audio-visual display. In a large café on St Mary's Square, I had an unlikely dish of fried chicken wings with a sauce to dip them in, and yes, could have had Yorkshire pudding with onion gravy. Through the open doors of the café I could see and hear street musicians, a jazz clarinettist and two-piece accompaniment pacifying the rather long queue for Jorvik.

What you see above ground, albeit in harmonious local brick, with All Saints in the background as you look north, bears little relation to what lies beneath pavement level. For when between 1976 and 1981 one of northern Britain's most important archaeological digs took place, it was found that damp and peaty soil had kept more or less intact an incredible amount of original Viking artefacts – houses, shops, workshops and warehouses. No fewer than four rows of buildings were found in virtually the same positions but below succeeding houses. And it was decided to use the great hole created by the archeological dig to recreate a Viking settlement with models, full-scale human figures, sounds and even smells – a time capsule, which the visitor enters in mechanized cars. At first sight you think you are

Clifford's Tower seen from near the public entrance to the Castle Museum. On the left is the Assizes Court and in the distance the spire of All Saints, Coppergate.

stepping on to a ghost train at a fair. In a way you are, but this is a very superior ghost train indeed. The journey is short and fairly sweet, if not sweet-scented. The smells are horribly authentic, and it is one man's special responsibility to augment Jorvik's already sweet smell of commercial success by means of small heated pots of oil-based liquids which, replenished daily, recreate the smells of everyday Viking life. I emerged from the depths and was accosted by a small elderly man with two children in tow. 'Is it good?' he asked. 'Is it worth waiting for?' As he was near the head of the queue, I replied, 'Definitely'.

Turn right past Jorvik with St Mary's Heritage Centre on your right and then left into Castlegate, along which, just a few yards on the left, is beautiful Fairfax House. I have seen some fine town and country houses on my travels, but Fairfax House stopped me in my tracks. It is sumptuous, effectively a late twentieth-century tribute to the Georgian age, its exquisite rooms renovated almost regardless of cost from a rundown original that was due to be razed to the ground. To say that the interior is the apotheosis of Georgian elegance is putting it mildly, for apart from the work that has gone into restoring moulded ceilings and decorative woodwork, the house contains intact one of the best ever collections of eighteenth-century furniture ever assembled in Britain. This belonged to Noel Terry, who for twenty-five years was Honorary Treasurer of the York Civic Trust. He was the great-grandson of the founder of Terry's, the confectionery manufacturer, long associated with the city. To appreciate what has been achieved here, pick up the glossy brochure at the modest desk where you pay to go in, for it contains just one 'before' photograph of a shabby corner of a bedroom with peeling paint and torn wallpaper.

As if there was not already enough to enjoy or to go back for time and time again, this walk through York gets better and better, for by turning left outside Fairfax House you emerge after just a few yards, still via Castlegate, into York's castle. This complex of buildings includes the original women's prison, the male debtors' prison, the Assizes Court and Clifford's Tower. As you emerge from Castlegate, and try not to be too distracted by a mass of parked cars, notice the new Crest Hotel on the right. It manages to be both huge and discreet, combining practicality (for a long time York was short of good quality accommodation) and clean attractive lines. On a good day it seems that half York's tourists climb to the top of Clifford's Tower, but the chances are that only a small proportion of them head straight for the exceptional Castle Museum, which was opened as early as 1938 mainly to house a collection of bygones, including complete shop-fronts, amassed by a Doctor Kirk of Pickering. Though perhaps taken for granted now by a young generation of tourists weaned on three-dimensional displays and holograms, this was the model for many historical museums in Britain. Its recreation of Victorian and later street scenes is still highly impressive. On leaving the Castle Museum, with the Assizes Court of 1777 on your left, turn left below Clifford's Tower and cross Tower Street and the public park which separates this from South Esplanade and the River Ouse.

Turn right along South Esplanade, which is as busy a bit of inner city riverside as I have come across, with several competing pleasureboat trips on offer. There is a good chance that anyone walking with a quickening pace towards the Ouse Bridge is heading for the King's Arms pub on King's Staith, outside which people like to spread themselves and watch the river traffic go by. It is perhaps appropriate that the Indian restaurant on the right before the King's Arms overlooks the river and warehouses, one or two of which will once have held, among other goods, exotic spices. Walk up the Ouse Bridge steps, cross the river, continue along Bridge Street and join Micklegate, with the Viking Hotel away to the right on the riverbank and, second right, George Hudson Street. This has only recently been renamed: for many years the 'Railway King' was in disgrace locally for having defrauded investors in his York and North Midlands Railway Company. I once had lunch with a York resident in the Viking Hotel, whose restaurant is right by the Ouse. 'Nice view,' I said, by way of polite conversation. 'Nice?' he said. 'It's horrible.' And the river is, admittedly, rather grey and uninspiring here. King's Staith and the Queen's Staith opposite are better.

Continue along Micklegate, roughly southwestwards, noticing particularly Holy Trinity Church on the left. Rather sombre and often overlooked, it is one of the most interesting in the city, for it incorporates Roman remains from the Temple of Mithras that stood opposite and, not least, still has a set of parish registers dating from 1538. Earlier yet, the church also has, for safekeeping, actors' scripts for the original York Mystery Plays, once mainly performed on the tops of open carts pulled in procession through the city but now performed every four years among the St Mary's Abbey ruins in Museum Gardens. It is recorded that the sum of fourpence was paid to the porter at Micklegate Bar when Richard II came to watch one of these plays in 1397. Immediately opposite the church is a very handsome house on classical lines built for John Bouchier (1710–1759), whose ancestor was one of the signatories of Charles I's execution warrant.

Weary walkers especially may feel at this point that they are leaving the best of the city behind, and it may come as a relief to ascend the walls at Micklegate (though this corner of York, too, is quite attractive) and follow the wall walk to the right above the road – that is, towards the north. The railway station is to the left and while

The classic view of York, from the wall walk just by the station. From here to the Minster you cross over the Lendal Bridge.

this is not a particularly beautiful stretch of York's walls there is quite a lot of interest and, not least, a particularly deep drop on the right-hand side, necessitating a safety rail. The station is considered by people who know about these things to be one of the finest in Britain, though it seems the curving tracks caused considerable problems. As the walls themselves start to curve, roughly parallel with the station front towards the north-east, ahead lie the Minster in full view, Lendal Bridge over the Ouse, and to the right the former headquarters of the North Eastern Railway, a most impressive red-brick building of 1907. This is the most photographed section of York's walls. Sometimes getting in the way of people out for a stroll, photographers position themselves in view of the Lendal Bridge with the Minster (minus scaffolding if they are lucky) in the distance.

Most people do not appreciate that as a historical treasure York's walls are locked and unlocked like any other ancient monument. There are fifteen gates and doors to deal with on York's $2\frac{3}{4}$ miles of medieval walls, and they have to be unlocked at eight in the morning and locked at dusk. Look down over the wall to the left through a gap in the parapet, where there is a scattering of gravestones set in grass between the walls and the Royal York Hotel. These mark the graves of victims of the last epidemic of cholera, in July 1832, who for reasons of hygiene, or what used to pass for that, had to be buried outside the city. A little further along towards the river, that is in the direction you are walking, notice, also on the left, a statue to George Leeman. He was three times Lord Mayor and a long-serving local MP. He was also the creative, energetic and much admired chairman of the North Eastern Railway Company. The elaborate crest adorning the railway headquarters is worth a second glance. It incorporates badges of the York and North Midland Railway, the York, Newcastle and Berwick Railway and the Leeds Northern Railway. In 1923 these all became part of the London and North Eastern Railway.

Here, it is necessary to descend the walls and cross the Ouse via the

Lendal Bridge, but a much recommended detour is to the National Railway Museum, for which it is better to drop down by the railway headquarters and make your way via Station Rise beyond Leeman's statue and thence up Leeman Road. The museum attracts a million people a year, and the procession of visitors up Leeman Road sometimes resembles a suburban station approach when commuters are on the move. It is a moot point whether the dull and very functional approach is a good or a bad thing. It certainly makes for a contrast when you arrive in the massive main exhibition hall – like stepping into a train buff's dream sequence, set mainly around two original locomotive turntables. I had only one reservation: nothing moved. If the organizers could devise even a 100 yd trundle across the outside yard in a third class carriage, *circa* 1870, they would never look back. This glorified engine-shed cuts ordinary commuters down to size. Unimpeded by station platforms, even six-footers are knee high to mirror-bright piston rods, though specially constructed walkways allow one to gaze into luxurious carriage interiors, which would of course have been more familiar to railway company directors and Russian princesses than *hoi polloi*, and would also put most modern five star hotels to shame.

I have rarely seen Lendal Bridge anything other than very busy, almost as if it were the only river crossing. It has had a chequered history. The first bridge was begun in 1860, took a year to build and collapsed into the Ouse, killing five men. The present bridge was opened in January 1863, replacing a ferry run by another Leeman, namely John, since 1831. He was compensated for his loss of revenue by a gift from the City Council of a horse and cart and £15. Look to the right as you cross the river, on whose north bank stands the Guildhall, a heavily restored fifteenth-century building, which is seen more closely at a later stage in the walk. At night it is illuminated, and the still waters of the Ouse reflect the moored pleasureboats and the

Part of the St Mary's Abbey ruins. Continuing a centuries-old tradition, the York Mystery Plays are performed here in the open every four years.

pristine and un-pockmarked castellation of a structure that would not disgrace a toy fort.

A couple of hundred yards over the river turn left into the Museum Gardens, again so centrally situated as to be very well frequented by local people and visitors, especially as it incorporates within its boundaries the Yorkshire Museum, the remains of St Mary's Abbey, the Roman Multangular Tower and attached wall, and the King's Manor, which was built as a residence for the abbot of St Mary's and later became headquarters of the Council of the North, instituted by Richard iii. There is also, and this sometimes takes casual visitors by surprise, an early observatory – I overheard one visitor approaching it express the hope that it was actually a public lavatory – and at the western extreme of the gardens, the Hospitium Museum, a solid repository for all kinds of stone artefacts, including Roman remains for which the city has not yet found an appropriate home.

Leave the Museum Gardens by the gate beyond the St Mary's Abbey remains, and turn right into the very charming Marygate, which gives the impression of having been overlooked by the city and most of its visitors. Tree-shaded and scented with flowers in summer, it contains, not least, the pretty church of St Olave's. This has the oldest foundation date (pre-Norman Conquest) of no fewer than twelve churches in Yorkshire dedicated to Olave, Norway's patron saint, although much of the building dates from the eighteenth century. It stands right on the road, greatly enhancing Marygate. At the top of Marygate, which is on a slight but noticeable hill, turn right into Bootham and thus towards Bootham Bar and, on the right, Exhibition Square. This contains the City Art Gallery, which is a haven of air-conditioned peace and quiet on a hot day, and, to the side of that, the main entrance to the King's Manor, which is opened occasionally to the public and backs on to the Museum Gardens.

Bootham Bar is reckoned to be the most attractive of the city's gates and usually seems to have by far the most tourists milling around it. This ancient gateway was first established by the Romans and is thus easily the oldest of them all. The original barbican, a double gateway whereby people passing through the first gate could be held for inspection between two separate towers, stood here as late as 1832, though now the only survivor of a barbican in York is at Walmgate. As with other city gates, notably Micklegate Bar, the severed heads of criminals and traitors were frequently displayed here, sometimes for weeks or even months at a time.

Between Bootham Bar and Monk Bar lies my favourite stretch of the city wall, but this can be incorporated into the walk at a later stage. Better, for the time being, to turn right down St Leonard's with the De Grey Rooms, housing York's Tourist Information Centre, on the left and, just a few yards beyond that, the Theatre Royal, a successful and popular repertory theatre which, though originally built in 1744, was substantially remodelled in 1967. At the bottom of St Leonard's look left towards the Minster dominating the eastern end of Duncombe Place and across the road to the Assembly Rooms, which alone indicate York's prowess as virtual capital of the north. Built in 1731, these rivalled anything to be had in Bath, for example, and provided a focal point for society at a time when London was effectively a provincial centre, and travel to the capital from this distance was quite impractical.

Turn right down Museum Street and then left into Lendal, passing

Bootham Bar was built on one of the original gateways to the Roman fortress. The archway is Norman but much of the rest was altered or rebuilt in the eighteenth and nineteenth centuries.

the Judge's Lodging on the left, a substantial red-brick building, now a hotel. This was originally the house of a prosperous local doctor but it was bought by the county magistrates as a residence for the Assize judges in 1806. At the end of Lendal, where it opens out into St Helen's Square, the Mansion House stands on the right, facing the square. It is imposing behind its seemingly low iron railings, and democratically right on the street. York was the first city, even including London, to have an official residence for its Lord Mayor, though the building, constructed in 1725–7, was originally intended to be a record office. Not the least of the rare and valuable plate it contains is a silver chamber pot bequeathed by a local resident in 1668! This three-storeyed building, impressive by any standards, is a fitting place of residence for the Lord Mayor during his year of office. Or is it three-storeyed? Actually, the top storey is a fake: the windows are not real but merely part of a second-storey assembly room. Immediately before the Mansion House, however, look for a narrow turning which appears to be a car park or something mundane but is in fact the approach to York's Guildhall (previously seen from the Lendal Bridge), which was built in 1447–8 and restored after being badly damaged during the Second World War. The alleyway once led to a landing stage on the Ouse and, in Roman times, a ford. Limestone for the Minster is said to have been landed here and conveyed towards it up – yes – Stonegate.

From St Helen's Square, bear left and then immediately right past St Helen's Church into Stonegate, a tourist honeypot along which – and I was reminded of sound effects in the Jorvik Viking Centre – three separate buskers were performing just out of earshot of each other. Unfortunately the Paul McCartney look-alike was not a Paul McCartney sound-alike. In a bookshop I mentioned in conversation that I supposed the name Stonegate derived from the fact that stone for the Minster was carried along here, but was politely told that the name was in use before the Norman Conquest. York's first printing presses stood here and one of the alleyways that ran off Stonegate was once known as Bookbinders' Alley. Stonegate was York's first pedestrianized street and contains the city's oldest pub, the Old Starre Inn. Cross High Petergate/Low Petergate and in Minster Yard turn left, with the immaculate Minster towers looming above. Follow Minster Yard round towards the west front. But if time allows detour left and right along, respectively, High Petergate and Low Petergate, for these are busy and tempting shopping streets. If you are not looking for souvenirs, time your detour for six in the evening when the shops have closed and the crowds have melted away.

For several years on end I only seemed to see the Minster with scaffolding superimposed on it, most recently because of lightning that set fire to the south transept roof – now completely replaced – but also for a long period after 1967 because of a massive scheme that was launched to strengthen the foundations and ensure the great church's survival into a third millenium. The Minster is full of superlatives: the largest lantern tower in Britain, looking from a distance like part of a substantial abbey that any country town would be proud of; an exceptionally light and delicate interior, some of it dating back to 1287, and outstanding even among Europe's greatest cathedrals; more medieval stained glass than anywhere else in the country; and the biggest east window in the world, which was completed in 1408, and contains 2,000 sq. ft of original glass. Its

Stonegate with some of its traditional residents – the Olde Starre Inn, buskers and tourists.

immense popularity has led to some overcrowding. So, if possible, time your visit so as to miss the summer Saturday afternoon pilgrimages. In any event fading light on, say, a winter day, brings out the Minster's fine stained glass to great advantage.

Exiting on the south side of the Minster, turn left along Minster Yard to College Street, on which is St William's College, built in 1466 as a home for Minster chantry priests. One of the small shops here was George Hudson's draper shop. I was tempted by a tea shop also incorporated into the black-and-white timbered, tiled and stone building, but pressed on bearing right, passing the extremely handsome York Diocesan Board of Finance, into Chapter House Street and from there, drawn by the ethereal sound of madrigals along Chapter House Street, towards the Treasurer's House. I was lucky enough to be in the Treasurer's House at the best possible time, which is almost always at the last moment before they decide visitors will not have enough time to see the house properly, and so had the place virtually to myself. Perhaps most visitors were in the garden listening to the music. Certainly twenty or so singers seemed to have about 250 people in the attractive, enclosed garden more or less at their feet. It is almost worth the modest entrance fee to visit this reputedly haunted house for the view from the rear landing window of the Dean's Garden and a stretch of wall which proved to be a fitting end to an exceptional walk.

Turn left out of the Treasurer's House down the unassuming backwater called Ogleforth, originally Ugel's Ford, probably an uncovered sewer, then left again into Goodramgate. On reaching Monk Bar, ascend the stone stairway to the top of the wall and follow this round to towards Bootham Bar, not forgetting to look down into the Treasurer's House. For some reason it seems less frequented by visitors than other stretches of the wall, despite intriguing backyard views to left and right – imposing to the left where manicured greenswards seem to demand clerical tea parties, more intimate to the right, where guesthouse owners grow roses in any spare time they

can manage. It is true that the wall has been substantially renovated and 'improved' over centuries, but the earth mound was Roman and even by AD 300 there was a stone wall of sorts, reinforced with polygonal bastions and multangular towers. Here, simply retrace your steps to Monk Bar and descend from there to return towards Heworth Green via Monkgate, or for an extra 'walk round the block' continue to Bootham Bar then walk along High Petergate and past the Minster and thus back to Monk Bar.

It is rather a shame that York's walls are not accessible after dark, because, as if it did not have enough going for it in the first place, the city is famous for its ghosts, and a moonlit night on the walls could do wonders for the imagination. York's ghost tours are an established part of the tourist scene, but the tour I experienced one weekend did not include the walls. Perhaps the best part of it was being encouraged to linger in unlikely corners and also being led into the deepest recesses of three- and four-hundred-year-old pubs long after most of York's admirers had caught the train home from that much admired railway station. At the time of writing another major hotel is being planned for the city centre, which is good news, because more than any other city, York demands at least two days of anybody's time, and a week would not be excessive.

INDEX

Page numbers in *italic* refer to the illustrations

Aaron the Jew's House, Lincoln, 94
Abbey Green, Bath, 20–21, *21*, 22
Abbey Square, Chester, 80
Abbeys: Bath, 18, *21*, 22, *23*, *24*
   Shrewsbury, 167
Abbot's House, Shrewsbury, 164
Adam, Robert, 18
Adam and Eve pub, Norwich, 118
Albion Inn, Chester, 76
All Saints Church, York, 178, *179*
All Souls College, Oxford, 132, *136*,
   138
Allen, Ralph, 20
Anne, Queen, 15
Anne of Cleves, 61
Arthur, Prince, 58
Arts Theatre, Cambridge, 39–40
Ashmolean Museum, Oxford, 125,
   125, 131, 139
Assembly House, Norwich, 109
Assembly Rooms, Bath, 15
Assembly Rooms, York, 183
Augustine Steward's House,
   Norwich, *114*, 115
Austen, Jane, 16, 18, 25
Avon, River: Bath, 18–19
   Salisbury, 144, *144*, 145, 153,
   153

The Backs, Cambridge, *26–7*, 30,
   43–4, 45
Bailgate, Lincoln, 96, *96*, *97*, 97,
   100
Balliol College, Oxford, 126–7,
   126
Barnes, Robert, 39
Bartlett Street, Bath, 16
Bath, *8–25*, 12–25
   map, *10–11*
Bath chairs, 16
Bath Oliver biscuits, 18, 25
Bath Place, Oxford, 130
Bath Preservation Trust, 14
Batt, Christopher, 149
The Bear, Oxford, *135*, 137
Bear Steps, Shrewsbury, 162–3,
   163
Beaufort, Margaret, 41
Beaufort Hotel, Bath, 17–18
Beaumont Street, Oxford, 125
Becket, Thomas, 50, 55, 60
Beckham, Humphrey, 149
Beecham, Thomas, 130
Belasset of Wallingford, 92
Bell and Crown, Canterbury, 63
Belmont, Shrewsbury, 168

Bilney, Thomas, 39
Bishop Lloyd's House, Chester, 79
Bishop's Palace, Lincoln, *84–5*, *98*,
   100
Blackfriars, Canterbury, 57–8
Blackfriars Hall, Norwich, 111
Blackwell's Bookshop, Oxford, 139,
   139
Bladud, 14
Bluecoat School, Chester, 71
Bodleian Library, Oxford, 130, 131,
   132
Bonewaldesthorne's Tower,
   Chester, 73
Boole, George, 99
Bootham Bar, York, 183, *183*, 185,
   187
Borrow, George, 80, 116
Botanic Garden, Oxford, 133–5,
   133
Botolph Lane, Cambridge, 36
Bouchier, John, 180
Brasenose College, Oxford, *136*,
   138, *138*
Brayford Pool, Lincoln, 88, *89*, 95
Bridewell Museum, Norwich, 110–
   11
Bridge of Sighs: Cambridge, 32, 33,
   41, 42
   Chester, 71
   Oxford, 130
Briton's Arms, Norwich, 111, *113*
Brown, Alderman Charles, 75
Browne, Sir Thomas, 108, 111
Brunel, Isambard Kingdom, 70
Bryant, Sir Arthur, 151
Buckingham, Duke of, 145
Burne-Jones, Sir Edward, 40, 139
Butchery Lane, Canterbury, 58, 63
Butcher Row, Shrewsbury, 164,
   164
Buttermarket, Canterbury, 50, 58,
   59

Caius College, Cambridge, 36, 38–9,
   39
Cam, River, 30, 31, 32–3, *33*, 45
Cambridge, *26–45*, 30–45
   map, *28–9*
Canterbury, *46–63*, 50–63
   map, *48–9*
Canterbury Centre, 63
Canterbury Heritage Centre, 53
Cardinal's Hat, Lincoln, 91
Carfax, Oxford, 137
Castle Gates House,

   Shrewsbury, 166, 167
Castle Hill, Lincoln, 95
Castle Museum, York, 180
Castle Street, Shrewsbury, 166–7
castles: Canterbury, 51, 52
   Chester, 74
   Lincoln, 88, 91, 94–5
   Norwich, 109–10, *110*
   Shrewsbury, 158, 165, *166*
   York, 179–80
Catharine Place, Bath, 14
cathedrals: Canterbury, *46–7*, 50,
   57, *58–60*, 60, *61*, 62
   Chester, 70, 74, 80–82, *81*, *82*,
   83
   Lincoln, *84–5*, 88, 89, 91, 92–4,
   93, 96, 99–100, 101
   Norwich, 116–17, *116*, *117*, 119
   Oxford, *134*, 135
   Salisbury, 149–51, *150*, *151*,
   152, 153
   Shrewsbury, 168
   York Minster, *170–71*, 174, 176,
   181, *181*, 183, *184–5*, *186*
Catherine of Aragon, 58
Cavell, Edith, 114
Charles I, King, 70–71, 78, 160,
   167, 180
Charles II, King, 63, 111, 132, 148
Chaucer, Geoffrey, 51, 53, 55, 57,
   58
Cheese Cross, Salisbury, 145
Chester, *64–83*, 68–82
   map, *66–7*
Chester Heritage Centre, 78
Chester Royal Infirmary, 73
Chester Visitor Centre, 68
Chillenden, Prior, 62
Choristers' Green, Salisbury, *151*
Christ Church, Oxford, 43, 124,
   134, 135, 137
Christ Church Gate,
   Canterbury, 58, *59*, 63
Christ Church Meadow, Oxford,
   124, 135, 137
Christ's College, Cambridge, 36, 42,
   42
Circus, Bath, 12, 14–15, *15*
City Hall, Norwich, 108, 109
Civil War, 70–73, 78, 100, 160,
   167
Clare Bridge, Cambridge, 30, 32,
   44, 45
Clare College, Cambridge, 44, 45
Clarendon Building, Oxford, 131,
   132

Clifford's Tower, York, 174, 179–80, *179*
Clitherow, Margaret, 177
Clive of India, 161–2, *161*
Clive House Museum, Shrewsbury, 161–2
Close, Salisbury, *140–41*, 149–52
Cobb Hall, Lincoln, 95
Colegate, Norwich, 119
College of Matrons, Salisbury, 152
Colman's Mustard, 106, 110
Constable, John, 144, 153
Convocation House, Oxford, 131, 132
Cook, Nell, 62
Coppergate, York, 178
Cornhill, Lincoln, 89–90
Cornmarket, Oxford, 137, 139
Corpus Christi, Cambridge, 34, 36–7, *37*, 41
Corpus Christi, Oxford, 137
Cotman, John Sell, 109, 116, 119
Cotton, Leonard, 53
Cow Tower, Norwich, 118
Coward, Noel, 106, 107
Cranmer, Archbishop, 126, 127, 132
Crest Hotel, York, 180
Cripps Building, Oxford, 41
Crome, John, 109, 116, 119
Cromwell, Oliver, 40
The Cross, Chester, 77, *77*, 78
Cross Bath, Bath, 22–4
Cross Keys Chequer, Salisbury, 146
Crystal Palace pub, Bath, 22

The Dana, Shrewsbury, 166
Dane John Gardens, Canterbury, 51–2, *51*
Danvers, Henry, 135
Darwin, Charles, 165, *165*, 169
De Wint, Peter, 88, 99, 101
Deadman's Walk, Oxford, 135
Dee, River, 73, 75, *75*, 76
Defoe, Daniel, 12, 80–82
Deloraine Court, Lincoln, 97
Dernstall House, Lincoln, 91
Dickens, Charles, 14, 50, 57, 63, 169
Divinity School, Oxford, 131–2
Domesday Book, 153, 177, 178
Donne, John, 130
Downing College, Cambridge, 34, 35–6, *35*

Eagle pub, Cambridge, 37
Eardley, Sergeant, 166
Eastbridge Hospital, Canterbury, 55
Eastgate, Chester, 68, 69–70, *69*
Eastgate, Lincoln, 97, 100
Eastgate Hotel, Lincoln, 97–9
Edgar, King, 22
Edward, the Black Prince, *46–7*
Edward III, King, 152
Edward VII, King, 79, 146
Elizabeth I, Queen, 50, 58, 113
Elizabeth II, Queen, 25, 53, 145
Elm Hill, Norwich, 111–13
Elm Hill Riverside Gardens,

Norwich, 113
Emmanuel College, Cambridge, 36
Empire Hotel, Bath, 19
English Bridge, Shrewsbury, *154–5*, 158, 167
Erpingham, Sir Thomas, 116
Exchequergate, Lincoln, 96, *96*, 99
Exeter College, Oxford, 138–9

Fairfax House, York, 174, 179
Falcon Inn, Chester, 78
Falstaff Inn, Canterbury, 57
Fawcett, Henry, 146
Fellows Building, Cambridge, 45
Fielding, Henry, 149
Fiennes, Celia, 108
Fitzsimmons, Alderman, 51, 52
Fitzwilliam Museum, Cambridge, 34–5
Fitzwilliam Street, Cambridge, 34, 35
Francis Hotel, Bath, 24, 25
Frederick, Prince of Wales, 25
Friary Court, Salisbury, 149
Fry, Elizabeth, 106–7

Gamul, Sir Francis, 78
Gentleman's Walk, Norwich, *102–3*, 109
George III, King, 95, 145
George Street, Bath, 16
Gibbs, James, 45, 138
Glory Hole, Lincoln, *90*, 91
Godshall Lane, Chester, 82
Gonville and Caius College, Cambridge, *see* Caius
Grand Parade, Bath, 18–19
Gray, Thomas, 34
Great Hospital, Norwich, 117–18
Great Pulteney Street, Bath, 17, 18
Greestone Stairs, Lincoln, *100*, 101
Greyfriars, Canterbury, 53–4
Grope Lane, Shrewsbury, 162, *162*
Grosvenor Museum, Chester, 70, 74–5
The Groves, Chester, 75
Grumbold, Robert, 36
Guildhalls: Bath, 18
  Lincoln, 91
  Norwich, 108, 109
  Salisbury, 146
  York, 182, 184

Halle, John, 147
Handbridge, 75
Handel, George Frederick, 149
Harnham Mill, Salisbury, 153
Harrison, Thomas, 74
Hartley, L.P., 114
Harvard, John, 36
Haunch of Venison, Salisbury, 146
Hawksmoor, Nicholas, 138
Henry II, King, 99
Henry III, King, 90
Henry VIII, King, 40, 42, 43, 45, 61, 63, 135, 149
Hertford College, Oxford, 130–31
High Bridge, Lincoln, 90–91, *90*
High Streets: Canterbury, 55, 58

Lincoln, 89
  Salisbury, 152, *152*, 153
Hill, John, 160
Hill's Lane, Shrewsbury, 160
Hobson, Thomas, 36
Holburne, Sir Thomas, 18
Holburne of Menstrie Museum, Bath, 17, 18, *19*
Holy Trinity, York, 176, 180
Holywell Music Room, Oxford, 130
Holywell Street, Oxford, 130
Hospitium Museum, York, 183
Housman, A.E., 166
Hudson, George, 174, 180, 185
Hugh of Avalon, 99, 100
Huguenots, 55, 106, 111, 113

Ignatius, Father, 113
Institute of Mathematics, Oxford, 129
Ireland's Mansion, Shrewsbury, *161*
Ivie, John, 148

Jacob's House, Salisbury, 151
Jacobsen, Arne, 130
James I, King, 91
Jesus College, Cambridge, 36, 40
Jesus College, Oxford, 139
Jews, 92, 94, 133, 135
Jew's House, Lincoln, 92, *92*
John A'Port House, Salisbury, 146, 149
John Halle's House, Salisbury, 147, *148*
Johnson, Samuel, 135–7
Joiners' Hall, Salisbury, 149
Jolly, James, 16–17, 25
Jorvik Viking Centre, York, 178–9, 184
Judge's Lodgings: Lincoln, 96
  York, 184

Keble College, Oxford, 124, *128*, 129
Kent War Memorial Garden, Canterbury, 60–61, *61*
Kett, Robert, 110, 111, 115, 118
King Charles Tower, Chester, 70–71
King Edward VI School, Norwich, 116, *117*, 119
King Street, Canterbury, 63
King's Arms, Salisbury, 148
King's College, Cambridge, 30, 37, *37*, 38, 40, 44–5
King's College School, Cambridge, 30–31
King's Manor, York, 183
King's Parade, Cambridge, 37–9, *38–9*, 45
The King's School, Canterbury, 50, 51, 62–3, *63*
Kingsland Bridge, Shrewsbury, 168–9

Lady Peckett's Yard, York, 178
Latimer, Hugh, 39, 126, 132
Laundress Lane, Cambridge, 32

Laura Place, Bath, 18
Laurens, Henry, 148
Leeman, George, 181
Leeman, John, 182
Lendal Bridge, York, 181, *181*, 182
Lewis, C.S., 129
Lincoln, *84–100*, *88–101*
    map, *86–7*
Lincoln City and County Museum,
    101
Lincoln College, Oxford, 138
Lincolnshire College of Art and
    Design, *100*, 101
The Lion, Shrewsbury, 168
Little St Mary's, Cambridge, 33–4
Little St Mary's Lane, Cambridge,
    33
Llewellyn the Great, 165
Lunn, Sally, 19

Maddermarket Theatre, Norwich,
    106, 107, *107*
Magdalen College, Oxford, 124,
    133
Magdalene Bridge, Cambridge, 40–
    41
Magdalene College, Cambridge, 36,
    40, 41
Maid's Head Hotel, Norwich, 113–
    14, *113*
The Maltings, Salisbury, *144*, 145
Mansion House, York, 184
Margaret's Buildings, Bath, 14
markets: Norwich, 102–3, 108
    Oxford, 138
    Salisbury, 145–6
    York, 177
Marks and Spencer, 20
Marlborough Buildings, Bath, 12
Marlowe, Christopher, 57
Marlowe Theatre, Canterbury, 57
Marygate, York, 183
Mathematical Bridge, Cambridge,
    31, 32
Maynard and Cotton's Hospital,
    Canterbury, 52–3
Mercery Lane, Canterbury, 58, 59
Merchant Adventurers' Hall, York,
    174, *177*, 178
Merchant Taylors' Hall, York, 176
Merton College, Oxford, 124, 126,
    135, 137
Merton Street, Oxford, *120–21*
Michaelgate, Lincoln, 92, 93
Micklegate, York, 180, 183
The Mill pub, Cambridge, 32
Milsom, Daniel, 16
Milsom Street, Bath, 16–17, 25
Minster Yard, Lincoln, 98, 99–100
Mompesson House, Salisbury, 151,
    151
Monck, Nugent, 107
Monk Bar, York, 174, *175*, 176,
    183, 185, 187
Monkgate, York, 174, 176, 187
Morgan's Mount, Chester, 71–3
Moritz, Pastor, 124
Morris, William, 40, 139
Morrison, James, 79

Morton, H.V., 114
Multangular Tower, York, 183
Museum of Costume, Bath, 15
Museum of Oxford, 137
Museum Gardens, York, 183
Mustard Shop, Norwich, 110

Nash, Richard 'Beau', 15–16, 17,
    19, 24, 25
National Railway Museum, York,
    174, 182
National Trust, 108, 151
Neighbour, Dr Philip, 151
Nelson, Lord, 116
New College, Oxford, 124, 132,
    133, 135
Newnham College, Cambridge, 31
Newport Arch, Lincoln, 97
Newton, Sir Isaac, 32
Nine Houses, Chester, 76
North Eastern Railway Company,
    181
North Parade Passage, Bath, 19–20
Northgate, Chester, 64–5, 71
Northgate Street, Bath, 17–18
Northgate Street, Chester, 78, *80*
Northumberland Place, Bath, 24
Norwich, *102–18*, *106–119*
    map, *104–5*

O'Brian, Patrick Cotter, 14
Octagon Chapel, Norwich, 119
Old Council House, Shrewsbury,
    167
Old Dee Bridge, Chester, 75, *75*
The Old George, Salisbury, 153
Old Grammar School, Shrewsbury,
    165, *165*
Old Market Hall, Shrewsbury, *161*,
    162
Oliver, William, 25
Oriel College, Oxford, *136*, 137
Our Lady's Row, York, 176
Ouse, River, 174, 180, 181–3, 184
Oxford, *120–39*, *124–39*
    map, *122–3*
Oxford Information Centre, 137
Oxford Playhouse, 125

Palace Plain, Norwich, 119
Palace Street, Canterbury, *62*, 63
Palladio, Andrea, 18
Parade Gardens, Bath, *8–9*, 19
Parade Shopping Centre,
    Shrewsbury, 167
Parker's Piece, Cambridge, 35
parking: Bath, 12
    Cambridge, 30
    Canterbury, 50
    Chester, 68
    Norwich, 106
    Oxford, 124
    Salisbury, 144
    Shrewsbury, 158
    York, 174
Pavement, York, 178
Peckett, John, 178
Pembroke College, Cambridge, 30,
    33, 34

Pembroke College, Oxford, 129,
    135–7
Pembroke Street, Cambridge, 36
Pepys, Samuel, 22–4, 41, 153
Peterhouse, Cambridge, 30, 34, *34*
Pied Bull pub, Chester, 80
Pitt, William, 33
Pitt Building, Cambridge, 33
Poor Priests' Hospital, Canterbury,
    53, 54
Poore, Bishop, 146, 149
Popjoy's Restaurant, Bath, 24
Pottergate, Lincoln, 99
Pottergate, Norwich, 108
Poultry Cross, Salisbury, 144, 145,
    146
Pride Hill, Shrewsbury, 164–5
Prince Rupert Hotel, Shrewsbury,
    164, 167
Princes Street, Norwich, *112*, 115
Pugin, A.W., 40, 147
Pull's Ferry, Norwich, 117, *118*
Pulteney, Sir William, 165
Pulteney Bridge, Bath, 17, *17*, 18,
    19, 90
Pump Room, Bath, 15, 21, *22*

The Quarry, 169, *169*
Queen Elizabeth Guest Chamber,
    Canterbury, 58
Queen Square, Bath, 24–5
Queens' College, Cambridge, 31, 32,
    33
The Queen's College, Oxford, 132–3
Queen's School, Chester, 73

Radcliffe Camera, Oxford, 43, 130,
    132, *136*, 138
Ralph Allen's House, Bath, 19–20
Randolph Hotel, Oxford, 125–6
Raverat, Gwen, 31
Red Lion Hotel, Salisbury, 147
Rembrandt, 35
Richard II, King, 96, 180
Richard III, King, 183
Richardson, Ralph, 145
Ridley, Nicholas, 126, 132
Robinson College, Cambridge, 30,
    31
Roman Baths, Bath, 21–2
Roman Pavement, Canterbury, 50–
    51
Roman remains: Chester, 68–9,
    74–5
    Lincoln, 94, 95, 97
    York, 180, 183
Roodee, Chester, 73–4, *73*, 82
Round Church, Cambridge, 40
Rowley, William, 160
Rowley's House and Museum,
    Shrewsbury, 158–60, *160*,
    169
Rows, Chester, 68, 76–9, *79*
Royal Arcade, Norwich, 109, *109*
Royal Crescent, Bath, 12–13, *13*,
    17, 25
Royal Crescent Hotel, Bath, 12, *13*
Royal Mineral Water Hospital,
    Bath, 15, 24

Royal Museum and Art Gallery, Canterbury, 58
Royal Photographic Society, 17
Royal Victoria Park, Bath, 12

St Alkmond's Place, Shrewsbury, 162–4, 163, 169
St Alkmund's Church Shrewsbury, 158, 159, 163, 167
St Andrew's Hall, Norwich, 111
St Andrew's Plain, Norwich, 111
St Ann Street, Salisbury, 149
St Augustine's Abbey, Canterbury, 61–2
St Bene't's Church, Cambridge, 37
St Catharine's College, Cambridge, 36
St Catherine's College, Oxford, 130, 133
St Chad's Church, Shrewsbury, 159, 169
St Clement's Church, Colegate, Norwich, 119
St Crux Passage, York, 177
St Edmund Hall, Oxford, 132, 135
St Edward's Church, Cambridge, 39
St Edward's Passage, Cambridge, 39
St George's Church, Norwich, 115
St Giles, Oxford, 127, 129
St John Baptist, Chester, 68
St John Maddermarket, Norwich, 107
St John Street, Oxford, 125
St John's Alley, Norwich, 107, 107
St John's College, Cambridge, 40, 41–2, 41, 43
St John's College, Oxford, 127, 127–9
St Martin's Gate, Chester, 73
St Mary Magdalene, Lincoln, 96
St Mary's Church, Shrewsbury, 167
St Mary's Abbey, York, 182, 183
St Michael's Arcade, Chester, 77–8
St Mildred's Church, Canterbury, 52, 53
St Nicholas Church, Shrewsbury, 165
St Olave's Church, York, 183
St Peter Hungate, Norwich, 111
St Peter Mancroft, Norwich, 108, 108, 116
St Peter's Church, Chester, 77, 79
St Thomas Becket, Salisbury, 145
St Thomas's Hospital, Canterbury, 55
St Thomas's Square, Salisbury, 145
St William's College, York, 170–71, 176, 185
Salisbury, 140–53, 144–53
    map, 142–3
Salisbury and South Wiltshire Museum, 151
Sally Lunn's House, Bath, 19, 20
School Gardens, Shrewsbury, 165
Schools Quadrangle, Oxford, 131
Scott, Sir Gilbert, 82

Selwyn College, Cambridge, 31
Severn, River, 154–5, 158, 167, 169
Sham Castle, Bath, 20
The Shambles, York, 176, 177
Sheldonian Theatre, Oxford, 131, 131
Shrewsbury, 154–69, 158–69
    map, 156–7
Shropshire Regimental Museum, 165–6
Shropshire Union Canal, 71, 71, 73
Sibthorpe, Colonel, 92, 101
Sidgwick Avenue, Cambridge, 30, 31
Sidney, Sir Henry, 167
Sidney, Philip, 165, 167
Sidney Sussex College, Cambridge, 35, 36, 40
Silver Street, Cambridge, 31–2
Simon of Sudbury, Archbishop of Canterbury, 55–7
Skipper, George, 109
The Square, Shrewsbury, 160–61, 162, 163, 166, 168
Steep Hill, Lincoln, 88, 92, 94, 94, 96, 97, 97, 100, 101
Steward, Augustine, 115
Stirling, James, 31
Stonebow, Lincoln, 88, 91, 91, 97
Stonegate, York, 184, 185
Stour, River, 54, 55, 56, 57
Stour Street, Canterbury, 52–3
The Strait, Lincoln, 92
Stranger's Hall, Norwich, 106–7
Suckling Hall, Norwich, 111
Sun Street, Canterbury, 63

Taylor, Sir Robert, 146
Taylorian Institution, Oxford, 127, 146
Telford, Thomas, 165, 166
Tennyson, Alfred, Lord, 98, 99
Terry, Noel, 179
Theatre Royal, Bath, 24
Theatre Royal, Norwich, 106, 109
Theatre Royal, York, 183
Thimbleby's Tower, Chester, 68
Three Old Arches, Chester, 78
Thrower, Percy, 169
Tolkien, J.R.R., 129
Tom Tower, Oxford, 135
Tombland, Norwich, 114, 115–16, 115
Tower House, Canterbury, 57
Town Hall, Chester, 79, 80
Town Mill, Salisbury, 145, 153
Treasurer's House, York, 174, 185–7, 187
Trim Street, Bath, 24, 25
Trinity Church, Chester, 79
Trinity College, Cambridge, 40, 42–4, 43
Trinity College, Oxford, 127, 129, 139, 139
Trinity Hall, Cambridge, 26–7, 44
Trinity Lane, Cambridge, 44
Trumpington Street, Cambridge,

30, 33
Tyler, Wat, 52
Tyndale, William, 130

Union Passage, Bath, 24
University College, Oxford, 126, 138
University of Kent, 51, 53
University Library, Cambridge, 30
University Museum, Oxford, 129
Upper Borough Walls, Bath, 18
Usher Art Gallery, Lincoln, 91, 101

Victoria, Queen, 18, 25, 44, 69, 101, 145, 146
Victoria Art Gallery, Bath, 18
Vikings, 178–9

Wadham College, Oxford, 129–30, 139
Walton, Isaak, 52
Walton Street, Oxford, 125
Washington, Rev. Godfrey, 34
Water Lane, Shrewsbury, 167
Water Tower, Chester, 72, 73
Watergate Row, Chester, 79
Waugh, Evelyn, 130
Weavers' Houses, Canterbury, 55, 56
Welsh Bridge, Shrewsbury, 158, 159, 162
Wensum, River, 113, 117, 118, 119
Wensum Street, 113, 113, 115
Wesley, John, 119, 138
Westgate, Canterbury, 53, 55–7, 57
Westminster, Duke of, 68
Whewell, Dr, 44
Whip-ma-Whop-ma-gate, York, 177–8
White Hart Hotel, Lincoln, 96–7
White Hart Hotel, Salisbury, 148
Whitefriars monastery, Norwich, 119
William the Conqueror, 52, 94–5
William of Orange, 19
William of Wykeham, 132
Witham, River, 88, 90
Wolseley, Sir Garnet, 109
Wolsey, Cardinal, 43, 91, 135
Wood, John the Elder, 12, 25
Wood, John the Younger, 12
Woodforde, Parson, 114
Worcester College, Oxford, 124–5, 129
Wren, Sir Christopher, 33, 43, 130, 131, 131
Wren Library, Cambridge, 43
Wyatt, James, 137
Wyle Cop, Shrewsbury, 167, 168
Wynter, John, 51

York, 170–87, 174–87
    map, 172–3
York City Art Gallery, 183
York Minster, 170–71, 174, 176, 181, 181, 183, 184–5, 186
Yorkshire Museum, 183